Circling Marilyn

Circling Marilyn

Text Body Performance

Clara Juncker

University Press of Southern Denmark 2010

Printed by Special-trykkeriet Viborg a-s
Cover Design by Donald Jensen
Cover Photo: Polfoto
Photos: Polfoto
University of Southern Denmark Studies in Literature vol. 56

ISBN 9788776744809

This book has been published with generous support from:
University of Southern Denmark
Ingeniør N.M. Knudsens Fond

University Press of Southern Denmark
Campusvej 55
DK-5230 Odense M
Phone: +45 6615 7999
Fax: +45 6615 8126
www.universitypress.dk

Distribution in the United States and Canada:
International Specialized Book Services
5804 NE Hassalo Street
Portland, OR 97213-3644 USA
www.isbs.com

Distribution in the United Kingdom:
Gazelle
White Cross Mills
Hightown
Lancaster
LA1 4 XS
U.K.
www.gazellebooks.co.uk

For Lo

Table of Contents

Introduction: Circling Marilyn

Marilyn Monroe lived her life as a sex queen, a tragedy, and a story. As a member of what a reviewer labels a "tragic pop-culture sorority," she inhabits "a storied life," with factoids, creative license, lies and truth intermingling in the fictional works, biographies, memoirs, and plays that adjust or revise her according to textual needs and intentions.[1] Among the fiction writers trying to trim Marilyn of qualities unfit for stereotype, Alvah Bessie created in *The Symbol* (1966) an irrational film star obsessed with attracting and servicing men. In 1973, Norman Mailer drooled over the strawberry-and-ice cream icon in his novel-biography *Marilyn*, and he returned to her in *Of Women and Their Elegance* (1980). Other (auto)biographers have followed, from Marilyn's half-sister Berniece Baker Miracle to Arthur Miller's friend Norman Rosten to Mailer himself, again. In "Strawhead," a one-act "memory play" staged for two weeks in 1986 at the Actors Studio in New York, Mailer cast his 23-year-old daughter Kate as the woman who never wanted him for her Daddy.[2] In *Diary of a Lover of Marilyn Monroe* (1979), the Danish politician Hans Jørgen Lembourn elbows himself in among Marilyn's male companions, as does Graham McCann, the author of *Marilyn Monroe* (1988), who belongs to the breed he and Mae West declare to be "no angels," though his interest in Marilyn remains academic.[3]

Movie biographies such as *Goodbye Norma Jean* (1976) or *Marilyn and Bobby: Her Final Affair* (1993) present, as McCann's notes, "the predictable thesis that Monroe was doomed long before Hollywood began 'irritating' her." McCann sees most Marilyn biographers as "death's secretaries," who write a depressively predictable story about a tragic heroine rising from orphan and foster child to sex symbol and movie goddess, only to fall into suicide or murder. He sums up: "The biography is a kind of 'pinball machine': the plot is planned; the supporting cast (Norma's mother, Jim Dougherty,

Joe DiMaggio, Natash[ia] Lytess, Arthur Miller, the Strasbergs, the Kennedys) are positioned beforehand, often 'static' in terms of personality; finally, 'Marilyn' is fired into this narrative by the author, made to bounce off each figure until the game is completed." In 1986, McCann accused Marilyn authors of sexism and voyeurism and searched the horizon for feminist analyses of her life story.[4] In 1994, film scholar Jackie Stacey still found few feminist analyses of Hollywood stars.[5]

In *Marilyn/Norma Jeane* (1986), Gloria Steinem set out to rescue the star from male biographers in general and Norman Mailer in particular, but she peels off Marilyn only to find Gloria. Walking out of a movie theater showing *Gentlemen Prefer Blondes* (1953), the adolescent Steinem identified with Marilyn's vulnerability and self-doubt, if not with her magnetism. Decades later, she worked with photographer George Barris on an illustrated Marilyn biography, since the dead actress no longer could set the record straight, as she had intended. Steinem took her place, and from Barris's photos and Marilyn's flesh she created a feminist text, *Ms. Magazine* style.[6] From Mailer's sexism to Steinem's feminism, Marilyn became an electric jolt aimed straight at "the aesthetic gut of the drug-deadened American belly."[7] In the phrase of Sir Laurence Olivier, who directed and co-starred with Marilyn in *The Prince and the Showgirl* (1955), she was "exploited beyond anyone's means."[8] Or, as Marilyn herself chose to put it, "If I didn't fight I would become a piece of merchandise to be sold off the movie pushcart."[9] American novelist Joyce Carol Oates became as possessed by the blond actress as everybody else. "I believe I was trying to give life to Norma Jeane Baker," she explains, "and to keep her living, in a very obsessive way, because she came to represent certain 'life elements' in my own experience and, I hope, in the life of America."[10] In her novel *Blonde* (2000), Oates invented an alternative Marilyn through fragmentation and multiplicity and asked the glamorous star to speak up and present the supporting cast in her own voice.

Circling Marilyn: Text Body Performance replaces the pinball machine with the circle in creating Marilyn with a difference. The circle evokes, of course, the fans and photographers who surrounded Marilyn in public, as during the (in)famous Manhattan night when

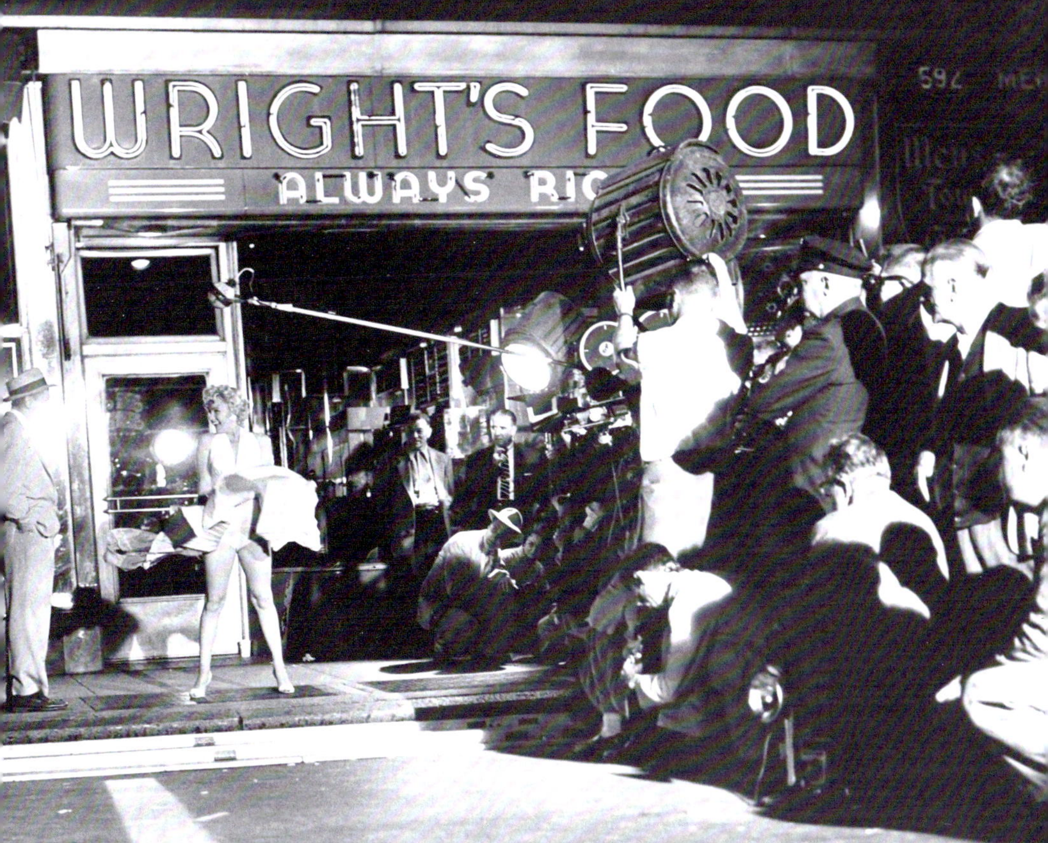

Circling Marilyn

her white dress ballooned up her hips and waist and drove the circle of New York men watching to higher temperatures than the hot air rising from the grate. The circle suggests, moreover, the Method acting that the New York-based Lee Strasberg taught Marlon Brando, Paul Newman, Marilyn Monroe, and others. This circle appears in Constantin Stanislavsky's *An Actor Prepares* (1936) and in Oates's epigraph in *Blonde*: "In a circle of light, in the midst of darkness, you have the sensation of being entirely alone. . . . It is what we call Solitude in Public. . . . During a performance, before an audience of thousands, you can always enclose yourself in this circle like a snail in its shell. . . . You can carry it with you wherever you go, on the stage or off."[11] The image of Marilyn installed in a circle describes both her solitude, in public and everywhere else, and the acting technique that in (post-)feminist readings of her became her source of strength.

The circle fits Marilyn as an American icon. Living and dying in the West, Marilyn surrounded herself with pioneers: Hollywood innovators, art photographers, writers, sport fans, or Mafia criminals, who explored frontiers of post-war America and circled their wagons around her. They became her source of protection as well as the dominance she could not escape except in death. Decades after her suicide or murder, vultures circle her body ready for their prey. Marilyn became a victim of those consuming her, but the circle indicates as well an elusive Marilyn that will not be defined. Those looking for the real Marilyn may search the right places and still not capture her essence or aura. *Circling Marilyn* has incorporated this elusive aspect of the blond actress into its structure by circling her from multiple angles and perspectives, overlapping, hybrid and process-oriented. Instead of lassoing her, like the cowboys in Arthur Miller's script for *The Misfits* (1961), *Circling Marilyn* tries to let (her) go by allowing a space within and between chapters and sections where she might roam.[12]

Marilyn may escape altogether, and circle us from above, looking and laughing as Marilyn Medusa. From up there, she would engage in the gaze reversal film and literary critics associate with feminine power and deconstruction. Unlike the endless biographies on Norma Jeane Baker or Marilyn Monroe, which narrate her tumultuous life and career, *Circling Marilyn* abandons the project of locating the "real" Marilyn. Instead, it moves into "Marilyn country" and contemplates Marilyn from different angles. It recognizes and celebrates the kaleidoscopic personality of Marilyn the individual and Marilyn the star, if this distinction is possible, or even desirable.

Academic Marilyn has enrolled in colleges everywhere. In the distinguished company of Barthes, Jameson, Lyotard, Habermas, and Haraway, she appears in an English course on "Postmodernism and Contemporary Culture" at Princeton University, in an Art course on "The Complete Marilyn Monroe" at the University of Leeds, and in a History course on "The Fifties: Fear, Sex and Discontent" at the University of Wisconsin. In a Women's Studies course at Wittenberg University, Ohio, the blond actress sits next to feminist scholars and writers of all colors—Audre Lorde, Susan Bordo, and Margaret Atwood—and a couple of other performers: Lillian Russell, Jamie Lee Curtis. Like Elvis, Academic Marilyn lends herself to the study of social and political practices, historical periods, gender and ethnicity, cultural theory, and media.

As a celebrity study, *Circling Marilyn* engages with work by film critics and cultural studies scholars, including Richard Dyer, James Naremore, Thomas Austin, Martin Barker, Barry King, Ann E. Kaplan, and Jackie Stacey. Its interdisciplinary perspective activates psychology, sociology, environmental studies, history, film, and sports, but its first love remains literature. The book began not with Marilyn but with Arthur Miller, Joyce Carol Oates, and Norman Mailer, or with Mailer's mentor, John Dos Passos, who also inspired Oates in *Blonde*, though she objects to the label "nonfiction novel." A contemporary chronicler in her own right, she explains that the "line of descent" of her Marilyn novel "may derive from John Dos Passos's 'U.S.A.' with its lively, inventive portraits of 'real people' mixed with fictional characters."[13] Like Dos Passos and Oates, *Circling Marilyn* has no particular investment in "historical veracity," to use Oates's term, [14] but it trespasses onto historical terrain, where Marilyn finds herself in the company of Don DeLillo, Robert Russo, Philip Roth and other writers who draw historical figures into fiction to articulate contemporary issues and concerns. *Circling Marilyn* stresses the American actress as representation, as a universal signifier with an elusive, ever-changing signified. As S. Paige Baty emphasizes in *American Monroe: The Making of a Body Politic* (1995), Marilyn changes according to decade, context, and author, from the '50s bombshell or the '90s post-feminist to the millennium monster.[15] In *The Many Lives of Marilyn Monroe* (2004), Sarah Churchwell creates her as metaphor: "The many lives of Marilyn Monroe are a talking cure for our lingering, persistent fears about sex, knowledge, the female body and earth."[16] To her list might be added American superpower, last frontiers, reality, and language itself. No wonder the actress took to Dom Perignon and pills.

Marilyn returned from the dead to haunt the present project as an uncanny presence, or absence. She is clingy, to be sure, and pulls at an author from every angle. Bloated, dead, hair soaked in blood or vomit, she insists on having her way, staying alive, dying, inflicting pain or pleasure, and getting something in return: love, a second or thirteenth chance, and attention, attention and attention. She is the chaos we try to stave off, the monstrous self we hide, the uncanny other who returns with our anxieties and desires. Sarah Churchwell identifies this Marilyn with "the unruly, symbolic, figurative world of the unconscious," and also Oates felt her pull.[17] The author of *Blonde* remains vague about the cost of her involvement with Marilyn, buried in a general statement and ellipsis: "I don't recommend, for anyone, writing a psychologically realistic novel about any 'historic' individual who is said to have committed suicide. It's just too . . . painful."[18] *Circling Marilyn* is different, perhaps, because it circumvents psychological realism and allows both its author and its glamorous subject space for escape, for solitude, and for silence. Its readers might enjoy Marilyn without paying her price, though she might, given a chance, seduce them.

In the first lines of Vladimir Nabokov's novel *Lolita* (1955), Humbert Humbert plays both with the appetizing nymphette of the title, with their mutual seduction, and with the name that will haunt him: "Lo-lee-ta: the tip of the tongue taking a trip of three steps down the palate to tap, at three, on the teeth. Lo. Lee. Ta."[19] In her own linguistic never-neverland, Marilyn belongs to us forever, and to the name she came to resent. Though we might play with the academic respect of Monroe, her glamor and her gloom belong to Marilyn. Like Elvis, Diana, Madonna, and Bill, who will not live on as Presley, Spencer, Ciccone, or Clinton, she cannot be separated from the name known to everybody, as Anthony Summers writes, "from Connecticut to the Congo."[20] Like Marlon, Marilyn has the right sound: mmmmmmmmh. Eager for seduction and attention, like most tricksters, Marilyn lives in our words.

I Text

Everybody's Marilyn

Everybody but Marlon Brando has talked or written about Marilyn Monroe. In 1995 S. Paige Baty counted seventy books exclusively on Marilyn, and the number keeps rising.[21] Wherever they situate themselves on the fact/fiction continuum, biographies of Marilyn gesture through their titles towards essence and mythmaking. Surely the myths surrounding the blond actress warrant her biographers' interest: the mad mother, orphanage and foster families, teenage wedding, nude calendar scandal, celebrity marriages, Mafia relations, the Kennedy brothers, drug addiction, alcoholism, mysterious death, FBI files, and more. Edwin P. Hoyt began his *Marilyn: The Tragic Venus* (1965) because of "a continuing interest in money, power and fame," and Norman Mailer continued the story of "a lovely if seldom simple woman" with a simple title: *Marilyn* (1973).[22] Other records of Marilyn's life and death include Fred Lawrence Guiles's *Legend: The Life and Death of Marilyn Monroe* (1984), Anthony Summers's *Goddess: The Secret Lives of Marilyn Monroe* (1985), S. Paige Baty's *American Monroe: The Making of a Body Politic* (1995), Barbara Leaming's *Girl-Woman* (1998), and Joyce Carol Oates's *Blonde* (2000).[23] The desire to get to the bottom of Marilyn also inspired Victor Adam's *The Complete Marilyn Monroe* (1999), an encyclopedic text that records Norma Jeane's and Marilyn's intriguing activities.[24] Even "Marilyns," a poem stressing the futility of essentializing its subject, leads readers into general categories in its "Instructions for Use": "mask, mother, everywoman, nun–/Choose one. This is a factory run."[25] In a review of Barbara Leaming's "uneven" biography, Michiko Kakutani writes that the legend of Marilyn Monroe "has been burnished, deconstructed, transmogrified and commodified. Her life has not only generated the usual biographies and pop tributes, but it's also spawned novels, plays, songs, movies, academic papers, gender studies and at least one opera."[26]

This mythologizing of Marilyn began with Marilyn. In *My Story*, ghostwritten by Ben Hecht and serialized in part during May through August, 1954, she lays the foundation for myths to come, and for the life and death that would last forever.[27] When Marilyn released this unfinished autobiography, she had just married Joe DiMaggio, the baseball hero, and visited Korea alone during their honeymoon to Japan in 1954. Marilyn describes as the high point of her life the performances she gave for the American soldiers stationed abroad. They reacted so enthusiastically to the song "Do It Again" that the title had to be changed to "Kiss Me Again." According to *My Story*, Norma Jeane and Marilyn both suffered from fragile identities, from the inner void that proved fatal to both. Marilyn articulates the role she was expected to play by (her) men, her fans, and her contemporaries: "People had a habit of looking at me as if I were some kind of mirror instead of a person. They didn't see me, they saw only their own lewd thoughts. Then they whitemasked themselves by calling me the lewd one."[28]

Though Marilyn poses as victim, she herself constructed the myths she lived. As Laura Miller writes in *The New York Times*, "her stardom, however much she came to resent it, was the product of years of determined striving . . . ."[29] Marilyn ben Hecht, as Norman Mailer dubs the author function of *My Story*, has arranged "a rainbow of tear-washed factoids" in American Dream fashion.[30] She foreshadows subsequent PR work with tales of the orphaned Norma Jeane bathing last in dirty water used by five or six other foster family members, fanatically religious foster parents, accusations of theft, a rape by a wealthy boarder, the arranged teenage marriage to Jim Dougherty, her unrequited love for her music coach, Fred Karger, who remains anonymous in *My Story*. The path to success involves as well a name change and is dotted with influential men like Fox producer Joe Schenck, Fox President Darryl Zanuck, and Marilyn's agent, Johnny Hyde. Sexual favors have carefully been swept away from Marilyn's road to fame. At the end of the rainbow we find the American Hero, marriage, honeymoon, and the detour to Korea.

The many anecdotes in *My Story* contribute to Marilyn's self-mythologizing. Norma Jeane used to watch the brightly lit R.K.O. Radio Pictures sign from her orphanage window. She hated the blue skirt and white blouse of the orphanage uniform, but at the age of twelve, she glimpsed her potential when she went to math class in a too-tight, borrowed sweater. Marriage to Jim Dougherty was "like being retired to a zoo" and taught her absolutely nothing about sex.[31] Hollywood will pay a thousand dollars for a kiss and fifty cents for your soul. Marilyn loves to linger in the bathtub, because Norma Jeane deserves a treat. She is always late (up to nine hours at the end of her career), but she only wants to feel loved and missed. Men are too talkative, and women, too resentful. Throughout *My Story*, vulnerability and self-destruction lurk behind sex appeal and success: "I was the kind of girl they found dead in a hall bedroom with an empty bottle of sleeping pills in her hand."[32]

Marilyn ben Hecht dishes up factoids as poisonous as the sleeping pills Marilyn always kept at hand. She explains to Arthur Miller that Ben Hecht had asked her for interesting stories about herself and that she had simply met the challenge: "Well, I was boring, and I thought maybe I'd tell him about them putting me in the orphanage, and he said that was great and wrote it, and that became the main thing suddenly."[33] Miller never quite sorts out whether Marilyn wished to present herself as an orphan or whether she merely remembered a temporary stay in the orphanage. He makes clear, however, that both scenarios implied to Marilyn that she was worthless. In Miller's view, Ben Hecht exploited Marilyn's background, "for if you were worthless and so innocently babylike too, you were a defenseless sex object, or if you preferred, a free spirit with no one in the world to account to for your actions."[34]

Marilyn's laid-back approach to facts inspired writers in her wake. In *Marilyn*, Norman Mailer created his own collection of factoids so as to advertise, yes, Norman Mailer. He had originally contracted to write the preface for a photo collection by Larry Miller, one of the three lucky photographers present during swimming-pool takes for *Something's Got to Give*, when Marilyn took off her flesh-colored bathing suit. She was fired from the set two short months before she died. Based on Fred Lawrence Guiles's first biography of the star, *Norma Jean* (1969), Mailer's preface exploded into a "novel biography" and ninety thousand words. Mailer shoots his Mailerness across the pages and photos of Marilyn until the two are entwined like lovers swimming in alphabet soup: "For a man with a cabalistic turn of mind, it was fair and engraved coincidence that the letters in Marilyn Monroe (if the 'a' were used twice and the 'o' but once) would spell his own name leaving only the 'y' for excess . . . ."[35] Norman needs Norma, and Mailer, Marilyn, though the commercial success of his fictionalized biography failed to impress Larry Miller, who saw Marilyn reduced to "Mailer in drag."[36] Mailer's "angel of sex" has no identity or character. She consists of moist, shiny surfaces and crevices available for male inscription. Libido oozes out of her; she gives off "a skin-glow of sex," while inside her lurks "a blank eye for power unattached to any notion of the moral."[37] As a projection of male (Mailer's) desire, she becomes "a womb fairly salivating in seed" and "breasts pop[ping] buds and burgeons of flesh over many a questing sweating moviegoer's face." Mailer concludes: "She excited dreams of honey for the horn."[38]

Mailer tried through his writing to possess what in life had eluded him. He knows that Marilyn was famous for Chanel No. 5, but would never, he admits, "have a real clue to how it smelled on her skin."[39] *The Complete Marilyn Monroe* notes more brutally that though Mailer "tried hard to meet Marilyn, she was evidently not interested."[40] Also Gloria Steinem, who ran into the star at Lee Strasberg's Actors Studio in New York in the 1950s, mentions this snub with considerable glee.[41] Mailer compensates by recreating Marilyn from Larry Schiller's photographs and more personal fantasies. In the chapter titled "Snively, Schenck, Karger, and Hyde," all powerful men who pushed Norma Jeane towards stardom in exchange for sexual favors, Mailer constructs Marilyn's body in the way Norma Jeane Baker became Marilyn Monroe. Hollywood hairdressers bleached her a platinum blonde and gave her an upsweep, while Mailer speculates about a promiscuous sex life. To him, Marilyn looks "in these years like the most popular blonde in the most expensive brothel in Acapulco." Aware that in this period Marilyn will give more of herself than she can get back later, Mailer claims to know that "she cultivates her sexual sweetmeats in the sexlands of

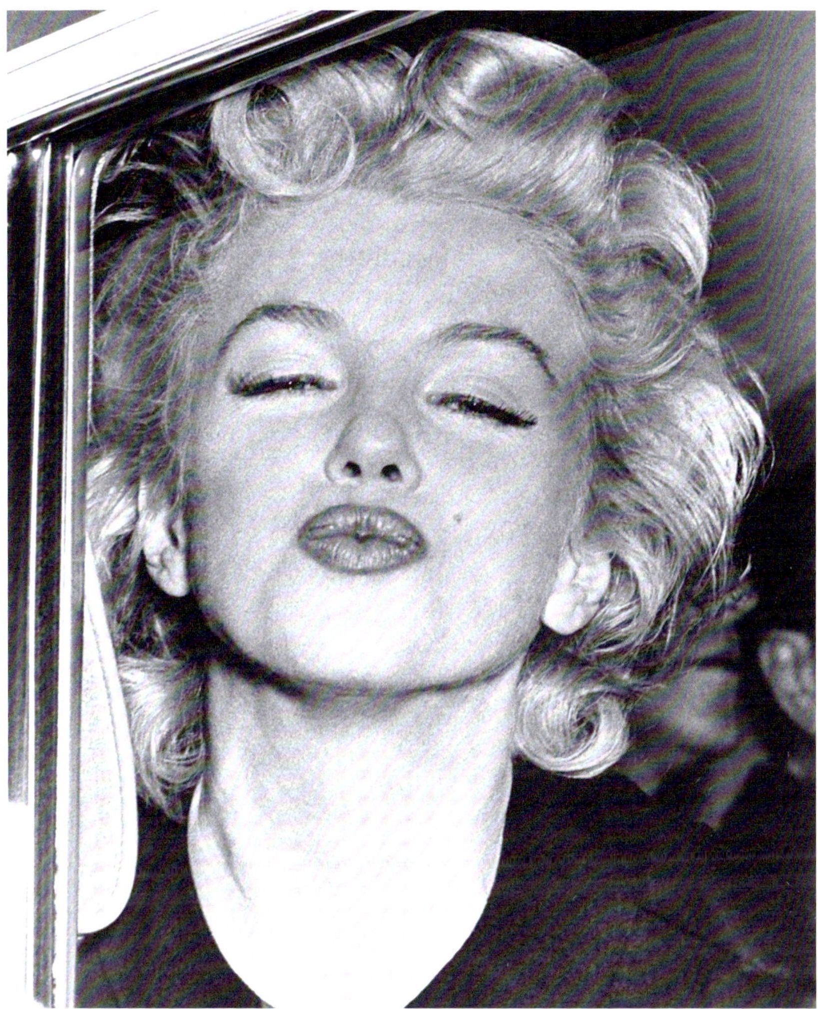

Everybody's Marilyn

swamp and plague."[42] The disease he associates with Marilyn's physicality extends to her mind, which he describes as a violated corpse: "whole parts of her psyche had been wounded, bruised, crushed, lacerated, amputated, thickened, and killed by then—the inside of her heart must have looked like a club-fighter's face."[43] Mailer is left, in the end, with Mailer, and the anxieties a feminized other might engender. Behind the mirror Marilyn hides as "a murderous emotional cripple," a masculinized club-fighter or "general of sex" with "the itch to kill love," or a schizophrenic with the personalities of a mouse and a monster.[44]

Shrewdly, Mailer identifies the contrary impulses in Marilyn's personality and moves her beyond the dumb blonde he chases. His own conflicting desires group him with anxious Puritan ministers sermonizing on devouring wombs, or in his own century, with the writer and activist Mike Gold, who in the 1920s predicted that one day, "the human female will devour the male in the moment of Love, exactly like a female spider or locust."[45] Despite or because of Marilyn's charms, "amputation or absurdity" hovers in her wake.[46] But Mailer's ninety thousand words help alleviate his castration anxiety. He confesses to having done no research whatsoever for his novel biography, which he based on the facts Fred Guiles presented in his first biography *Norma Jean*. Mailer introduced the murder theory, he later confessed, only to hit the jackpot.

With *Goddess: The Secret Lives of Marilyn Monroe*, Anthony Summers throws himself on dead Marilyn. He does, of course, a lot more. As an investigative writer, Summers conducted substantial research to write his story of Marilyn's marriages, and especially of her murder. Summers had previously written a monograph on JFK, titled *Conspiracy* (1980). He interviewed innumerable people and gathered obscure source materials relating to Marilyn's last months, when she was living alone in her Mexican-style house on Fifth Helena Drive in Brentwood. In *Goddess* he claims to have pieced together the puzzle of Marilyn's premature death. Marilyn got caught, he argues, in an intricate web of events that included FBI attempts to cover up her alleged affair with Attorney General Robert Kennedy, Mafia attempts to incriminate the Attorney General and stop investigations of organized crime, and Frank Sinatra's (in)famous Rat Pack and their Lake Tahoe parties. Marrying men to inhabit their identities, Marilyn dreamed of a Kennedy for her fourth husband. In Summers's story, Bobby arrived at Marilyn's house on the day she died to break off the relation that had become an embarrassment. Whatever happened in the interim, the Kennedys' brother-in-law, Peter Lawford, helped destroy compromising evidence before the arrival of Marilyn's psychiatrist, Dr. Greenson, and the Los Angeles police.

The titillating triangles—Marilyn, Dr. Greenson, and Eunice Murray (the housekeeper Dr. Greenson had planted in Marilyn's home); Marilyn, Frank Sinatra and Jimmy Hoffa; Marilyn and Jack and Bobby Kennedy—would ensure the popularity of Summers's biography among the forty or so books on Marilyn published before *Goddess*. His serious research justifies his sales numbers, not to mention the talk show appearances that followed. But like many an infatuated lover, Summers pursues his goddess into forbidden territory. As in numerous books on Marilyn, the illustrations in the biography follow its photogenic subject from Norma Jeane days into close-ups of the thirty-six-year-old, where the camera searches out signs of the Marilyn one-liner "Gravity catches up with all of us." Summers goes further than most by showing Marilyn's Brentwood home on the morning of August 5, 1962, abandoned toy tiger on the lawn and all. He also treats us to a close-up of the bottle of chloral hydrate that presumably helped kill the addicted star. We get to see her nightstand, littered with pill bottles and documents overflowing to the floor, proof that the neat little housewife Jim Dougherty knew was forever gone.

On the following page, Summers invites the reader-as-voyeur to contemplate a photo of Marilyn's remains after the autopsy. The caption states that the sagging of Marilyn's face this time does not originate in gravity, but in the coroner's scalpel. Also Summers's own pen cuts deeply into dead Marilyn:

> When Marilyn was wheeled away, the beauty was gone. A picture retrieved from police files—the only known surviving postmortem photograph—shows a sagging, bloated face, hair hanging limp and straight over the edge of the table. The facial muscles had been severed during the removal of the brain, and the remains sluiced with water once the doctor's work was done.[47]

Graham McCann writes about Summers's "*violent*" photo that "the corpse fills the space where Monroe no longer is" and thus "discourages us from fully appreciating her absence."[48] Obviously, Marilyn-as-Monster has returned to haunt the biographer, who takes up his pen in self-defense.

Like Mailer, Summers might kill off Marilyn so as to assert masculinity. He hears, after all, Marilyn's mocking, "too-long" laughter down the decades into his own "Age of Anxiety," when his new wife's family suspects "there was no life outside the subject of Marilyn Monroe."[49] Maybe he wished to rescue Marilyn from the fame she resented by restoring to her the mortality a fall from stardom would bring. After all, he ends his biography with a telegram from Marilyn to Bobby Kennedy, in which she counts herself among the "earthbound" stars, who demand only their "right to twinkle."[50] Or maybe Summers simply chose to chase his goddess like the paparazzi who ensured that the luminescence and vulnerability of Britain's Queen of Hearts would live forever, candle in the wind fashion.

Gloria Steinem, a well-known feminist and founding editor of *Ms. Magazine*, tried with her *Marilyn Monroe/Norma Jeane* (1986) to save the star from male biographers and rewrite Marilyn's story as herstory. She notes that most of the eulogies following Marilyn's death had male authors, as do, by her count, most of the forty monographs on Marilyn published before her own. Steinem believes editors' biases had played a role, since "they seemed to assume that only male journalists should write about a sex goddess."[51] Besides, before second-wave feminism, women worried about "being trivialized by association."[52] Were they to publicize their fascination with Marilyn, they were compelled into "admitting an identity with a woman who always had been a little embarrassing, and who had now turned out to be doomed as well."[53] Nonetheless, Steinem argues that for men and women both, "the ghost of Marilyn came to embody a particularly powerful form of hope: the rescue fantasy."[54] People simply wanted to rewrite the tragedy of Marilyn's life and death, with themselves cast as the savior. For Steinem to go public with her own rescue fantasy became a way to show that we've come a long way, baby.

This road began in 1953, when Steinem left the movie theater showing *Gentlemen Prefer Blondes*, "in embarassment," she recalls, "at seeing this whispering, simpering, big-breasted child-woman who was simply hoping her way into total vulnerability."[55] Steinem's rescue project sends her looking for the "real" Marilyn, the one behind the platinum hair, the wiggly walk, and the hourglass figure. Steinem's double title suggests that she peels off Marilyn Monroe and uncovers Norma Jeane Baker, misrepresented by male writers. Steinem returns, for example, to the rape of the eight-year-old Norma Jeane that most biographers have questioned. Biographer Fred Guiles bases his scepticism on the absence of male boarders in Norma Jeane's foster families, but Steinem spots the British actor who rented most of the little white house that Marilyn's mother could not afford alone. Steinem also reconciles the contradictory stories that earned Marilyn a reputation for being nonchalant with truth by stressing the emotional consistency of Marilyn's memories.[56] Steinem concludes that underneath the glamorous exterior hides somebody else. This other woman "hadn't liked It all along . . . . her apparent suicide stood at once as accusation and answer: no, Marilyn Monroe, the ideal sexual female, had not liked it."[57]

Though Steinem can no longer rescue Marilyn, she can take her place. Gloria's embarassed response to the actress in *Gentlemen Prefer Blondes* leaves a residue of bonding: "How dare she be just as vulnerable and unconfident as I felt?"[58] With her writing project, Steinem takes the position Marilyn had wanted. After she was fired from *Something's Got to Give*, Marilyn collaborated with photographer George Barris on an illustrated biography intended to "set the record straight."[59] Her death ended this ambition. Twenty-five years later, Barris was finally ready to publish his photos, and Dick Seaver of Henry Holt and Company began to look for a writer who would "help explain Marilyn as an individual and as an icon of continuing power."[60] Steinem volunteered to set the record straight, just as Marilyn had hoped to do.

Steinem shared with Barris "an empathy for [their] subject,"[61] but her own agenda propels Marilyn onto feminist terrain, since she uses Marilyn and her life to exemplify a more general suppression of women. When she gets to the sexual assault on young Norma Jeane, Steinem mentions that one in six women has been sexually abused in childhood. "Most were made to feel guilty and alone," she writes, "and many were as disbelieved by the grown-ups around them as Marilyn had been."[62] She explains to her readers that "as with most women, the decision to have or not have children was the major undercurrent of [Marilyn's] life." She brings up her "classic conflict" between a career and Joe DiMaggio's wishes.[63] Steinem finds that

Marilyn's search for love "was rewarded and exaggerated by a society that encourages women to get their identity from men—and encourages men to value women for appearance, not mind or heart."[64] In short, Steinem markets her convictions through Marilyn, whose body engenders a feminist text.

Steinem's feminism creates a niche among the host of biographers attracted to Marilyn, including Fred Guiles and Anthony Summers, whose biographies had come out within two years prior to the Steinem/Barris publication. Her feminist angle explains the gender-segregation of certain chapters—the short "Among Women" and the longer "Fathers and Lovers." In Steinem's text Marilyn's white poodle "Maf" arrives as a gift from a woman friend, whereas other biographers credit Frank Sinatra with the present and the name Marilyn gave it as a joke on Sinatra's Mafia connections. Steinem sees Marilyn's marriages through a feminist prism. DiMaggio tries to possess her—before, during and after the marriage—and Miller fares only slightly better: "In a world that equates womanliness with dependency on a man, he might be forgiven for finding Marilyn's extreme dependency extremely appealing—but now he was paying the price."[65] Her male psychiatrists, Steinem writes, "gave her a dangerous permission to remain dependent," failing as they did to "challenge Freudian assumptions of female passivity, penis envy, and the like."[66] Instead of a passive Marilyn, Steinem has her actively engage in contemporary politics, for example by reprinting in full a letter from Marilyn to Lester Markel, the Sunday editor of the *New York Times*. In this communication, which demonstrates to Steinem that "her political instincts were interesting," Marilyn speculates on presidential candidates and ends up preferring Justice William Douglas for President, with John F. Kennedy as Vice-President. With this constellation, Catholic voters would come around to Douglas, despite his divorce(s).[67]

Steinem seeks to liberate Marilyn from her "Body Prison," another chapter title, by casting her in the asexual roles of mother and child. Two pages into the text, she reminds us that "almost everyone who saw Marilyn anywhere near children has remarked on the direct, emotional connection she had with them."[68] She tells us of Marilyn's close ties to DiMaggio's son and Miller's children and stresses that she kept photos of all three stepchildren in her bedroom. Outside of dependency sections, Steinem highlights Marilyn's childlike behavior, though the feminist author follows the child around: "(Can we imagine a male movie star being praised for acting helpless, looking for motherly sex partners, and singing sensuously, 'My Heart Belongs to Mummy'?) Because she was a woman Marilyn was encouraged to remain a child."[69]

Steinem's hostility to Norman Mailer originates in gender politics, but she also uses the figure of Marilyn to vent a private resentment of his work and his person. She comments angrily and repeatedly on Mailer's obsession "with this long-dead sex goddess" and seeks to rescue Marilyn from "the sugary blonde Norman Mailer desired."[70] She points to Mailer's blind spots with undisguised relish. Discussing Marilyn's refusal to marry the dying Johnny Hyde, who could have made her a woman of independent means, Steinem notes that "Mailer treats her refusal as inexplicable. In fact, he missed the romanticism that governed her behavior and was the legacy of her Depression childhood."[71] Steinem informs us that she herself met Marilyn at the Actors Studio, whereas Mailer never got to see his sex queen, though he pushed his friend Norman Rosten for an introduction. "Though Mailer quotes from Rosten's slender book," Steinem writes, "he omits the account of his own rejection."[72] Though her vendettas against sexism and Mailerism overlap, Steinem vents her feminism through Marilyn. She promotes Marilyn not least to promote *Ms. Magazine*:

> If you also would like to contribute to the Ms. Foundation for Women, a tax deductible public charity, and earmark your contribution for the Marilyn Monroe Children's Fund, write: Ms. Foundation for Women, 370 Lexington Avenue, New York, New York 10017. Together, we can help Marilyn to help other children in the future.[73]

S. Paige Baty has also been haunted by Marilyn, her marketing potential, and the voices that insist on repeating her story. Baty writes about inhabiting a "Marilyn country," a metaphorical or actual plague-ridden city in which otherness and insanity reign.[74] She follows an American tradition from Frank Norris and John Dos

Passos in representing Hollywood as an infected site and seeks out Marilyn amidst underworld rubble. She finds an unholy hybrid of academia and mass culture, fact and fiction, as well as history and fantasy.

Like Steinem, Baty wishes to rescue Marilyn from all the male writers constructing her as erotic object. She dismisses the Danish Hans Jørgen Lembourn's *Diary of a Lover of Marilyn Monroe* (1979) as pure fabrication. Lembourn and Mailer portray Marilyn "as the object of the author's desire and the subject representative of American sexuality." These writers do not, in Baty's view, invite their readers to "enter Marilyn's textual body via a critique of pornographic scripting, but rather as the site of a shared or mass-mediated desire."[75] A decade after Steinem, Baty engages in a new version of the rescue fantasy, though the feminism of the 1970s and 1980s in Baty's text has turned into feminist postmodernism.

Steinem tried to rescue Marilyn by taking seriously her efforts to improve herself through books, but Baty elevates Marilyn much in the way a British university professor some years ago discussed "Academic Elvis" at a University of Warwick conference. He lectured on Elvis in a fairly impenetrable academic discourse, while two women in the audience from Nashville kept stressing that Elvis had been real nice to his mom, bought her a fancy car and everything. Baty, in turn, chooses chapter headings in Latin: "*In Medias Res,*" "*Ecce Signum,*" "*Vita Feminae,*" "*Amor Fatality,*" and "*Corpus Mysticum.*" She lends to the study of Marilyn a highly serious aura, though her titles suggest a Catholic devotion, or idolatry. They evoke the anecdote of Sir Laurence Olivier, who directed and co-starred with Marilyn in *The Prince and the Showgirl* (1957). During a taxicab ride, he heard Paula Strasberg, Marilyn's acting coach, flatter her blond employer *ad nauseam*: "You are the greatest woman of your time, the greatest human being of your time, you name it. You can't think of anybody, I mean—no, not even Jesus—except you're more popular."[76] Anecdotes aside, Baty's Latin restores to Marilyn intellectual dignity, as do the numerous, lengthy notes and the academic, poststructuralist diction of *American Monroe*. A random page in "*Amor Fatality*" thus lets us know that "Whereas the iconographic mode of remembering manifests a fluency through specific, often super- or ahistorical units operative outside of any particular structure, the cartographic mode underlines the importance of structure as content itself."[77]

Also the angle of *American Monroe* rescues the actress from her image of dumb blonde. Baty does not view Marilyn as a sexual icon but focuses on her primarily because she constitutes a site on which American political culture is written and exchanged. By linking Marilyn with knowledge and power, she propels the star from rumors of Kennedy indiscretions into respectable political and cultural terrain. She further deemphasizes sexuality by discussing Marilyn as a "representative character." Both Marilyn herself and Frederick Douglass a century earlier are symbols that "exist at the intersection of cultural production and consumption, circulating in specific times and places where they are made to mediate values to a given community."[78] By using passive voice, however, Baty retains a whiff of victim status, as the slave and the sexpot become the objects of communal systems of signification. In her sentence, the two share the vulnerability that made Marilyn Monroe.

Baty uses a number of authorial voices in discussing "her" Marilyn. Having listened to "the chroniclers of mass-mediated immortality," she has produced "a schizophrenic text" that makes itself heard in the voices of its author.[79] By occupying shifting authorial positions, she inhabits, as have other writers, a space identical to Marilyn's own. Baty pluralizes Marilyn: Mailer's, Guiles's, Steinem's, Summers's, Baty's. Like Steinem, Baty moves into Marilyn's territory—literally, by relocating to the outskirts of Los Angeles, and symboli cally by placing "her" Marilyn in the grey zone between academia and pop culture. Or has Marilyn swallowed Baty's life? Is "Marilyn" Mailer's monster or his mouse?

Baty's Marilyn becomes, like her author, a postmodern heroine, who thrives on hybridity. In *American Monroe* she combines high and low culture, presence and loss, indeterminable identities, and infinite positions on the time-space continuum. She has moved out of the 1950s and into simulacrum. As Baty stresses Marilyn's commodification, the "real" Marilyn vanishes, and a postmodern product materializes. She becomes in Baty's text representation itself, a story available for endless circulation and consumption. Baty's monograph carves still another niche in the Marilyn marketplace:

the academic superstore, where Arthur Miller found himself a shelf, but Joe DiMaggio did not.

DiMaggio and Marilyn

In the spring of 1952, Marilyn posed with Gus Zernial of the Philadelphia A's for a Twentieth Century Fox publicity shot. In the studio-approved photograph fed to all the Los Angeles newspapers, Zernial showed her how to hold the bat with his arms encircling her. In town for a charity game against the A's, Joe DiMaggio saw Marilyn dressed for her baseball lesson in a halter top, tight white shorts and seven-inch heels and felt sufficiently envious of Zernial to have a friend arrange a meeting with her. Soon afterwards, Marilyn walked into the Villa Nova, a restaurant on Sunset Boulevard, to have dinner with a man she did not know. She was two hours late and not too eager to meet the sports star waiting for her. "I don't like men in loud clothes, with checked suits, and big muscles and pink ties. I get nervous," she had told her business manager, David March, who set up the blind date. But inside the dark restaurant, she found a gentleman dressed in a gray suit that matched a touch of gray in his hair. She noticed the blue polka dots on his silk tie, one exactly in the middle of his tie knot. DiMaggio had stood up when she arrived, but remained silent and distant during the dinner. "I could see right away," Marilyn reports in *My Story*, "he was not a man to waste words. Acting mysterious and far away while in company was my own sort of specialty. I didn't see how it was going to work on somebody who was busy being mysterious and far away himself."[80] She was not sure who the baseball superstar was until Mickey Rooney, a big Hollywood name, asked for DiMaggio's autograph and eagerly drew up a chair, but her words suggest that she had much in common with her date. Like Marilyn, DiMaggio knew about dreams, about fame, and about self-promotion. He would expect Marilyn to play his game, however, and would end up losing his magic—and her. DiMaggio's Marilyn could not and would not be Mr. America's wife and ultimately left the field. Her countrymen booed or cheered, but they followed her into new risks and new tragedies. DiMaggio represented American heroism, *machismo*, and Old World ethnicity, but Marilyn opened up American futures.

As the greatest baseball player since Babe Ruth, or ever, DiMaggio embodied all-American manliness. Alone in the field with thousands of eyes following his every move, he would perform with stoic calm, interrupted only twice in his career with recognizable emotion. When he played for the San Francisco Seals, he was Dead Pan in the press box, and sixty years later, another Seals player would remember both his stillness and his elegance: "Then, the guy was a *statue*."[81] His 1941 hitting streak in fifty-six consecutive games made baseball legend. Richard Ben Cramer writes in *Joe DiMaggio: The Hero's Life* (2000): "DiMaggio was assumed to have complete and otherworldly mastery over his bat and balance, his swing mechanics, his thoughts and emotions, and of course, the strike zone." Briefly put, "in the Baseball Nation, there was everyone else, and there was DiMaggio."[82] Outside the diamond, he was beautifully dressed and groomed: expensively tailored dark suits, silk ties, gold cufflinks, manicured nails, every hair in place. He made the list of Ten Best Dressed Men in America and an artists' list of Ten Most Interesting Faces. Norman Rosten, Arthur Miller's friend, found that "Joe DiMaggio did not have a movie smile but a decency showed in his face." Rosten goes on to list DiMaggio's strengths: "He was a famous baseball player, a great American athlete, serious, dedicated, well-mannered, light years away from the showbiz sleaze."[83] Closer to the sleaze perhaps, Marilyn found his body, and his bedroom performances, perfect. In "The Silent Season of a Hero" (1966), a famously critical portrait of DiMaggio, Gay Talese describes an older DiMaggio, elegant as ever:

> At 51, DiMaggio was a most distinguished-looking man, aging as gracefully as he had played on the ball field, impeccable in his tailoring, his nails manicured, his 6-foot-2 body seeming as lean and capable as when he posed for the portrait that hangs in the restaurant and shows him in the Yankee Stadium, swinging from the heels at a pitch thrown 20 years ago.[84]

Not surprisingly, the hero label recurs in DiMaggio biographies and baseball records. He was an old-fashioned American hero living an American Dream, or so the story went. He had literally risen from newsboy to national baseball star in a New York second, and he had exuded an "All-Time Greathood" from the outset.[85] He was fiercely competitive, American hero fashion, as Cramer spells out in his biography: "His ambition couldn't be described with a line of numbers in a record book. He wanted to be, in any year, any town, on any day, any field—in every game, on every play, no matter who else was there—the best player in the park."[86] Joe DiMaggio had stamina and would play hung-over, injured, or sick. Even as an old man, he would get out of bed, cough up blood from his unmentionable cancer, and get into a taxi, a limousine, or a plane for the day's assignment. Cramer concludes: "That was want. That was DiMaggio. If you lost track of that hunger, that toughness, you lost his core."[87] Throughout his celebrity life, DiMaggio was living proof that the American Dream might come true. Especially during the Depression and WWII, he gave hope to millions of Americans. In the verse novel *Becoming Joe DiMaggio* (2002), Maria Testa tells the story of her father, Joseph Paul, who was born, we learn in "Dreams 1936," when "the Yankees had/a new center fielder/whose name sounded like music." Because of Joe DiMaggio, "For the first time/in a long time/Papa-Angelo had dreams/to go with his nightmares."[88] Glued to the radio, his grandson Joseph Paul learns the rules of baseball in Papa-Angelo's lap as the two listen to the magic sound of Joe DiMaggio hitting. In "The Streak," Testa writes of "the perfect number," 56: "Hits were the same as/hope/that summer."[89] Finally, in "Dreams 1951," Joseph Paul decides to become a doctor. "*It is still a wonderful thing/to dream of being/Joe DiMaggio*," he thinks, as he reaches out to touch his grandfather's cheek. "Papa mio," he said, "you are the one/who showed me how/to pick up his glove."[90] Melodrama aside, DiMaggio was not only Sports; he was, like Marilyn, the Promised Land.

He was also a Yankee. Money was important to DiMaggio, from his unsuccessful holdout in 1938 for a $40,000 contract, which ended with Yankee negotiators Jacob Ruppert and Ed Barrow signing him on for $25,000, to his final refusal to autograph for fans without his $6.00 fee. Ben Cramer refutes in the prologue of *The Hero's Life* the myth of the baseball rings stolen from DiMaggio's Hotel Lexington suite in the 1960s: "More likely he traded them for free lodging, food, transportation, services of every kind." His last public appearance on September 27, 1998, was not about rings, about history, about winning, or about a monument to Mickey Mantle. "That whole Joe DiMaggio Day," Cramer believes, was about "money, mostly money, as it mostly was with Joe."[91] As Marilyn noticed in 1952 inside the Villa Nova, Joe DiMaggio looked like a businessman, and he acted like one.

On the last day of his career, DiMaggio walked off the field alone, as he had done from day one. Alone with his challenges and failures, he was the Lone Ranger, but also a Hemingway hero of sorts. The Hemingway connection surfaces in the insistence on taciturn masculinity, and in the drinking and sportsmanship the two American champions shared. They both frequented Toot's Shor, DiMaggio's favorite bar, and they went to a boxing fight together, where fans crowded in on DiMaggio, and Hemingway for once took a back seat: "Yeah, I'm his doctor."[92] Hemingway wrote DiMaggio into *The Old Man and the Sea* (1952), and Cramer describes young DiMaggio with the Seals as a Hemingway hero: "He went at his outfield job like a Sicilian fisherman—alone out there in the weather, talking to no one, vaguely suspicious, treating anything that came his way as a threat."[93] Written in a prose indebted to Hemingway, Gay Talese's "Silent Hero" portrays a man's man, not given to female company except an occasional couple of "broads."[94] Those dining with DiMaggio at Reno's bar in San Francisco had learned "that he generally prefers male companions and occasionally one or two young women, but never wives; wives gossip, wives complain, wives are trouble, and men wishing to remain close to DiMaggio must keep their wives at home."[95] Though DiMaggio may have outdone Hemingway here, he too shows traces of what Hemingway critics call *el Nuevo Hemingway*, a figure immersed in gender experimentations and ambiguities, as in the posthumous *The Garden of Eden* (1986). After his break-up with Marilyn, DiMaggio retreated to a feminine space. He visited Isola delle Femmine or the Island of Women, off the main coast of Sicily, where fishermen's wives had lived while their husbands took off to sea. Biographers agree that the post-divorce relationship of Joe and Marilyn became supportive and asexual, though the idea of DiMaggio as a New Man seems as rocky as Isola delle Femmine itself. In *Of Women and Their Elegance*

(1980), Norman Mailer calls in Marilyn's voice her ex-husband "the greatest protector." "I would have been comfortable shaking hands with a tiger if Joe was around." "Of course," she continues, "after the tiger left, where did Joe and I go from there? It wasn't that he was humorless, he was Italian."[96] Like Hemingway, he was also accident-prone and frequently bed-ridden, but he did not believe in shrinks and depression, though he knew how to fire a gun.

Representations of DiMaggio as a gentleman, a hero and a businessman, as the epitome of Hemingwayesque masculinity, co-exist with portraits of him as dumb sportsman. Neil Norman and Jon Barraclough's play *Insignificance*, adapted to film in 1985 and released in book form in 1989, focuses on four "mythic" characters over a long night in New York City, 1953: McCarthy ("the Senator"), Albert Einstein ("the Professor"), and "the Actress" and "the Ballplayer," surely Marilyn and Joe. The Ballplayer is "a lamb in wolf's clothing, a sad and forlorn reminder of a glorious past."[97] He is also plain dumb, as in his first appearance outside Albert Einstein's hotel room, where his wife is hiding. Before they let him in, the Ballplayer thumps on Einstein's door and threatens to break in at the count of ten. The Actress moves to the door and yells: "You never counted past three in your life you dumb ox!" "Shit," the Ballplayer responds. The Actress: "One two three home; that's as far as you bothered to go."[98] Once inside the room, the Ballplayer disrupts a conversation about relativity theory, to the Actress's regret: "I suppose we could discuss something we all know about but that would limit us to the last nine world series and the names of the seven dwarves."[99] The Ballplayer prefers to talk about bubble-gum cards, especially those with his own picture on them. As Graham McCann writes in *Marilyn Monroe*, the Ballplayer is stupid enough to make "Monroe's love for DiMaggio seem altogether irrational and masochistic."[100]

Joyce Carol Oates takes up the dumb sportsman stereotype in *Blonde*. Like Joe DiMaggio, her Ex-Athlete lasts six months as Marilyn's husband, a few years as her stalker, and his and her lifetime as friend-protector and grieving ex-husband. But Oates casts America's famous baseball hero as a couch potato, an inarticulate hunk given to home-cooked Italian dishes, boys' nights out, sport on TV, and

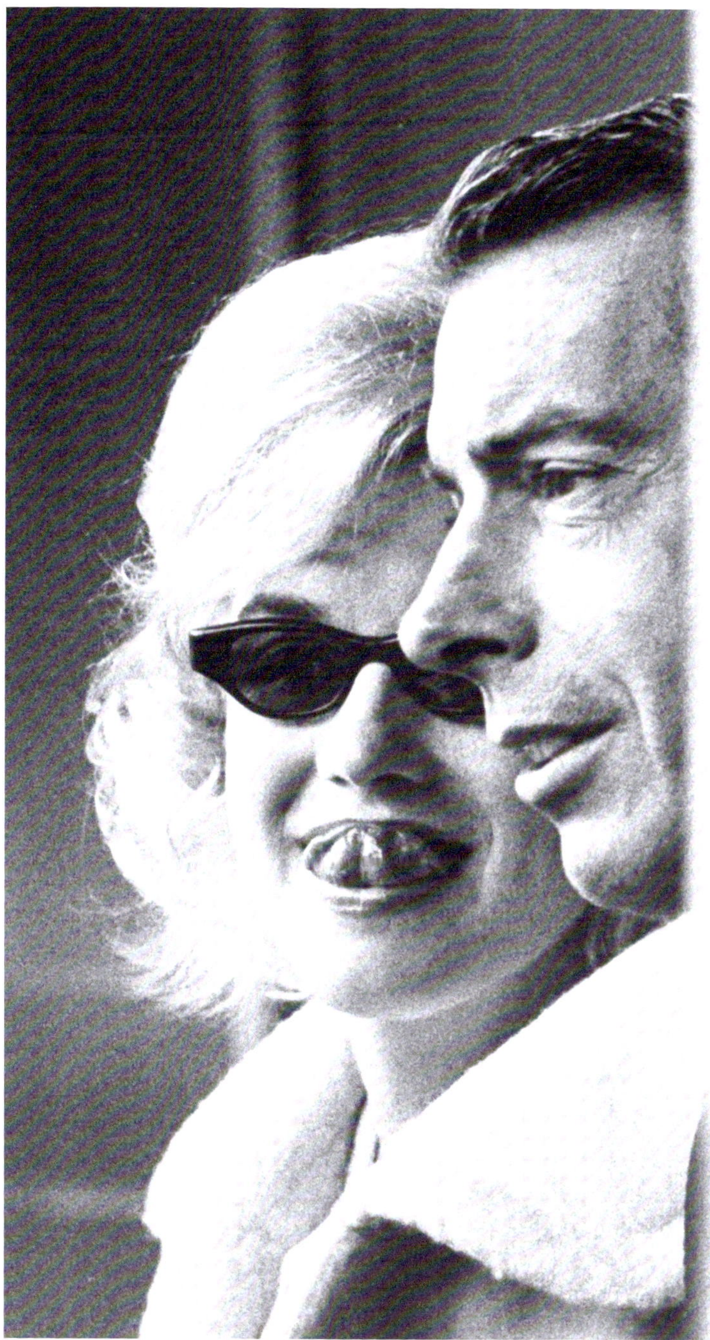

Disruptive Marilyn

wife-beating. After Marilyn's appearance in the white full-skirted dress on a Manhattan subway grating, the Ex-Athlete's practiced hands leap towards his wife at the Waldorf-Astoria: "*Whore! Are you proud? Showing your crotch like that, on the street! My wife!*—with the force of his final blow sending the Girl with No Name staggering against the silk-wallpapered wall, sweet as any home run."[101]

The relationship between Mr. and Mrs. America, as the press dubbed them, inspired hangers-on, fans, critics, and everybody else to choose side. Robert Kahn, the author of *Joe and Marilyn: A Memory of Love* (1986), sides with Joe. In a prose that matches Kahn's own, the front flap tells prospective readers about the importance of his work: "Roger Kahn describes the love, the joy, the heartbreak that was Joe and Marilyn, one of the great, poignant romances of this century." The flap continues: "Mr. Kahn gives us a DiMaggio who was almost as godlike as his legend on the diamond, but vulnerable and intensely human off the field." In contrast, Marilyn is sloppy, desperate and promiscuous. "She loved to wear tight, skimpy clothing," Kahn writes. "Married or single, she flirted with half the Western world."[102] Here and elsewhere, Kahn merges with DiMaggio in a shared condemnation of Marilyn's unabashed sexuality. When Kahn asks DiMaggio to talk about Marilyn for a short *McCall* article to be titled "This Was a Woman!" DiMaggio sends "a quick, courteous no" to the offer of $50,000. "Some things are not for sale," Kahn writes with admiration. "Like the memory of love."[103]

Mr. and Mrs. America did have a lot in common, including their physicality. DiMaggio's body is centerfield in most biographies, scrutinized, adored or lamented. In Cramer's work, we get to know everything about the young hero's arm strength and speed, his body a container for God-given gifts. Later on, DiMaggio's famous body battles against itself, as his heels turn sore, his shoulders ache, his ulcers act up, and his legs give in. His perfectly trained body simultaneously articulates and resists the ideal body image that also Marilyn projects. Even Talese's silent hero exudes strength or beauty, at least physically: "His gray hair was thinning at the crown, but just barely, and his face was lined in the right places, and his expression, once as sad and haunted as a matador's, was more in repose these days. . . ."[104] Marilyn, of course, would not reach this stage of middle-aged grace and distinction, but her conflicted physicality has become a cliché. She was the Body, after all, though it cost her considerable work and pain.

Joe and Marilyn displayed their bodies. They shared the knack for image control that helped them reach fame and hold on to it. Notoriously reticent, young DiMaggio posed for photographers peeling potatoes in his mother's kitchen—incidentally wearing dark pants, a well-ironed white shirt and a tasteful tie, only the missing jacket signifying relaxed domesticity. In another photo taken at home, he patiently shows his father a baseball glove and ball. Guiseppe DiMaggio looks at the glove across the chequered tablecloth that signals family intimacy and modest origins, though Joe's outfit, identical to the first, tells a competing story. Comparing him to Lou Gehrig, his Yankee predecessor, Cramer writes:

> The difference was that Joe was aware from the first moment, aware at every moment, of the hero game. He was alive to the power of the camera: he made himself available, he could smile, and he knew when to smile. With writers he was alert, as poised and pent as he was in center field. Positioning was the edge in both games.[105]

Talese freezes this performativity in "The Silent Season of a Hero." After his "lethal rejection" of the young journalist, DiMaggio sits down at a small table and displays himself in profile with studied composure: "He said nothing, just lit a cigarette and waited, legs crossed, his head held high and back so as to reveal the intricate construction of his nose, a fine sharp tip above the big nostrils and tiny bones built out from the bridge. . . ." Even Talese had to give it to Joe: "a great nose."[106] Like Marilyn, DiMaggio always felt watched, and like Marilyn, who could turn the star quality on and off, he never forgot the spectators' gaze. Helped by journalists guaranteed lifetime access, including Jimmy Cannon of the *New York Post*, DiMaggio had manipulated his public image to perfection. "The truth is," Marilyn writes in *My Story* about her husband, "we were very much alike. My publicity, like Joe's greatness, is something on the outside."[107] David Halberstam sums up:

> The essential portrait of DiMaggio which had emerged over the years was of someone as attractive and graceful off the field as he was on it. DiMaggio had rather skillfully contributed to this image—he was extremely forceful and icy in his control of his own image, as attentive and purposeful in controlling it as he was in excelling on the field, and he quickly and ruthlessly cut off any reporter who threatened to go beyond the accepted journalistic limits. Those limits were, of course, set by Joe DiMaggio.[108]

As she grew famous, Marilyn would approve or reject publicity shots, and as she grew troubled, her public and private performances would separate and clash. Also DiMaggio gave conflicting shows. Cramer notes that he wanted it both ways: "he wanted to be well known at what he was known for—and for the rest, he wouldn't be known at all."[109] Halberstam is more explicit: "the truth among those who knew him relatively well was somewhat different [from the "thoroughly likeable DiMaggio"]: he was said (privately by people who did not want to go on the record) to be an unusually self-absorbed man, suspicious, often hostile, and largely devoid of charm."[110] Halberstam's own prose reflects the secrecy surrounding DiMaggio, with its postponed information and quiet parenthesis. The famous baseball player knew how to perform, and knew about audiences. In the much-quoted conversation between Marilyn and Joe taking place upon her return from Korea and the adulation of thousands of American soldiers, Marilyn describes the crowds: "Joe, you never heard such cheering." DiMaggio responds: "Yes, I have."[111] Both Joe and Marilyn were performers, and both needed an audience. DiMaggio craved the refrain supplied by friends, acquaintances, and hangers-on: "*Joe, you look great.*"[112] The two stars shared their stardom, their mystique, and their awareness of cameras. Talese calls the older DiMaggio "a kind of male Garbo."[113]

The most famous scene in Joe and Marilyn's relationship became known as "the shot seen around the world." Marilyn was promoting *The Seven Year Itch* on the Lexington Avenue subway grating, with the hot air from below blowing up her skirt and revealing her legs, her underwear, maybe more. Did she change from see-through nylon to white cotton panties? Who asked her to? The story has been told and retold and taken various forms. The two men operating the wind and the subway sound machines have been photographed and interviewed, and the thousand men turning up for a sight they never forgot have told their stories. Friends and acquaintances of DiMaggio's have been hunted down. Marilyn enjoyed the attention and delivered a memorable performance—platinum hair bouncing, red lips laughing, skirt rising, head tilted backwards in orgasmic abandon. The male audience, the journalists, and the numerous camera men certainly enjoyed the show, which ended at 4:15 a.m., but DiMaggio hated what he saw. Walter Winchell, New York City's "best known insomniac and the nation's most famous columnist" knew Marilyn's husband on location would make a great story and fetched him from the St. Regis Hotel bar.[114] DiMaggio arrived to see camera lenses and lights aimed at his wife's crotch and hordes of men cheering whenever the wind from below sent her dress up over her ears. "What the hell is going on here," DiMaggio supposedly asked as he pushed his way through the crowds back to the bar. Director Billy Wilder would later remember "the look of death" on DiMaggio's face.[115]

His hostile reaction makes it to the *Insignificance* screenplay, which takes place on Manhattan, the night of the publicity shot. From his hotel window, Einstein watches the scene, which shifts to Lexington Avenue. The stage direction reads: "*The crowd still jostle for a better view. Standing back beyond the crowd is a tall, awkward man. His face is tight and angry as he watches the proceedings.*"[116] Soon, he is chasing the Actress's limousine. Unable to catch up with it, he sees her face "*small and frightened, like a rabbit's caught in headlights.*"[117] Later, the angry Ballplayer hammers on the door to the room where the Professor and the Actress are enjoying at least each other's conversation. The Actress threatens not to see him for a while if he keeps up his loud knocking on the door. "That's a very big joke," the Ballplayer responds. "I want to see my wife I just go to the movies. I want to see your underwear, I just walk down to the corner like all the other guys."[118] He admits to Einstein: "I could kill a man, you know? If she ever got it down to one."[119]

As in *Insignificance*, DiMaggio and Marilyn fight about space. Jealous, possessive and private, DiMaggio's behaviour relates to what performance scholars call "geopathology," the study of abnormal or diseased approaches to topography, climate, clothing, food habits, etc. He saw Marilyn's body as a domestic space, intended for private consumption and pleasures. On the couple's wedding day, January 14, 1954, Marilyn wore a dark blue suit with a white fur collar as a guarantee that absolutely no part of her famous body would show.[120] This wedding outfit gestures towards DiMaggio, who also took an interest in the clothing habits of his first wife, the showgirl Dorothy Arnold. Cramer records a 1942 quarrel between the two about a new bathing suit that Dorothy wore for a beach picnic with Lefty O'Doul, DiMaggio's friend and fellow ballplayer, and his wife June. Seeing this two-piece swimsuit, DiMaggio told his wife to put her blouse back on, or else: "No wife of mine is going to wear that in public." Despite the protests of Dorothy, Lefty, and June, he got the keys from Lefty, slammed the car door, and drove away, leaving the rest of the party to hitch a ride.[121] DiMaggio's choice of words reveals that something private has been made public, a key issue in performance studies, and in Marilyn's relationship with him.[122] They had a number of issues to "work out," she admits in *My Story*, her predilection for low necklines among them. "I wear no more low-cut dresses," she writes. "Instead they have a sort of collar. The neckline is an inch under my chin."[123] Though Marilyn Monroe is a frame or a body intended for visual consumption, DiMaggio sees her as generating trouble by exposing what ought to stay hidden. His wife is thus a disruptive force sabotaging his own performance of reserve and discretion.

DiMaggio's Marilyn belongs at home, in the domestic sphere. She cooked a bit in the San Francisco home and may have produced a dish or two of spaghetti and meatballs, though she irritated DiMaggio's competent sister Marie, who knew how to run a house and cook her brother's favorite meals. But Marilyn violates this domestic space by turning her labor into performance—for Joe, for his family, for the world to enjoy. Besides, she quickly tired of her role as cook and caretaker. Marilyn's notorious messes—in her car, in her bedroom, in their apartment—taxed DiMaggio, whose identity and masculinity revolved around control.[124] Her habits presumably inspired the violence most studies of the Marilyn/DiMaggio relationship mention. Marilyn was hard, if not impossible, to domesticate, though DiMaggio temporarily won the neckline argument.

He was left with his hatred of the movie industry, the Hollywood crowd, his wife's career, and her outrageous public performances. "Publicity was one of the problems in our courtship," she writes in *My Story*. She has to be "careful in writing about my husband," she knows, "because he winces easily." What seems normal to Marilyn is annoying to Joe, who is "against doing anything to encourage or attract publicity."[125]

Marilyn's famous body became a battlefield, with Joe eternally trying to gain access and control. He turned up in Canada with his buddy George Solotaire for the shooting of *Niagara* to watch his wife wriggling "her red-clad bottom in a skin-tight dress." Fred Guiles admits in his sober biography *Legend: The Life and Death of Marilyn Monroe* (1984) that "DiMaggio had begun to take a proprietory interest in Marilyn's fabulous breasts."[126] On her wedding day, Marilyn told reporters that she intended to remain in pictures. She also declared: "But I'm looking forward to being a housewife, too!"[127] Marilyn elasticizes public/private boundaries, and possibly those of dream/reality and truth/lie as well. She was "a whole host of contradictions," Guiles explains. "There was no way you could plan a life with her, since she might very well suggest that she was considering doing one thing and actually doing exactly the opposite."[128] Guiles seems to take on DiMaggio's exasperation here, though Marilyn consisted of "eighty per cent publicity."[129] But DiMaggio saw his wife differently. Her body was a domestic sphere, which he inhabited and patrolled. He hated Marilyn's male colleagues and directors; he hated her acting coach, Natashia Lytess, and he overlooked how seriously Marilyn worked on her movie star career. "He was soon to discover," Guiles writes in *Legend*, "that it came before everything else."[130]

In *Marilyn among Friends*, Sam Shaw and Norman Rosten agree that *The Seven Year Itch* "spelt doom for the Marilyn/Joe relationship," a word choice that suggests the apocalyptic or tragic outcome of their love. In the introduction, Shaw and Rosten vacillate between approaching their topic as melodrama, or as a Greek or American tragedy.[131] Critics have overall preferred the tragic vision, in a Greek-American blend. Marilyn is cast as the tragic goddess who had it all and wanted more until her desires killed her. DiMaggio appears as a hero who simply "was Sport."[132] Both crave eternal glory and honor. A St. Louis catcher, Joe Garagiola, recalls DiMaggio's "godly goodness" and felt at the time that if in church, "they'd have said: '*Joe DiMaggio*,'" then "we'd have said, '*Pray for us!*'"[133] But *hubris* and fatal flaws lead to DiMaggio's tragedy—the need for perfection, his love for Marilyn, his possessiveness, or envy. Marilyn, of course, would stumble and fall. Both DiMaggio and Marilyn had so much, had gotten it all by themselves, and then lost their happiness, each other, and ultimately everything else.

"What went wrong so quickly?" asks biographers Roger Kahn, Ben Cramer, Fred Lawrence Guiles, and half the western world. A shopping list of reasons turns up in most biographical accounts. Kahn offers the standard response to the famous break-up after 286 days of marriage: "He was neat. She was sloppy. He was repressed. She was hyperactive. Each was wilful. Each had a temper. Each was a star. Stars in collusion." He continues: "He felt San Francisco was his home. She insisted on living in Los Angeles. He liked days on the golf course and evenings spent in jock chatter with friends. She wanted him constantly to generate excitement." Others add to the list infidelity and physical violence. Nobody mentions sex. "If marriage was only bed," Marilyn declared, "we could have made it."[134] The two fought, undoubtedly, about roles and casting. He needed to demonstrate control of his life off the field, but Marilyn refused to be a prop and rejected his script. Sidney Skolsky, gossip columnist and Marilyn's friend, responded with horror when DiMaggio asked him to explain the divorce, though the truth might be simple: "How could I tell him he'd bored her? How could I tell a man his ex-wife became ex because she found him dull?"[135] Like many other commentators, Skolsky sided with Marilyn. At a press conference at North Palm Drive on October 6, 1954, the day DiMaggio left permanently, a teary-eyed Marilyn delivered a performance that helped her case considerably, including the slight stumbling that caused the grieving star to lean on her attorney, Jerry Giesler.[136]

DiMaggio was celebrated by crowds of American fans throughout his career and beyond, but as the second husband of Marilyn Monroe, he was cast as the Italian villain. Contemporary newspaper accounts dealt enthusiastically with his sports talents and his subdued and modest public persona, but in the context of America's blond actress, he often came across as chauvinistic, selfish, and abusive. Many Marilyn biographers have been unkind to DiMaggio, as have acquaintances, observers and journalists. From the outset, he was Dago to fans and fellow players, and then there were those spaghetti publicity shots. In "The Silent Season of the Hero," Talese presents an Italian male surrounding himself with inferiors and given to expensive suits, violent outbursts, and futile leisure pursuits. The baseball hero attends for money an All-American country fair, where a middle-aged chorus girl looks for a quick flirt and a man with wine breath feels his arm. These guests at the barn banquet sense an exotic aura not exclusively related to DiMaggio's "immortal" fame.[137] Somehow, DiMaggio is Sicily, or Italy, while Marilyn is 80% publicity and 100% American. DiMaggio represents an unknowable Italian other, with Marilyn as his blond American victim. In short, the couple dramatizes tensions within American life and thought from the Cold War period to the new millennium. In Oates's *Blonde*, DiMaggio remains the masculine, inarticulate and chauvinistic Italian, whose ethnic codes prevent Marilyn from constructing herself as star and as Woman.

Marilyn and Joe never talked about each other, as if the past they shared never existed. Lauren Bacall remembers Marilyn going with Joe during work on *How to Marry a Millionaire* and acknowledges in her comment the emptiness they shared: "It seemed like the ideal marriage except that it wasn't."[138] In Cramer's book, the myth that was Joe DiMaggio shrinks to lies "growing cheap."[139] In other representations, the myth has turned into nostalgia for more innocent times, as in Paul Simon's 1967 hit song about Mrs. Robinson: "Where have you gone, Joe DiMaggio? A nation turns it lonely eyes on you."[140]

Ultimately, DiMaggio represents a European-American past defined through ethnicity and community, while Marilyn offers a sanitized version of American futures. DiMaggio exudes something has-been: ex-husband, ex-athlete. Biographers agree that off the field, he never achieved much beyond being Joe DiMaggio.[141] They also record his aging, his physical and moral decay. Talese portrays him as a figure of the past, though "he tries hard to remain as he was—he diets, he takes steambaths, he is careful; and flabby men in locker rooms of golf clubs sometimes steal peeks at him when he steps out of the shower. . . .” DiMaggio has a young man’s body, but “his face is dark and lined,” Talese notes, “parched by the sun of several seasons.”[142] On the first page of Cramer’s *The Hero’s Life*, DiMaggio appears as “a sad figure.” He has shrunk, obviously, “that bent old man who took off his rings behind home plate and tottered off the field.” But there is something else as well. There is no microphone that works: “Maybe the hero had nothing more to say.”[143] DiMaggio’s silence links up with his father’s, and with the secrets and silences of the Sicilian DiMaggio fishermen. His association with the past has a European flavor, which intensifies after the break-up with Marilyn. DiMaggio returned first to his family of siblings and cousins in San Francisco and later, he traveled in Italy. “He was as elegant (and bygone),” Cramer sums up, “as private railroad cars.”[144] In contrast, Marilyn returns to work in Hollywood by limousine, cheerful, on time, and ready for new takes of *The Seven Year Itch* and a new future. As always, she would shutter each section of her past and move on, with few carryovers in her luggage. “The friends she would know as Mrs. Joe DiMaggio,” writes biographer Fred Lawrence Guiles, “were nowhere visible when she became Mrs. Arthur Miller.”[145]

Miller and Marilyn

Arthur Miller has written up the Marilyn phenomenon with special authority. Four years into their marriage, Marilyn and Miller barely spoke to one another when shootings for *The Misfits* began in 1960, but Miller had intended his film script, based on an earlier short story, as a love gift for his wife. Roslyn, the female lead—cast with an aging Clark Cable as her romantic interest—represents Marilyn’s best qualities. Maggie, the blond singer intent on tormenting the Miller persona in *After the Fall* (1964), represents her worst.[146] The play cost Miller considerable goodwill after the opening a year or so after Marilyn’s death in August 1962. He portrays Maggie/Marilyn as a control monster, who forces Arthur’s *alter ego*, Quentin, to dispense her deadly drugs and thus become her murderer. Miller’s autobiography *Timebends: A Life* (1987) also portrays his famous second wife, though readers must work their way well into the six hundred pages plus to get a glimpse of the actress who turned his existence upside down.[147] Miller joined the horde of people wishing to rescue Marilyn and risked his life in the process, though he might indeed have loved her vulnerability. Writers such as S. Paige Baty and Joyce Carol Oates have also problematized Miller's Marilyn. Ultimately, Marilyn became for him a surface on which to write his own life story.

In *Timebends*, Miller ascribes his initial success with Marilyn to a "lifelong timidity," which set him apart from routine predators of the male persuasion, Norman Mailer among them.[148] Mailer, the novelist, and Miller, the playwright, lived for a while in the same neighborhood, and in *Timebends* Miller describes young Mailer's appetite for women and work. In Miller's recollection, Mailer stopped him on Pierpont Street in Brooklyn and boasted that he could easily write a play like *All My Sons*, an assertion that made Miller laugh. It also compelled him to let readers of *Timebends* know that over the years Mailer tried in vain to write a successful play and that he never got to meet Marilyn. In fact, she avoided the novelist and asked him over only once, hard pressed and knowing that he could not accept the invitation. As Eve Kosowsky Sedgwick argues about erotic triangles in *Between Men: English Literature and Male Homosocial Desire* (1985), Mailer and Miller competed, with Marilyn in the middle, her body the prize for Most Successful American Writer. To the surprise of Mailer and the rest of the world, it was the stern and married Miller who swept the blond actress off her feet. The drama supports Sedgwick's thesis that strong desires between the two men subordinate the woman in the erotic triangle. Miller won the competition and got the prize.[149]

Three hundred pages into *Timebends*, Miller describes his first meeting with Marilyn. In 1951 he had travelled to Hollywood with Elia Kazan to market the screenplay for *The Hook*, though his collaboration and friendship with Kazan would collapse with the McCarthy hearings that followed. Miller first describes what S. Paige Baty calls "Marilyn country"[150] as a sexual landscape, more specifically a woman's body:

> Hollywood for me will always evoke a contradictory mixture of certain scents. A sexual damp, I have called it, the moisture in the clean creases of a

> woman's flesh, combined with a challenging sea-salt smell; the exciting air surrounding a voyage on water and the dead ozone inside a sound stage; raw gasoline and lipstick perfume . . . . [151]

Even before Marilyn has entered the void that Miller associates with Hollywood, he confesses that "the boy within smelled sexuality."[152] The timid Miller learns fast to recognize the close connection between sex and power that enabled moguls like Twentieth Century Fox President Darryl Zanuck to reap their rewards, also from Marilyn. Sex in Hollywood links up with power and influence, as Miller finds out: "I had never before seen sex treated so casually as a reward of success; the immemorial right of the powerful to bed women of choice, a right claimed by men of the world, from Darryl Zanuck to Mao Zedong . . . ."[153] The actress who in *The Asphalt Jungle* (1950) had seemed to Miller "the quintessential dumb blonde on the arm of the worldly and corrupt representative of society" now catches his attention with her figure:

> In this roomful of actresses and wives of substantial men, all striving to dress and behave with an emphatically ladylike reserve, Marilyn Monroe seemed almost ludicrously provocative, a strange bird in the aviary, if only because her dress was so blatantly tight, declaring rather than insinuating that she had brought her body along and that it was the best one in the room.[154]

Miller focuses on Marilyn's difference, which he comes back to in a later passage, when they go to a bookstore together so that Marilyn may obtain a copy of *Death of a Salesman* (1949), Miller's most famous play. Marilyn comes across a collection of poetry by e. e. cummings, and Miller notices that she moves her lips when reading. He gets overwhelmed by her exotic presence in this setting of books and words: "I could not place her in any world I knew; like a cork bobbing on the ocean, she could have begun her voyage on the other side of the world or a hundred yards down the beach."[155] Miller writes Marilyn as a foreigner in his own intellectual world, the bookstore—the only site in Los Angeles where he has influence and thus, by Hollywood standards, sex appeal. The bookstore becomes a contact zone, where different cultures clash, as Marie

Louise Pratt theorizes in *Imperial Eyes: Travel Writing and Transculturation* (1992).[156] With his panoramic view of the scene, Miller functions as Pratt's "seeing-man," the colonial representative who controls and wins the cultural encounter. While Marilyn pores over cummings's poems, Miller surveys the store and spots a customer who begins masturbating at the sight of Marilyn, oblivious to anything but her book.

Like the anonymous customer overwhelmed by desire, Miller focuses in both instances on Marilyn's body. In the tradition of radical writers like young John Dos Passos, he associates lower-class background with erotic appeal. His comments about Marilyn and the body she brings to the Hollywood party echoes Mailer's division of her into mouse and monster. Distracted by the famous hourglass figure, both Mailer and Miller fail to see that Marilyn with her complexities and inconsistences forms an infuriating whole. Miller stops initially at her toe, which he fondled throughout their first evening together. His reticence won Marilyn's heart: "I could not yet imagine that in my very shyness she saw some safety, release from the detached and centerless and invaded life she had been given."[157] The passive voice he chooses for Marilyn ignores her agency and suggests that Steinem had a point on the vulnerability issue.[158]

Miller benefits from the evening. He carries back to Brooklyn "the certainty that I could, after all, lose myself in sensuality." Typical of Marilyn's men, he writes his story on her body, as when describing his own passion: "This novel secret entered me like a radiating force, and I welcomed it as a sort of proof that I would write again . . . ."[159] Marilyn-the-mouse scares him, however, and his plane ride back to New York City turns into a flight: "I had to escape her childish voracity, something like my own unruly appetite for self-gratification, which had both created what art I had managed to make and disgusted me with its stain of irresponsibility."[160] Marilyn's appeal and personality seem voracious, but she reflects simultaneously Miller's own uncontrollable appetites. In Marilyn's embrace, Miller finds himself, but distorted: a monster.

Miller represents Marilyn as other, both when she fails to fit in at Hollywood parties and when she struggles to read poetry. Marilyn too aligns herself with the unconscious: "Marilyn lived in the belief that she was precisely what had to be denied and covered up by the conventional world."[161] Meeting Marilyn initiates Miller's inner war between the conscious and the unconscious, between order and chaos, and between the past and the future. In articulating his dilemmas, he draws on images of war and disaster, which suggest that his world is turned upside down: "My world seemed to be colliding with itself, the past exploding under my feet."[162] Miller's tumultuous word choice expresses the power he associates with Marilyn: a kind of flood that swallows up his crisis and frees him from independent choice. Marilyn exists in a space outside Miller's regular rationality:

> I could not understand how she had come to symbolize a kind of authenticity; perhaps it was simply that when the sight of her made men disloyal and women angry with envy, the ordinary compromises of living seemed to trumpet their fraudulence and her very body was a white beam of truth. She knew she could roll into a party like a grenade and wreck complacent couples with a smile, and she enjoyed this power. . . .[163]

In "Woman Can Never Be Defined" (1974), Julia Kristeva situates the feminine in a negative space, which she associates with the repressed. Woman belongs outside conventional linguistic systems, "at odds with what already exists."[164] In Miller's text, Marilyn occupies this negativity, since she does not reside within the systems Miller identifies. She embodies to Miller a dream of authenticity, but her negativity constitutes an explosive force that may threaten or destroy those around her. "It was impossible to guess what she wanted for herself when she herself had no idea," Miller writes in *Timebends*. "At the same time the mystery put its own burden on us, the burden of the unknown."[165]

In 1956 Miller resided temporarily at Pyramid Lake, Nevada, in order to obtain a divorce from his first wife, Mary Slattery. He describes the break-up as "an optimistic reaching for authenticity, a rebellion against waste,"[166] qualities he had earlier associated with Marilyn's body. More alien forces hover in the new Marilyn landscape. Miller repeatedly mentions the displacement he would dramatize in *The Misfits*, and the unknown or the unconscious yawns

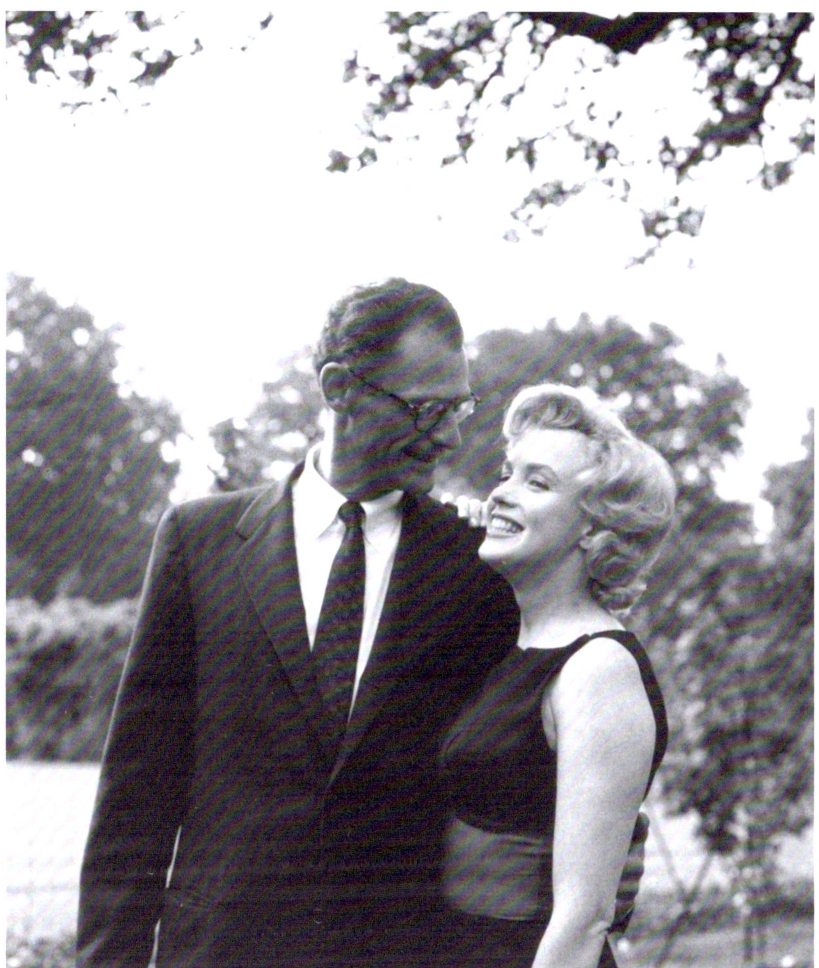

The Brain and the Body. Getty Images

ahead: "I had moved into the unknown, physically as well as spiritually, and the color of the unknown is darkness until it opens into the light."[167] Miller paid "the necessary price for what might truly be waiting just ahead, a creative life with undivided soul," and married Marilyn on July 1, 1956. Marilyn embodies his longing for unity, but, as his next sentence makes clear, his desire aims at his writing activities: "For the first time in months or maybe years, a fierce condensing power of mind moved in me, the signal to write . . . ."[168]

Like the men in *The Misfits*, who want Roslyn, the Marilyn character, to make them whole, Miller seeks to overcome his own divisions through his new bride: "To be one thing, sexuality and mind, appetite and justice, one."[169] In 1987 with *Timebends*, Miller finally answers the question that everybody had asked in 1956: Why did Egghead want to marry Hourglass?[170]

In the script for *The Misfits*, Norman Rosten recognizes a pattern "of male dependence." The male characters in the movie all want something from Roslyn, but they do not realize that "her needs are more desperate than theirs."[171] In the first week of their marriage, Marilyn and Miller had traveled to Great Britain for the shooting of *The Prince and the Showgirl* (1957), with Sir Laurence Olivier and Marilyn in the title roles and Olivier as director. Marilyn found Olivier condescending and whirled Miller into power struggles involving Lee and Paula Strasberg, her drama coaches; Milton Greene, her partner in the newly-established Marilyn Monroe Productions; her psychologist, flown in from New York City; and, of course, Olivier himself. Miller realized that life with Marilyn would be turbulent indeed. She meant chaos, as Miller hints in *Timebends* when describing her shopping in London: "When she visited Marks and Spencer a few weeks after arriving, the entire store was vacated of customers and closed for fear of an uncontrollable stampede of people trying to get a look at her. She shattered a thousand years of British imperturbability."[172] Also Miller lost his balance. Norman Rosten, a close friend, writes that "Miller was plunged into a world of daily crises, unspoken antagonisms, endless decisions, and with these new tensions came the necessity of providing Marilyn with almost constant support. It was a difficult, perhaps impossible, role for him."[173]

Earthquakes, tornados, wars and floods sweep across the psychological landscape of Marilyn country. It is an infected area, where insanity reigns. Paula Strasberg, the drama coach who drove Olivier crazy, plays in *Timebends* the role of insane mother. With an inexplicable power over Marilyn, she replaces the psychological space usually inhabited by Gladys Mortensen, who tried to kill Norma Jeane, her daughter, and since then had lived inside mental institutions in California. In Miller's analysis, Paula Strasberg completed the vicious circle and created a suffocating situation that allowed what Miller calls "the real, murderously deranged mother" to influence Marilyn's mind at a distance of ten thousand miles.[174] Marilyn country, in short, means the inner morass that, fame and power notwithstanding, threatened to overcome Marilyn and Miller. He writes that "the swamp of doubt within her showed no sign of drying up."[175]

The flowers of sickness grow luxuriously in the lives of the lovers who have both risked everything to face not the ideal, but each other. These "strange blossoms" with "ancient roots" spring from the roles the two have written for each other.[176] Miller plays the savior who cannot save, and Marilyn, the soft, sensuous muse demanding monstrous texts. Miller explains: "In the void that had opened up between these dreams and reality worked the immemorial worms of guilt."[177] To please his wife, he started working on the script for *The Misfits*, within a genre he detested. The film version of his original short story became the sacrifice he made to save his marriage. It focuses on a group of restless men, who must learn that butchering wild horses for canned food violates the sanctity of life. The Nevada desert, where men and horses roam, metaphorically represents the wasteland that Miller and Marilyn inhabit together. What David Miller in *Dark Eden: The Swamp in Nineteenth-Century American Literature* (1990) calls "desert" places reflects the inner swamp that Miller must escape on his own.[178] As Rosten writes in *Marilyn*, "*The Misfits* is the one work that may tell more about the Miller-Monroe story than most analytical conjectures."[179]

While Miller still lived his rescue fantasy, he tried to save Marilyn from Marilyn. Far from infectious Hollywood, she might pick flowers, save fishes, have babies, and move around the furniture in the rented cottage in Connecticut. Miller toys with the idea of an ordinary Marilyn, but he finds out that without Marilyn the star not much of Marilyn remains: "An ordinary person and hardly able to spell—what would she do with herself?"[180] Marilyn herself resorts to champagne and sleeping pills. Miller recognizes his own reflection in the "ordinary Marilyn" fantasy:

> The shocking egotism of my thought stared me in the face—her stardom was her triumph, nothing less; it was her life's achievement. How would I feel if the condition of my marriage was tractability, the surrendering of my

> art? The simple fact, terrible and lethal, was that no space whatever existed between herself and this star. *She was "Marilyn Monroe," and that was what was killing her*. And it could not be otherwise for her; she lived on film and with that glory forsworn would in some real sense vanish.[181]

Miller has realized in *Timebends* that only Marilyn can save Marilyn, who was already consuming daily doses of death. The savior is an accessory to murder. By repressing or ignoring her demonic past, he denies herself: without the monster, no Marilyn. As Miller concludes his reflections, "Innocence kills."[182] The statement refers both to Marilyn, who survives on an innocence she does not possess, and to Miller, who rescues and represses.

Miller's *After the Fall* dramatizes the roles the couple lived. It takes place in the mind of Quentin, the protagonist, in a tripartite brainscape, where memories and figures flare up and die away. Miller writes in the initial stage direction that he aims at "*the surging, flitting, instantaneousness of a mind questing over its own surfaces and into its depths.*"[183] The play represents Miller's first effort to settle the accounts of his second marriage, to dive into the unconscious and try to figure out what happened between Marilyn and himself. The Maggie character in *After the Fall* seems familiar indeed. Though she appears on stage in disguise, with wig and sunglasses similar to those Marilyn used to avoid her fans, Maggie's voice, tone, body, sexuality, childhood, exploitation, career, fame and demons match those of the blond actress, who in the play has become a singer. Also Marilyn's void looms ahead. Maggie often signs herself Sarah None, a name she can always recall.

In the last scenes of *After the Fall*, Maggie is desperately swallowing sleeping pills and forcing Quentin to hold the medicine glass and keep track of how many pills remain. By begging Nembutals of her husband, she makes him death's retainer. Quentin refuses to play the part she has written for him, and Maggie responds by swallowing another handful of pills. Towards the end of the play, we have reached the craters of Quentin's unconscious, where the war between the spouses threatens the life of both combatants. The Marilyn figure flirts with death, and also the rational Quentin has reached the abyss: "Maggie, I only tell it to you so you'll understand that the question is no longer whether you'll survive, but also whether I will. Because I'm backed up to the edge of the cliff, and I haven't one inch left behind me."[184] Quentin abandons the savior role, because he must save himself. To Maggie, he has become evil personified, the incarnation of betrayal, broken dreams, and revenge. Quentin backs off from this dance of death, though Maggie maintains that it "takes two to tango, kid."[185] He knows that his wife wants to die, but he also knows that he does not have the strength to stop her.

Quentin makes one last attempt to kill the innocence strangling them both. He tries to face the truth that his rescue mission is illusory and that the two have merely exploited each other. Also Maggie might live by not faking innocence:

> "You eat those pills like power, but only what you've done will save you. If you could only say, I have been cruel, this frightening room would open! If you could say, I have been kicked around, but I have been just as inexcusably vicious to others; I have called my husband idiot in public, I have been utterly selfish despite my generosity, I have been hurt by a long line of men but I have cooperated with my persecutors . . . ."[186]

Maggie responds to this truth with more pills. Quentin wants to stop her, but she resists. Suddenly the two are rolling around the floor in a struggle of life and death. Both are monsters now. Maggie's "*strength is wild and no longer her own, and, strangely, she is smiling, almost laughing.*"[187] She is a laughing Medusa, a murderous monster destroying men and unborn children. Also Quentin has changed. Not only does he squeeze Maggie's wrists; "*he lunges for her throat and lifts her up with his grip.*" His language echoes Maggie's: "Drop them, you bitch! You won't kill me." While Quention tries to strangle her, Maggie feels "*as though facing a wild, ravening beast.*"[188] In *The Misfits*, Marilyn delivers the line: "Husbands and wives are killing each other." Rosten hears it as "a line written by Miller and delivered by her with an intensity that vibrated throughout the film, as though a confessional understood by both."[189] In *After the Fall*, the two killers reflect one another, but the beauty they saw has turned into a monster.

Marilyn and Miller wrote each other into the story of life stories. Barbara Johnson argues in "My Monster/My Self" (1982) that the autobiographical impulse originates in the desire to (re-) create a being in one's own image. She calls this motivation "the desire for resemblance," in her view "the autobiographical desire par excellence."[190] The autobiographer might discover a monster in the process of writing life history, and, like Victor Frankenstein in Mary Shelley's novel, deny any resemblance to the creating self. More than loss of eyesight is at stake. As it covers his eyes, the monster in *Frankenstein* says to its creator: "*Thus I take from thee a sight which you abhor. . . . but my form is a filthy type of yours, more horrid even from the very resemblance.*"[191] Miller uses the same imagery of sight and blindness in his Marilyn portraits, and he too creates a monster or two. His Marilyn is a product of "filthy creation,"[192] and Miller must look at himself in the mirror with abhorrence.

Miller could not endure this sight. He is surprised that audiences and readers equate Maggie and Marilyn, since, according to Miller, *After the Fall* attempts to depict a world of ethical and political dilemmas. The play, he argues, thematizes "how we—nations and individuals—destroy ourselves by denying that this is precisely what we are doing."[193] Miller was working on *After the Fall* and realizing that Maggie would have to die as Marilyn was approaching her own end at Fifth Helena Drive in Brentwood. In his commentary, however, he moves the dramatic center from the private to the political battlefield, where monsters roam freely. Marilyn and Miller's life together nonetheless evokes Shelley's *Frankenstein*. As Johnson writes, "both characters reach an equal degree of alienation and self-torture and indeed become indistinguishable as they pursue each other across the frozen polar wastes."[194]

Though Miller fails to catch up with Marilyn and ultimately lost the desire to try, he gets a great deal of sympathy, if only because of writer-reader identification. In "Biographical Boundaries: Sociology and Marilyn Monroe" (1991), Graham McCann notes that Marilyn biographers, most of them men, tend to identify with Miller and move into the space he occupied in Marilyn's story.[195] After all, Miller shares their intellectual and writerly lives. Adam Kirsch finds that Chris Bigsby's definitive biography of Arthur Miller, published in 2009, makes the implicit statement that Miller's life ended when he was forty-seven years old and the remaining half of his life was a "superfluous coda."[196] Kirsch agrees uneasily that the playwright's marriage to Marilyn "broke the spring of his imagination," but not everyone agrees. One comment to Kirsch's review in *The New Republic* suggests that Marilyn did not ruin Miller's career but he ruined hers.

Joyce Carol Oates writes her fictional biography *Blonde* "as an epic, uniquely American."[197] The Miller character in *Blonde* hopes through his marriage to Marilyn to "*rewrite the story of both our lives. Not tragic but American epic!*"[198] Despite their common project, Oates exposes the Playwright when he undertakes third-degree interrogations of Marilyn about her activities with Lee Strasberg, her drama coach. In Oates's text, Miller becomes a generic husband, given to jealousy, vanity, stinginess and pride. Marilyn angers the Playwright, for example, by revising and complicating the one-dimensional Magda role she rehearses at Actors Studio. That the Playwright hopes to find his manhood through Marilyn suggests as well Oates's gender critique. His manhood had died in his first marriage because "that woman's aging raddled flesh" had repelled him. As he whirls himself into a skating ring and the Blond Actress's embrace, he believes that his manhood "would be resurrected now," though, as Oates makes clear, "this was a scene of a kind the Playwright himself could not have written for it lacked irony, subtlety."[199] Nonetheless, Oates's Miller is capable of self-scrutiny and emotional generosity, since Joe DiMaggio, Darryl Zanuck and JFK embody the male chauvinist of her feminist fairy tale. In 1956 Rosten had assigned to Miller the more difficult part: "It was a fairy tale come true. The Prince had appeared, the Princess was saved." Meanwhile, on the next page in Rosten's book, the princess feels her perfect body coming apart.[200]

A famous photograph of Marilyn and Miller is shot in a never-never-land of spring trees and cherry blossoms. The dignified Miller is smiling, so that the creases contributing to his intellectual sex appeal deepen. Marilyn exudes little-girl happiness with Daddy's protective arm around her waist, but she has expertly positioned her body in profile: the hourglass solicits attention. Together they have survived on book covers, in newspapers, in biographies, for more than five decades. Their fans and readers find themselves reflected in the ideal—the perfect brain and the perfect body—but recognize as well their monstrosity, their demons, and their transgressions. The playwright and the star appear in other stories of other lives. In the last pages of *Timebends*, the aging Miller is working at his Connecticut property, where he has lived with Inge Morath, his third wife, for four decades, surrounded by the coyotes outside his writing cottage: "I am a mystery to them until they tire of it and move on, but the truth, the first truth, probably, is that we are all connected, watching one another."[201] Though Miller's autobiography ends in the virgin landscape of an American dream, Marilyn's nightmare hovers between the lines. Maybe fans and readers circle them like coyotes, reflections of Miller inventing himself: "I am, I suppose, doing what they are doing, making myself possible and those who come after me."[202]

But Miller could not let Marilyn go. His play *Resurrection Blues*, which premiered in Minneapolis in 2002, gives up on reviving God and Messiah in their own country, but in 2003, he brought Marilyn back to life one last time.[203] His last play, "Finishing the Picture," focuses on Marilyn's medicine and alcohol addictions. Drunk and drugged, the Marilyn character, called Kitty, is lying in a hotel bed during shootings for *The Misfits*, while her friends and associates try to get her to work. They include a director resembling John Huston and acting teachers based on Lee and Paula Strasberg.[204] The center of attention remains off-stage, since the blond actress never herself appears in the play, but through her disturbing negativity, she destabilizes those who do. As in Peter Greenaway's film *The Pillow Book* (1997), Miller combines the roles of lover and calligrapher, writing his texts on Marilyn's (absent) body.

II Body

Marilyn's Bodies

In 1956, Norman Rosten wondered, along with everybody else, what exactly his friend Arthur Miller and Marilyn Monroe saw in one another. "Why did the Brain want to marry the Body? What did the sexy blonde want from the ascetic-looking writer?" he asks in *Marilyn: An Untold Story* (1973). His slim volume on the full-figured actress who had snatched up the married playwright records the author's fascination with Miller's bride.[205] Marilyn lives on as Body not only in Norman Rosten's and Norman Mailer's and all the other monographs on her life and death, and not only because of her famous curves. She began jogging in Los Angeles before anybody else and used as her bible Mabel Elsworth Todd's *The Thinking Body* (1937), an early fitness book that explored the impact of physiological and psychological processes on body movement.[206] Marilyn possessed the indescribable aura, "shine," or charisma Richard Dyer associates with movie stars, and she epitomizes the category of stars he identifies through physicality.[207] Unlike actors such as Al Pacino, William Hurt and Tom Hanks, who inspire discussions of "technique" and "seriousness," Marilyn belongs with hunks such as Sylvester Stallone and Arnold Schwarzenegger, who invite body-fixated representations, despite other talents and activities. According to Billy Wilder, who directed *The Seven Year Itch* (1955) and *Some Like It Hot* (1959), Marilyn has "flesh-impact."[208] Marilyn saw things differently: "People didn't take me seriously . . . or they only took my body seriously."[209] The actress inevitably means Body, and she continues to mystify those looking for her, perhaps because she vacillates between various bodies. Her first major movie, *Niagara* (1953) made, as Carl E. Rollyson, Jr., puts it in *Marilyn Monroe: A Life of the Actress* (1986), "her face, her figure, her voice, and the way she employed them, the subject of the screen." *Niagara* fore-

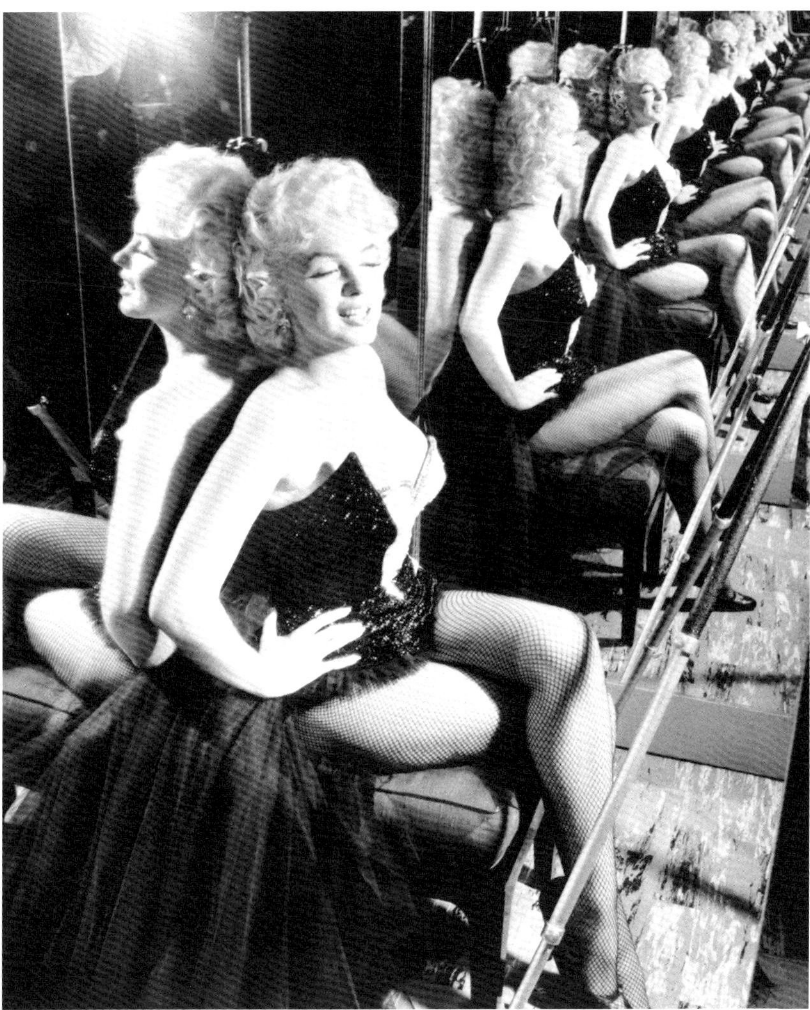

Marilyn's bodies

shadowed, in short, "the many 'Marilyns' to come."[210] The actress inhabits most of the body typologies that Arthur W. Frank identifies in "For a Sociology of the Body: An Analytical Review," his contribution to Mike Featherstone's *The Body: Social Process and Cultural Theory* (1991): the disciplined body, the mirroring body, the dominating body, and the communicative body.[211] Eternally elusive, Marilyn becomes both everybody and nobody.

Numerous academics have, like Miller, responded to Marilyn as Body. Anthony Summers got his share of respect and attention when he unveiled the mysteries surrounding Marilyn's marriages and especially her death, but he literally uncovers her body to the point of reproducing the photograph of dead Marilyn after the coroner has finished with his scalpel. Graham McCann writes in "Biographical Boundaries: Sociology and Marilyn Monroe," another essay in Featherstone's *The Body*, that "Summers cannot resist trying to 'find Marilyn'—even to the extent of entering the morgue. It is a particularly great misfortune that Summers should find it necessary for his narrative to include a photograph of Monroe's corpse."[212] McCann still finds Marilyn's physique intriguing. He begins his article with the response Marilyn gave to a reporter who had asked if her breasts had been enlarged: "Those who know me better, know better."[213] Himself the author of a monograph on Marilyn, McCann lingers in his article on the body of biography. He finds his Marilyn project a "risk-laden, complicated analysis" for an academic to undertake, apparently because of his colleagues, who embarrass him with a "sneaking feeling…that I must have a 'soft spot' for Monroe."[214] He proceeds with a series of body metaphors to get closer to Marilyn and the genre he investigates: "How can a biographer re-present and remember a person? *Is* there a body lurking beneath the text, between the lines, somewhere in the library? Is the only body present my own? Do biographers wear falsies?"[215] In drawing the contours of biography, McCann goes straight to curvaceous Marilyn and puts his own body next to hers. He writes in "The Body in the Library," a chapter in his Marilyn biography: "When I attempt to examine my interest in Marilyn Monroe (not selfishly but sincerely), I am necessarily involved in an effort to examine and defend my interest in my *own* experience, in my own body, in the moment and passages of my life I have spent with (and without) my subject."[216]

Everybody associates Marilyn with body, but nobody succeeds in holding on to her. Berniece Baker Miracle, one of the two half-siblings Gladys Mortensen abandoned or gave up before the birth of Norma Jeane in 1926, tries in her Marilyn biography to squeeze her famous sister into conformity. She portrays in *My Sister Marilyn: A*

Memoir of Marilyn Monroe (1994) a nice, family-oriented and ordinary girl much like Berniece herself. Marilyn's half-sister legitimizes her biography with her wish to present "the truth" behind the myth: "I have always wanted most keenly to erase the myth that Marilyn had no family to love her. . . . So I decided to break my silence. I wanted Marilyn's fans to see the human Marilyn behind the public image and to understand the complicated relationship she and I had with our mother."[217] This wish to reach behind the mirror to find the real Marilyn competes in the memoirs of Berniece Baker Miracle with a desire to reproduce herself in a younger, more attractive version. The big sister focuses on resemblances, also in their relations with the problem-haunted adults surrounding both the sister in Florida and the sister in California. The cover photo of Berniece's book shows the two siblings on the beach, both in bikinis—reflections holding on to each other. Only the observant spectator will notice the practiced pose of one of the sisters, who stands on tip-toe to make her legs look longer. Her bikini top is tighter also: Marilyn to the right!

Marilyn may have left the 1950s beach behind and held on to life and death in subsequent decades, but she continues to escape embraces, possibly because she has not one body, but many. Andy Warhole, for one, knew that Marilyn must be "understood . . . in the plural."[218] In theorizing social bodies, Arthur W. Frank introduces four dimensions within which a body operates in relation to other objects: control, desire, other-relatedness, and self-relatedness. In terms of **control**, our bodies are not necessarily as predictable as we would like them to be. We may know what we want our bodies to do, but bodies do not always obey us. They retain a will of their own and force us to accept a "degree of contingency" in their performance.[219] As for **desire**, a body may either be lacking or producing, defined either through incompleteness or through excess and plenitude. Frank emphasizes that this dimension—as well as the others—include a "flip-point," where one end of a continuum turns into the other.[220] A body may thus alternate between sub-body and superbody status, between lack and productivity. Also the **relation to others** helps define our corporality as either monadic (closed) or dyadic (open). A closed, western body like that of a medieval nun may thus flog herself so as to contain the sin within, whereas an open or dyadic body situates itself as a contact point for self and other in a relation of "mutual constitution."[221] Finally, the dimension of **self-relatedness** uncovers whether or not we associate or distance ourselves from our bodies, whether we exist in or despite of our bodies. These four dimensions—control, desire, other-relatedness and self-relatedness—constitute the matrix within which Frank theorizes the body. Though he stresses that real bodies operate in a conceptional mess that typologies of the body cannot hope to emulate, he sets up four styles of body usage: **the disciplined body, the mirroring body, the dominating body,** and **the communicative body**. Over the dead bodies of queer scholars such as Judith Halberstam, the author of *Female Masculinity* (1998), Frank identifies the dominating body as exclusively male and thus off-limits to Marilyn.[222] Otherwise, she inhabits all of his body types and moves into one more: **the *fin de siècle* body**.

The Disciplined Body

Like the other body types, the disciplined body responds to the continua of control, desire, other-relatedness and self-relatedness. It seeks in terms of control to eliminate the threat of its contingency through predictability, which it approaches by following a regimen such as a diet or a fitness program. As long as this regimentation remains successful, the body is predictable to itself. When internal control fails to check the physical contingency, however, the disciplined body may resort to domination in a need to control other bodies, rather than its own. When it comes to desire, the disciplined body associates itself with lack. It lacks, Frank explains, itself.[223] While regimentation does not alleviate lack, it prevents total disintegration. The sense of lack must be conscious in order to sustain control, so the disciplined body tends to place itself in a hierarchical structure in which it remains subordinated. The lack produces subordination, which subsequently reproduces lack. As for other-relatedness, the disciplined body is monadic. It may perform among others, but it does not sustain relations with them. Frank calls it "a virtuoso in the practice of the regimen."[224] Should the disciplined body begin to break its isolation and relate to others, it may do so by force, since it needs to impose its own regimen on other bodies. Discipline here flips into domination. Finally, in relating to itself, the disciplined body uses disassociation. It endures humiliation, because it has distanced itself from its physical surface; it exists within but not of the body. In this process, it distances itself emotionally and experientially from other bodies: "Unable to receive affection, it will be equally unable to give it."[225]

Marilyn's body has not struck all fans as disciplined. With unabashed political incorrectness, Norman Mailer describes her as "so desirable as to fulfill each of the letters in that favorite word of the publicity flack, *curvaceous*, so curvaceous and yet without menace as to turn one's fingertips into ten happy prowlers." To Mailer, Marilyn is as sweet and drippy as ice cream. "Take me," she smiles to Mailer. "I'm easy. I'm happy. I'm an angel of sex, you bet."[226] While the self-advertising novelist licks Marilyn's soft spots, Joyce Carol Oates uncovers in *Blonde* her predictability and control. In her early starlet days, Norma Jeane Baker runs like a clockwork: she starches and irons her shirts and skirts, she visits studios, she auditions, she takes dance classes, acting classes—the regimen of the disciplined body fills her days. Also, Marilyn Monroe loves control. All accounts of the star in the studio mention the multiple takes and re-takes she went through, again and again and again. As her directors knew and dreaded, she insisted on getting a scene just right. On the set the predictability and control she sought flipped into domination, while despairing fellow actors and directors obeyed the whims of Hollywood's most popular blonde, or those of acting coaches Natasha Lytess and Paula Strasberg. Tony Curtis, who as Joe woos Marilyn's character, Sugar, in *Some Like It Hot*, never forgave Marilyn her delays and re-takes, which forced himself and Jack Lemmon to suffer for hours in women's clothes and make-up. Only the seduction scene with Sugar and Joe on Osgood's boat was completed in one take, but Curtis had not enjoyed the encounter. Kissing Marilyn, he declared, was "like kissing Hitler."[227] When Marilyn lost her grip and lived for pills and champagne only, she dominated instead Arthur Miller, who found himself reduced to pill-dispenser. As a screen for her death drives, he could save her only by saving himself. Clark Gable did not last as long. He waited patiently for his *Misfits* co-star in the hot

Nevada sun, but died of a heart attack eleven days after the film was completed. Marilyn blamed herself, as did others.[228]

Academics, novelists, or novel biographers all recognize in Marilyn the lack of desire that Frank associates with the disciplined body. Mailer dwells on nineteen-year-old Norma Jeane's one-month fling with André de Dienes, a young photographer, because the affair raises the issue of Norma Jeane's desire. Did she have her first orgasm with Dienes, or did she merely tell him that she did? Mailer finds that she seems less interested in sex than her screen image suggests. He ascribes half of her passion for Fred Karger, the music teacher who would not marry her, to his mother, Mary Karger: "it was a mother she needed first, and marrying into the Karger family would have suited her most intimidating psychological needs as perfectly as a superb vehicle will resuscitate an aging actress."[229] Mailer mentions as well that testimony from later lovers indicate that "she was more likely to sleep with her brassiere on (for fear her breasts would sag) than to lie in abandon on an orgiastic bed."[230] Joyce Caroll Oates agrees. She describes in *Blonde* a woman who lacks desire and on her first wedding night "wished it was over so she could cuddle in her husband's arms and sleep, sleep, sleep." Her Marilyn is disoriented by sexual intimacy: "she couldn't see herself to know what was going on."[231] Like other disciplined bodies, Norma Jeane and Marilyn compensate for lack by situating themselves in hierarchies beyond their control: traditional marriages, model agencies, the Hollywood studio system, Cold War politics. The domination they encounter reinforces, as Frank predicts, their sense of lack and inferiority, as when Norma Jeane in *Blonde* visits the Hollywood mogul Mr. Z. Oates barely disguises the President of Twentieth Century Fox, Darryl Zanuck, accustomed to sexual obedience:

> I was on my hands & knees on the soft fur rug (Russian fox, Mr Z wld boast later) & my sharkskin skirt shoved up to my waist & panties removed . . . . I would not remember Mr Z afterward except the small glassy eyes & dentures smelling of garlic & the sweat-film on his scalp visible through the wiry hairs & the hurt of the Thing of hard rubber, I think greased & knobby at the end shoved first between the crack of my buttocks & then up inside me like a beak plunging in *In*, *in* as far *in* as it will go . . . .[232]

Afterwards, the hobbling starlet passes Mr Z's "sharp-eyed & disdainful" secretary: "I thanked her too ashamed to raise my eyes to hers."[233] She hides alone in the powder room for an indefinite period of time.

Photographs of Norma Jeane or Marilyn with other people do exist, but both visual and verbal representations of her suggest isolation and aloofness. Norman Rosten opens his book with Marilyn leaning against a tree in a posture that "seems to suggest a deep inner loneliness."[234] In the words of McCann, "Monroe was isolated for others and from others."[235] She appears on a California beach with her half-sister Berniece; she dances with Marlon Brando; she appears in a window with Joe DiMaggio; she arrives at a party with Arthur Miller; she entertains with him Karen Blixen and Carson McCullers. But most photos depict a woman alone, as in André de Dienes's Norma Jeane photos, as in the nude calendar shots, as in George Barris's beach series taken shortly before Marilyn's death, as in numerous Larry Schiller photos. When photographed with others—Paula Strasberg, Carl Sandburg, Clark Gable—she stares into space or retains an aloofness confirming the monadic destiny of the disciplined body. Rollyson comments in his biography on the self-containment of Marilyn's photo poses, and McCann blames in his monograph the studio for reinforcing her image as "the woman in isolation."[236] In Oates's *Blonde*, young Norma Jeane, alone in a Hollywood movie theater, bonds with the female lead: "Close-ups of the Fair Princess seem too intimate. We want to stay on the outsides of others, not be drawn inside."[237] As a star, Marilyn later performs among others, though Jean Negulesco, the director of *How to Marry a Millionaire* (1953), spotted her aloofness: "it is difficult to come close to her. She becomes vague. She puts up a curtain between herself and people."[238] Marilyn relates most effectively to her fans, who, with a few exceptions, remain distant and anonymous. Mailer describes in the chapter "Lonely Lady" how Marilyn after the shooting of *The Misfits* slid into "the longest depression of her existence."[239] Within a week in November 1960, she had returned to an empty New York apartment, announced her separation from Arthur Miller, learned that her lover Yves Montand had returned to Paris and his wife, Simone Signoret, and been informed about

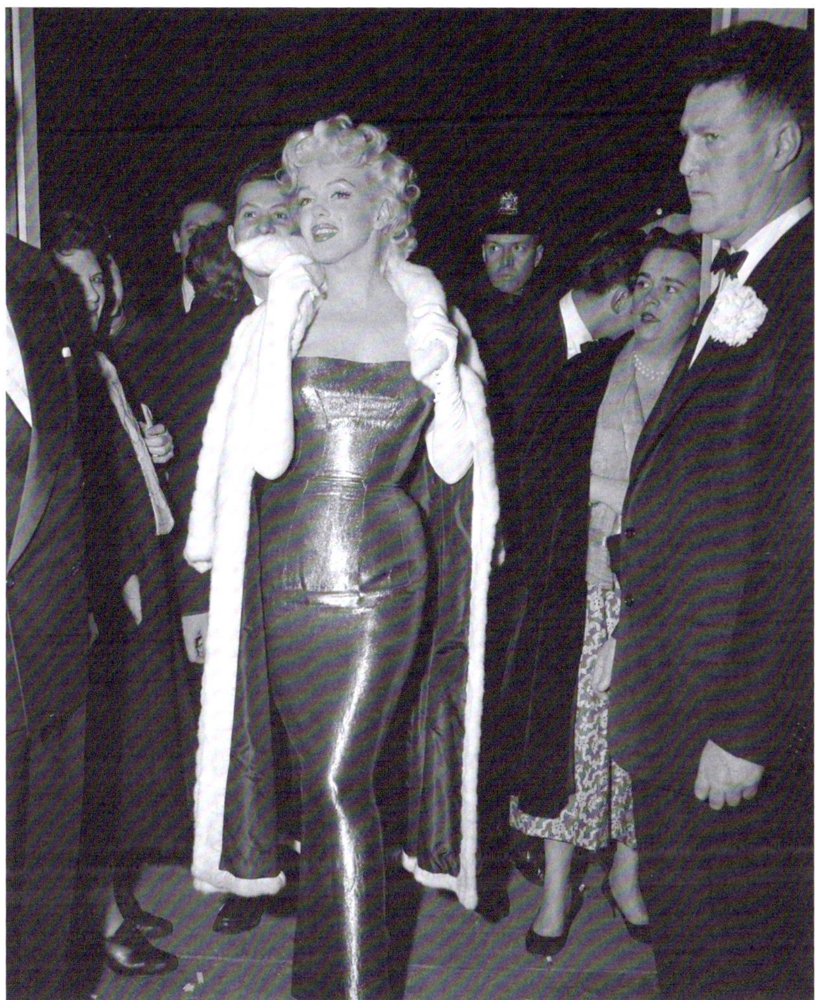

Marilyn's disciplined body

Clark Gable's heart attack and Kay Gable's pregnancy. As Mailer puts it, "the days of dwindling are at hand."[240] Marilyn has not yet died alone in her small house in Brentwood, but she reaches out to those around her with the force and determination characteristic of the disciplined body's approach to others. In *After the Fall*, Miller positions Maggie in bed alone, behaving not like Mailer's mouse but like his monster. She feeds herself on bennies and champagne as well as on the Miller persona's bottomless guilt. Later still she will place phone calls to a Kennedy, a girlfriend, a doctor, or an associate and impose upon her surroundings her own habits and needs.

Marilyn cannot get close to herself. Emotionally, she cannot communicate with others; she exists as mere surface and tends to retreat even further away from her own skin. Like the ascetics who can tolerate pain and degradation because they merely observe their bodies, Marilyn cultivates the disassociation that will allow physical intimidation or humiliation, as in the encounter with Mr. Z: "I dont need to shut my eyes to 'go blind' you'd learn in the Home when you're 'blind' time passes strangely floating & dreamy in a way.... Already I was forgetting Mr Z."[241] Joyce Carol Oates focuses on this detachment in young Norma Jeane's psychology, influenced by Gladys Mortensen's life lessons: "girls aren't strong enough; girls aren't big enough; your body is fragile and breakable, like a doll; your body *is* a doll; your body is for others to admire and to pet; your body is to be used by others, not used by you; your body is a luscious fruit for others to bite into and to savor; your body is for others, not for *you*."[242] Without the feminism that gets Oates going, Mailer explains Marilyn's detachment not with gender roles but with acting strategies. "A good actor," he writes, "can be the equal of a movie projector and a screen; if the projector is his will and the screen his skin, a total display of sexual energy can mean no more than that the energy within is void."[243] Mailer explains the blond starlet's "secret catlike search through sex" in the years prior to her discovery as part of a Method acting technique that has the actor become the role, "be possessed," so to speak. He also gives less flattering explanations for Marilyn's alleged promiscuity over this "choppy period."[244]

Oates sees Marilyn as the sexually exploited starlet, who resorts to disassociation when facing what Frank calls "mortification practices."[245] Occasionally, Oates compares Marilyn to the country that invented her, in the process depriving the star of what substance she may have left. Oates's Blond Actress thinks when seeing her own blue eyes reflected in the brown eyes of a Jewish photographer: "*I'm only an American. Skin deep. There's nothing inside me, really.*"[246] Everywhere in *Blonde*, Marilyn invents her identity through mirrors and camera lenses. She can turn her identity on and off and feel most truly herself when basking in the gaze of others. Rollyson suggests in his chapter "Becoming a Star" that we "imagine how Monroe became accustomed to polishing parts of her reflected image, so that she was deflected from the deeper sense of self she claimed to be seeking."[247] McCann describes the same phenomenon in *Marilyn Monroe*: "Since her early sessions as a model, she acquired a taste for posing and holding poses; everything was, at times, an opportunity to freeze a gesture, to instill a mood; in these brief, beautiful moments of timelessness Monroe became her own statue."[248]

The Mirroring Body

The mirroring body always reflects its surroundings. It thrives in the realm of consumption and holds as few surprises as a McDonald's cheeseburger. The disciplined body seeks predictability to stave off the threat of contingency, but the mirroring body produces desire so as to avoid a consciousness of lack. Its primary activity remains consumption, but not consummation. When the mirroring body encounters an object, it seeks to make the object part of its self-image. The body reflects itself in the object, which becomes a mirror rather than a purchase. Since the objects are always already mirroring the body, or "pre-assimilated" to the body,[249] the mirroring body fails to acknowledge an outside reality, which, as in Jean Beaudrillard's *America* (1988), becomes hyperreal. With regard to other-relatedness, the mirroring body exists in monadic isolation, unchallenged by an image outside of itself. As Frank puts it, "consumption is the monadic reproduction of the body through its assimilation of a world which exists only for its own assimilation."[250] The mirroring body responds to itself with narcissistic fascination. As body surface, it lives for decoration: it is a site for ornaments, for clothes, for physical expression. A grimace and a smile function as empty signifiers, since pain or joy have been reduced to image, with no referent. In the advertising world of the mirroring body, a grimace may signal the consumption of drugs, not physical or emotional pain. The mirroring body fails to connect with its interior. In Frank's formulation, "its inner organization is like a closed circuit appliance: only authorized personnel may open it."[251]

In her disciplined mode Marilyn retains control through various regimens such as ironing, auditions, bubble baths, or jogging, but the mirroring Marilyn becomes predictable through her surroundings. The wives of Jim Dougherty, Joe DiMaggio, and Arthur Miller never met. Mrs. Dougherty darned socks, sewed in buttons, cleaned the house, and served carrots and peas for the color effect. In bed, she played in Mailer's view the role of Dougherty's "most responsive bride."[252] Mrs. DiMaggio tried her hand at Italian dishes, but often dined out, dressed demurely, faked an interest in sports, and spread her clothes all over the place. Mrs. Miller acted the "Jewish Princess."[253] She took out books on Jewish rituals and the Holocaust, moved to Connecticut, flirted with politics, and preferred theater to film. Mailer sums up Marilyn's tendency to reflect those around her: "She was the measure of her surroundings. There is hardly a posed photograph in which she does not appropriate something of the background by the curve of her limbs—she is the mirror of the mood about her and may have had a tendency to return each man his own sexual goods . . . ."[254] Marilyn's tendency to inhabit the personalities of her men originates in her wish to consume them, to make them part of her own (lack of) identity. Oates lists in *Blonde* an impressive list of Marilyn's lovers up until her twenty-seventh birthday, but the blond actress's conquests serve her consumptive rather than her consummated needs. She finds and throws away her men as she shops for dresses, hairstyles, and identities, so as to make her lovers help her self-imaging. As Rollyson sees it, "she was quite aggressive in dismissing the significance of her feelings for Dougherty, as though her real life only began with the moment of her photographed self's incarnation."[255]

As a mirroring body, Marilyn links herself with desire, but not with her own. To arouse a consciousness of lack, she has to arouse desire endlessly, a task for which the blond bombshell was well equipped. During her honeymoon with DiMaggio, she leaves her groom and Seoul to entertain the First Marine Division on a winter location and hangs outside the helicopter so as to suck up adoration. Every wiggle of her shoulders sets off wails in the troops. Marilyn reports on this happiest of occasions: "I didn't feel a thing, except good."[256] During the famous publicity stunt with Tom Ewell for *The Seven Year Itch*,

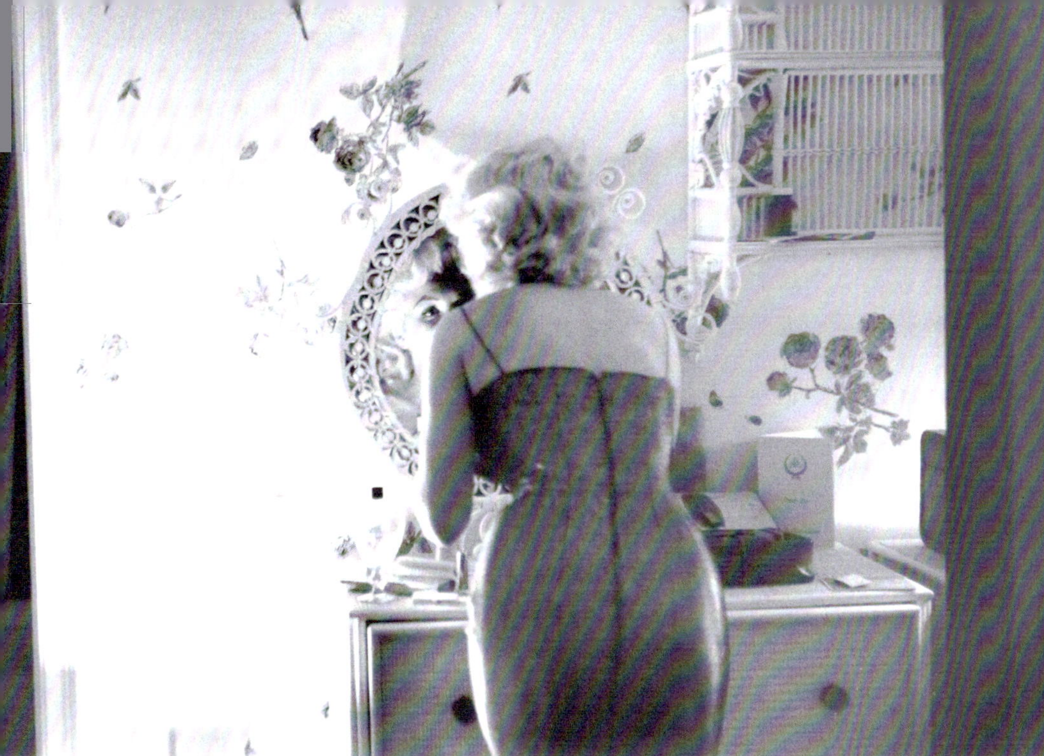

Marilyn's mirroring body

Marilyn laughs as her white dress billows up with each rush of hot air from the Manhattan subway grating, but she responds more to the whistles of the crowd than to the fuming DiMaggio. Even as Marilyn tires of Miller, she needs him to need her. As Maggie holding back Quentin in *After the Fall*, she "*turns on the phonograph and goes into a hip-flinging, broken angle step around him.*" She implores her husband to make love to her despite his frustration: "I mean, you gonna wait till I'm old? Or what? I mean what is it?"[257]

The mirroring Marilyn is as lonely as the disciplined Marilyn and cannot break her monadic isolation. She opens herself up to an exterior reality, which she proceeds to appropriate for her self-reflection. Her relation with the outside world consists of projection and introjection. In Frank's words, "One size fits all, and all fits the one body."[258] Rollyson comments on her "self-referential" gestures in performing "Diamonds Are a Girl's Best Friend."[259] Posing for photographs, she "frames herself in her own appeal, emphasizing her smiling, open-mouthed self-intoxication."[260] Monadic closure prevents her from recognizing other images than her own. As Maggie in *After the Fall*, she casts Quentin as her accomplice; as Hollywood's whore, she considers her producers pimps; as Marilyn the orphan, she sees Clark Gable as her father.

Marilyn's reaction to Gable's death shortly after the completion of *The Misfits* signals her narcissism, or her inability to relate to herself. She sends a host of sleeping pills into her physical interior but cannot otherwise deal with her depths. Only the surface of her body exists as a text on and with which she may write herself: with clothing, with peroxide, with make-up, and with physical expressions. The menstrual blood that flows through Oates's *Blonde* and Marilyn's skirts and pants in most biographies springs from an incomprehensible and uncontrollable interior space. Always a surprise, it ruins the creamy white outfits with which Marilyn signals her innocence. She enacts a personality change from Norma Jeane to Marilyn by manipulating surfaces: bleached hair, short curls, and eternal bubble baths supposed to wash away her past. As Oates has Norma Jeane think in the darkened movie theater of her childhood, "*my skin is my soul. There is no soul otherwise.*"[261] Audrey Flack fills her painting *Marilyn* (1977), reproduced in Rollyson's biography, with "symbols of self-transformation": mirrors, lipsticks, powder puffs, make-up brushes, jars of all kinds.[262] Mailer notices the blond actress's "skin-glow of sex."[263] As a mirroring body, Marilyn throws back at her novelist-biographer his own obsessions.

The Communicative Body

Everybody writing on Marilyn comments on her sex-appeal. It stole the picture from more famous names, as in the early *Love Happy* (1949) with Groucho Marx, where, Mailer notes, "the famous undulating movement of her hips is now unveiled for the first time on film."[264] Marilyn's sensuality suggests as well the communicative body of Frank's typologies. Unlike the disciplined and mirroring bodies, the communicative body is in the process of creating itself. As an ideal body type, it escapes attempts to theorize it, but it may be approached through the fragments of its emergence, as in dance and performance. The communicative body sees contingency not as a problem; contingency links it with another about to become: a lover, or a child. Frank theorizes male sexuality as monadic, centered on its own desire, but he sees female sexuality as dyadic, opening towards something or somebody outside of itself. Dyadic contingency, he argues, enables the body to "realize itself diffusely."[265] While the mirroring body desires monadic consumption, the communicative body wishes for dyadic expressiveness. It produces a world in which it partakes. In a process of dyadic sharing, this body type uses itself to articulate what it finds outside itself: sorrow, pain, pleasure, etc. Through dyadic sharing, the body experiences contingency as a possibility for further "diffuse realization."[266] Unlike other bodies, the communicative body associates diffusion not with dissolution but with potentialities of expression and pleasure. In relating to itself, then, the communicative body operates with realization rather than representation. It realizes its own body within institutions and discourses that no longer subjugate or define it, but function as modes of (self-)expression. They have changed from constraint to creativity.

The F.B.I. file of Marilyn's lovers up till 1953 suggests an emerging communicative body. The F.B.I. agents who put together the interminable list might have uttered snide remarks unrelated to the twenty-seven-year-old star's communicative skills, though, as Oates writes in *Blonde*, "the most scandalous were yet to come."[267] But Marilyn invents herself physically and sexually through a chaotic love life. Like other communicative bodies, including dancers and performers, she shows herself only in fragments or flashes. She becomes an unpredictable body allied with unpredictability. Unlike her other body types, this Marilyn sees contingency as potentiality. Her alliance with chance, what Hélène Cixous calls "chaosmos," drives husbands, colleagues and producers up studio walls.[268] Norman Rosten finds that "anything could happen with her around, wherever it was. Explosion. No match, just her and air. Spontaneous combustion."[269] But Marilyn's unpredictability accounts as well for her humor, her special angle. When a journalist asks her over the phone what she has on, she answers, famously, "Nothing but the radio."[270] She takes odd approaches to housekeeping, as when the young Mrs. Dougherty brings a cow out of the rain and into her neat living-room, where it will not suffer. Mrs. DiMaggio throws

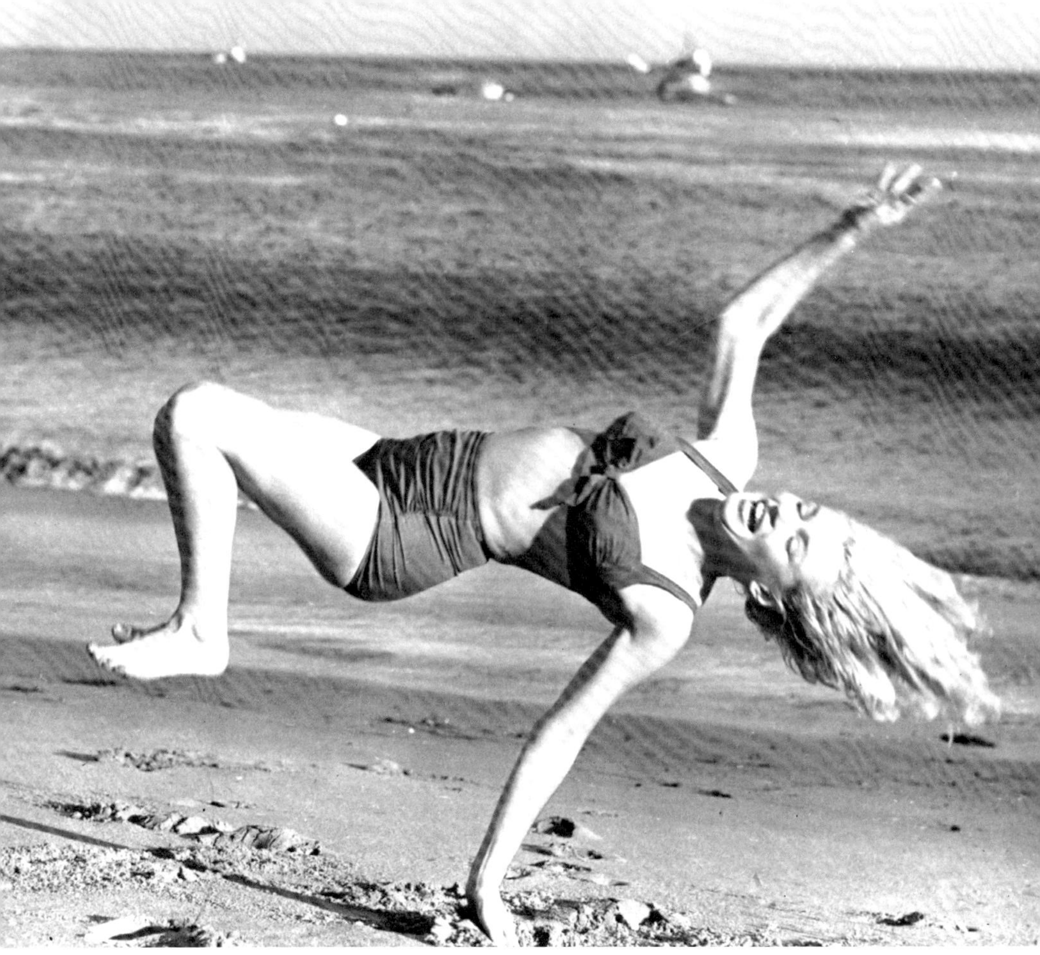

Marilyn's communicative body

underwear, sleeping pills and beauty creams among the baseball hero's alphabetically arranged bathroom things. And then, of course, Marilyn arrives late everywhere. Her unique conception of time allowed for bodily and other surprises. Rosten concludes: "You had to be on her time. She never got the time thing straightened out: It was a built-in, psychic time, Marilyn time. Possibly Einstein time."[271]

Marilyn's contingency links her to lovers in a dyadic diffusion that allows her to realize herself most fully as she merges with others. Desire becomes dyadic and expressive rather than monadic and consuming. Dyadic other-relations account as well for the love of children that no Marilyn biographer or novelist fails to mention. In *Blonde* Norma Jeane Dougherty endlessly walks baby Irina, whose mother is a depressed World War II widow. One miscarriage after another would disrupt her dreams of wife- and motherhood in Arthur Miller's rented Connecticut cottage. Oates's blond actress hangs out at playgrounds watching other people's children, and Marilyn dies with photos of DiMaggio's and Miller's children in her room. As a communicative body, Marilyn becomes the children around her, incidentally Miller's explanation for her unusual *rapport* with young people. In short, Marilyn uses herself to express her world. Whatever hems her in—men, marriage, Method acting, medical practices, studios—becomes enabling rather than constraining means of self-expression. Biographers such as Rollyson comment on Marilyn's "diffidence and remoteness, the impression she created that she was not 'all there'. . . ."[272] Obviously, she came across as void, distraught, or diffuse, but diffusion suggests as well "various possibilities of pleasure and expression."[273] We end up with the chaosmos and charm that articulated Marilyn and keep her biographers busy.

Frank gives up theorizing the communicative body and concentrates on its practices. He locates its ideal form mostly in performance. Dance uses contingency as a source of inspiration; dance produces rather than consumes desire. It is communal, since it involves an invitation to other bodies. And dancers must relate to their own bodies to be dancers. Nonetheless, the ideal of dance may quickly, Frank writes, plunge "back into a reality in which this ideal is rarely reached." In his worst case scenario, dance may simply be(come) male fantasies imposed on female bodies.[274] Anybody who has watched Marilyn wiggle her behind in front of the cowboys circling her in *The Misfits* would follow this argument, yet Marilyn's body—disciplined, mirroring, communicative—might also speak of a cultural crisis. As her famous *derrière* moves faster and faster, she boogies from one body type into another and teases the gazes of cowboys and audiences into postmodernity. Like Laura Anderson, Carolee Schneemann and Don DeLillo's Lauren Hartke in *The Body Artist* (2001), she deconstructs the culture that formulates women's bodies and keeps them "in subordinate categories of embodiment."[275] Schneemann says about *Eye Body* (1963), a piece in which she uses her body to extend her "painting-constructions," that she wished "to 'conceive' of [her] body in manifold aspects which had eluded the culture around [her]."[276] Like Marilyn, she inhabits not one body but many, and she too runs the risk of becoming pornography. Like performance artists and other postmodernists, both Marilyn and Schneemann occupy a space that "threatens and undermines society at the same time as it is the fullest expression of society's unspoken desires."[277] Once again in western culture, the body embodies simultaneously constraint and possibility.[278]

The *Fin de Siècle* Body

Like the body artists appearing in millennium cityscapes, Marilyn inhabits a *fin de siècle* body. Bryan S. Turner argues in "Recent Developments in the Theory of the Body" for parallels between cultural crises in the late seventeenth and the late twentieth centuries, despite the vast political, social and economic differences that prevent him from pressing the comparison to the limit. His descriptions of baroque ceilings that "drip with pink, abundant flesh" nonetheless call forth the contours of Marilyn's rippling curves, which critics and fans initially found exaggerated, too much. Lisa Cohen articulates excessively Marilyn's excess:

> Marilyn Monroe has: too much written about her—too much sex about her. There was too much breath in her voice and there were too many drugs in her body. Too much vulnerability, too much trouble, too much exposure. She read too many books, she had too many abortions, she put too much bleach on her hair, she had too much interest in acting, too much willingness to undress, too much talent, too much tardiness, too much anxiety, too much foster home, too much JFK—and these days there is too much paraphernalia associated with her. Her clothes were much too tight; her house was much too messy; her life ended much too soon. Too white, too childlike, too stupid, too manipulative, too sincere. Too awkward too undulating too intelligent too pathetic too diligent too lonely too lazy too funny—too, too much.[279]

Like Marilyn herself, Hollywood producers, and twentieth-century postmodernists, the baroque ideologues and artists reached their audiences by over-stimulating the senses.[280]

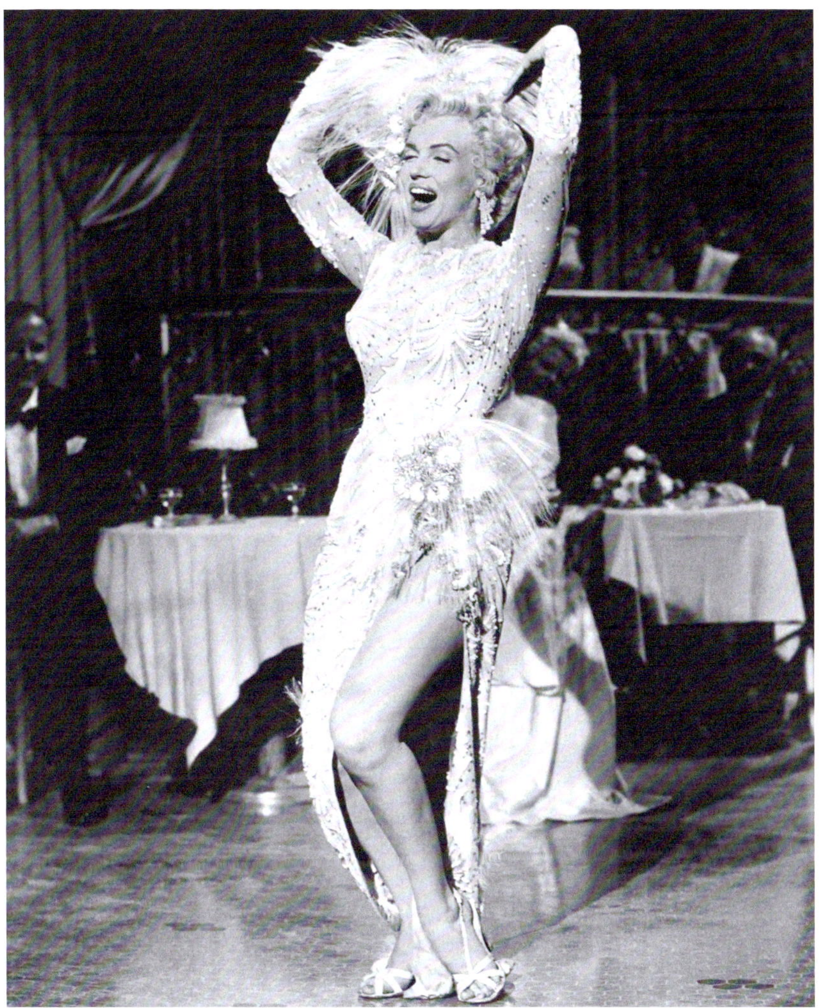

Marilyn's fin de siècle *body*

As in baroque art, where high culture meets low in a blend of styles, Marilyn combines in her body and texts various histories and art forms. She sings, dances, moves, and acts in and outside dramatic performances, and she merges comedy and tragedy, comic strip and theater. She leaves the Hollywood studios behind to enroll in Lee Strasberg's acting classes, and she plays the dumb blonde while setting up her own production company. She exchanges a baseball hero for a playwright. She mixes West Coast and East Coast, orphanage and privilege in her Kennedy affairs. As in the high art of baroque, Marilyn always lands among kitsch.

Marilyn's body exudes an air of "contrivance, of constructionism, and artifice." The baroque artists dwelled on the ruin as an allegory of human decay and melancholy; they repeatedly challenged notions of "natural order." [281] Similarly, dead Marilyn symbolizes human fear and waste, a sense of nature violated. Blond, beautiful and dead, she becomes the everybody or nobody she claimed to be, with the mystery and constructedness of her suicide or murder thrown in for good measure. Anthony Summers's biography lingers on her decline and death for more than half of its pages, and the addicted star does not know either when enough is enough and thus lends herself well to melodrama.

The angel of sex embodied the combination of spirituality and sensuality that appears in the baroque blend of the sacred and the secular. This combination constitutes in Turner's view a form of perspectivism: "By bringing the sensual to the forefront of effects in order to break down the space between art-object and subject-spectator, the baroque transformed the human body into rippling, creamy, palpable flesh."[282] Turner comments on Rubens's bourgeois women models exhibiting "a virtual delirium of flesh," much in the style of Mailer writing about Marilyn, or about Mailer.[283] Marilyn's own creamy body thus pushes itself to center canvas or screen in *fin de siècle* culture, because she too blends virgin and whore, the sacred and the secular. In the process, she empowers the spectator otherwise distanced from artistic and political expressions. Marilyn's ripe figure lives on in millennium culture, where it embodies (and deconstructs) the spectator democracy of postmodernity.

Marilyn's bodies provide academics and other spectators with the entertainment demanded in postmodern culture. She represents the competing impulses of the world she inhabits as a disciplined, a mirroring, a communicative or a *fin de siècle* body. In her multiple forms she upholds and dismantles the ideologies she performs. With her much-advertised interior void, she acted the roles and functions around her and danced the matrices of control, desire, relation to others and selves in dizzying constellations that intrigue those looking for her. As a disciplined body, she is Miller's and Mailer's monsters, an isolated star intent on dominating and controlling herself and others. As a mirroring body, she stares into mirrors and camera eyes, only to find the world she reflects in narcissistic assimilation. As a communicative body, she invents herself and others through the sums of their performances, and as a *fin de siècle* body she enacts the discourses whirling through and around her. "Each writer," McCann notes, "has set out to strip the myth bare, to retrieve the body from the literary embodiment, to find the flesh and blood of Marilyn Monroe."[284] Elusive as ever, she teases the biographers trying to reassemble her "with pictures, paper and paste." They do not succeed. McCann concludes that "where the body is absent, a heartbeat is far away: there is no body beneath the page we are holding."[285] Looking at not just the body he mentions, but many, we might get closer to Marilyn's representations, but not necessarily to that particular gorgeous blonde who wanted to die and didn't. Only those who know her better, know better.

III Marilyn Performing

Oates's Actress

In June of 1999, Joyce Carol Oates wrote two pages for the book-signing sessions that would follow the publication of her Marilyn Monroe novel *Blonde* (2000), roughly at the time the actress would have turned seventy-five. "On the Composition of Blonde" records the prolific Oates's original intention to write a novella focusing on the girlhood and early career of the long-dead actress. The project was to have ended on the day she accepted her studio-invented name, Marilyn Monroe. But like others before her, Oates succumbed to the rescue fantasy that she alone might help the movie star help herself. She confesses: "I came to feel that Norma Jeane had no one but me to tell her story from the inside."[286] With *Blonde*, Oates tried like Maurice Zolotow, Ben Hecht, Norman Mailer, and others, to give Marilyn a voice of her own and produce what Graham McCann in *Marilyn Monroe* calls "an imaginary memoir."[287] "It was my wish to express the inner, poetic, spiritual life of Norma Jeane Baker," Oates writes in "Composition." "How it felt, how it feels, to have been her. Not to look at her, but to be her."[288]

Blonde recycles Marilyn's endlessly marketable story, in some readers' view, endlessly. In *The New York Times*, Michiko Kakutani complains of "pages and pages of the sort of heavy-breathing romance-novel prose one would think beneath a writer of her distinction."[289] Close to eight hundred pages of small print, *Blonde* seeks to add weight to Marilyn's renowned body through its thorough treatment of her life and death. Oates writes in her "Author's Note" that she consulted *Legend* by Fred Guiles and *Goddess* by Anthony Summers, as well as *Marilyn Monroe: A Life of the Actress* by Carl E. Rollyson, Jr.[290] She points to other "subjective" texts about Marilyn as myth, including *Marilyn* by Norman Mailer, but many voices echo in her text, not least the breathy whisper of Marilyn's *My Story*.[291]

Oates insists on fiction as her form, a claim prompting the *New York Times* reviewer to state that she "is using the life of Marilyn Monroe as a substitute for inventing an original story."[292]

Oates's Marilyn inhabits an infected, gothic underworld, where the fluid identities of the Blond Actress reflect the postmodern surfaces defining her. Marilyn performs and is performed, as images of actors, acting and moviemaking whirl around and through her. Oates constructs her star through porous boundaries between life and movie, between fact and fiction, and between genre and gender divisions. Her readers become an audience of feminine and feminist voyeurs, at times indistinguishable from author and subject, as male figures invade and violate physical, psychological and literary terrains. Marilyn herselves dissolve along lines of race and gender. She takes on whiteness, redness and blackness in constellations that also separate femininity from female bodies. Ultimately, Marilyn articulates the chaos of millennium existences, as well as the dreams and disasters that haunted the twentieth century. With her famous walk, she strolls into the twenty-first—late as always.

Before Oates, other women writers had followed Marilyn's steps and missteps. In "The Death of Marilyn Monroe" (1963), Diana Trilling looks at the star from a universalist perspective and interprets Marilyn's life and death as a tragedy "inherent in human existence in civilization."[293] We wish to contemplate sex directly, without illusions, Trilling argues, but "civilization" will permit us to confront sex only in mediated form. Marilyn mediates between sexuality and audience exactly because she performs. She acts *as if* she offers to her fans the real thing.[294] In *Marilyn Monroe* (1973), Joan Mellen rejects Trilling's argument by stressing the actress's victimization by patriarchal systems. Like Gloria Steinem, she finds the image Marilyn projects, not to mention her film roles, to be demeaning.[295] In *From Reverence to Rape* (1974), Molly Haskell undermines Mellen's views by pointing to the extra nuances—comedy among them—that Marilyn brought to her blond bombshell performances. As Haskell saw her, Marilyn rescued many stupid scripts from themselves.[296]

Oates became as obsessed with Marilyn, dead and alive, as everybody else. "I felt the barriers dissolving between myself and Norma

Jeane as Norma Jeane, the actress, felt barriers dissolving between herself and her screen roles. I felt her fingers encircling my wrist."[297] Oates and Marilyn grip each other tightly; both try to justify American lives and careers. The writer constructs the actress as a cultural icon, her life "an epic, uniquely American," and the fictional biography a portrait of an "emblematic American artist who lost her way."[298] Mailer found Marilyn's death to give "a lavender edge to that dramatic American design of the Sixties," and Oates contemplates the second half of the American century through the prism of Marilyn's life and death.[299] She shares this effort with writers such as John Berendt, Don DeLillo, Philip Roth, Tim O'Brien, and Toni Morrison, who all take up brands of American history and historiography in their millennium works.[300]

Like Berendt in *Midnight in the Garden of Good and Evil* (1994), Oates situates the Blond Actress in gothic terrain, where vice, crime, and mental disorders flourish. According to Gladys Mortensen, Norma Jeane's mother, the girl's father used to call Los Angeles the "City of Sand." Mother and daughter inhabit a place unfit for humanity and must suffer the Devil's punishment for their foolishness and pride: "Earthquakes, fires, and the air smothering us."[301] Hollywood, in short, is familiar to Oates, whose "aesthetics of ugliness" caused her to out-write Mailer on topics such as boxing and serial killing. Gladys adds to the "menace" and "chaos" by attempting to lower Norma Jeane into scalding bath water and getting herself strapped to a stretcher and taken to a mental institution. In the air above Los Angeles hover the fires of 1934 as "demonic cloud formations at sunset above the Pacific."[302] Down below, Oates's cityscape fills with the ruthless predators Marilyn meets on her way up the Hollywood ladder, Mr Z, the thinly disguised Fox President Darryl Zanuck among them. With a cocktail of Dom Perignon, drugs galore, wife beaters and sharpshooters, Oates's Blond Actress moves in an underworld of sex and death. Like the other writers of the (late) twentieth century, Oates tries in *Blonde* to make sense of America through biography and history. In the process, her own identity as an American writer gets scrutinized. In "Composition," Oates includes the actress's often-quoted words: "I guess I never believed that I deserved to live. The way other people do. I needed to justify my life." Oates adds: "Perhaps I identify with these words?"[303]

With her question mark, Oates echoes Marilyn's notorious insecurities and her fluid, perhaps downright absent notions of identity. In *Blonde* and elsewhere, Norma Jeane Baker changes into Marilyn

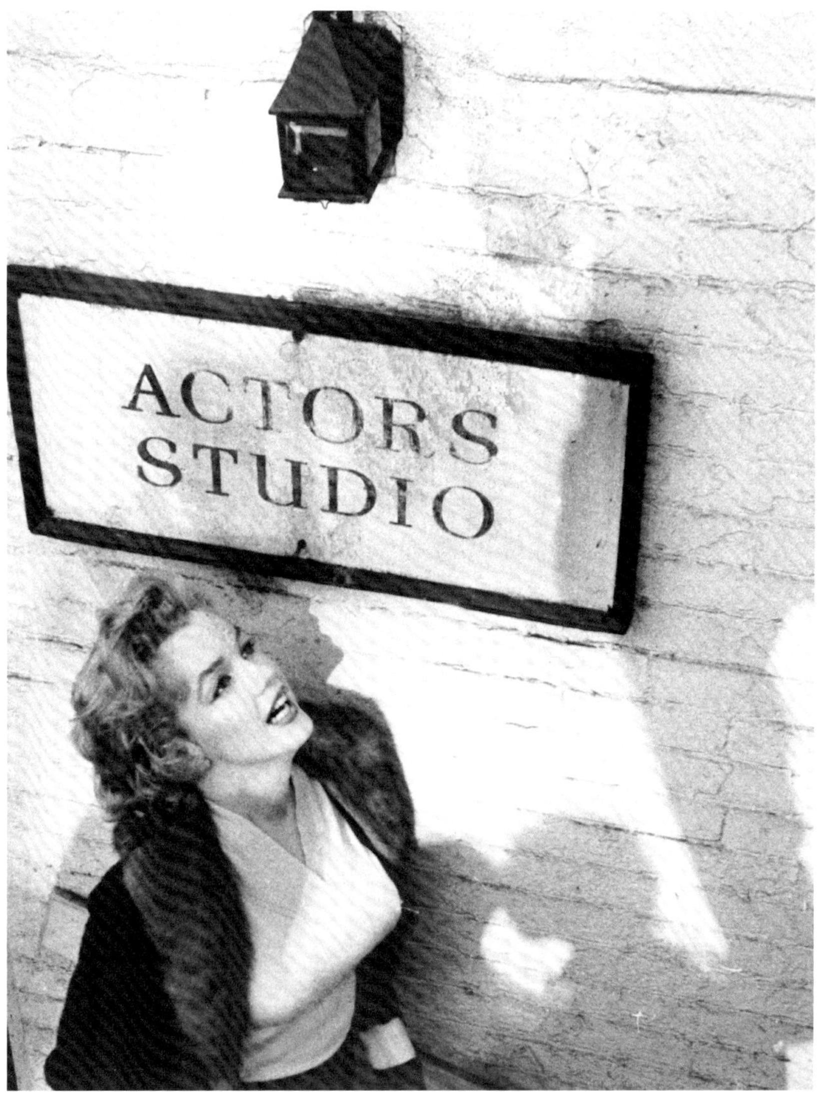

Marilyn performing

Monroe, who is first Norma, then Marilyn to Arthur Miller. She declares herself to be Cherie and then Roslyn Tabor, in the "Reno-*Misfit*-hell"[304] of 1961, when her playwright-scriptwriter-husband and her director, John Huston, watched her come apart in the Nevada desert. Apart from this profusion of name changes, Oates employs a series of metaphors that destabilize what solid notions of identity and reality her readers may cherish. Marilyn constitutes with her fragile or absent sense of self a perfect postmodern sign. Her favorite poem in "Little Treasury of American Verse" remains Emily Dickinson's "I am Nobody!" and Oates stresses both Norma Jeane's doll-face and her love of dolls. Gladys, incidentally, would outlive her daughter "as a doll baby might be fitted snug inside a larger doll ingeniously hollowed out for that purpose."[305]

Oates's many references to ice, glass and mirrors link Marilyn to performativity. Gladys's laughter sounds to six-year-old Norma Jeane like an ice-pick stabbing into ice blocks; later in the day, the girl feels happiness like "broken glass" in her mouth.[306] As in O'Brien's *In the Lake of the Woods*, sheets of water come to represent postmodern hybridity, with surface and depth surging into one another. In the "Dancing in the Dark" episode set on the Central Park ice ring, the embrace of Marilyn and Miller, as well as the Blond Actress's glittering hair and the "deep sadness" in her eyes, bring together surface and depth.[307] Most obviously, Oates keeps referring to Norma Jeane and Marilyn's "magic friend in the mirror." Her inspiration for this constant play with surfaces and mirrors might be Carl Rollyson, Jr., one of her sources. In *Marilyn Monroe: A Life of the Actress* (1986), he discusses the typology of the Hollywood blonde, including the Marilyn figure in Ken Russell's film *Tommy* (1977). "The elevation of this goddess, like much cheap magic," Rollyson writes, "is done with mirrors, with reflecting surfaces that have no depth, no resonance; they represent, instead, only the shadow play of self-realization, the suggestion of a complete identity that bemuses the insubstantial, cryptic individual, the crippled self."[308] The mirror allows for self-recognition and holds together a fragmented identity made possible only through the gaze of others, or through the camera. Rollyson quotes Mailer's statement about Marilyn as "the magnified mirror of ourselves" and relies on mirrors and camera eyes to present to us the life of the actress: "films perform as mirrors which throw back to audiences images of stars that have already been reflected by other films, mirrors."[309]

Oates uses Rollyson's metaphors throughout *Blonde* to highlight the performance that always already constitutes her protagonist: "always there was Norma Jeane's Magic Friend in the Mirror. Peeking at her from a corner of the mirror or staring boldly, full-faced. The mirror could be like a movie; maybe the mirror *was* a movie."[310] This doubling comes about also through Marilyn's astrological sign, Gemini, and gets dizzying when the Blond Actress takes up with Cass Chaplin, himself a Gemini. Cass looks like his famous father and becomes Marilyn's twin lover, the two engaging in an erotic triangle with Eddy G—, who, as Cass declares when Marilyn surprises the two men in bed together, is "my twin too."[311] The Geminis, as we know them, contribute to the incessant imaging and performativity of *Blonde*: both are sons of famous actors, both are actors themselves, and both are fictional additions to Marilyn's biography. The cinematic metaphors in *Blonde* help construct the performative self that Norma Jeane and Marilyn embody: Life the Movie!

Oates skates across Marilyn's many surfaces, from Norma Jeane to her mirror to the mirror-as-movie and back to the curly-haired girl who has learned that "*whatever isn't in the spotlight isn't observed*," or, for that matter, lived.[312] Since film can be edited, erased, run backwards and forwards, Oates creates a time zone of her own, in which Marilyn has moved out of the 1950s and into postmodernity. As S. Paige Baty argues in *American Monroe* (1995), she has become a circulating discourse without referents.[313] The '50s bombshell responds to our longing for the past, which leads, as Norman K. Denzin suggests, "to its reenactment and effacement in contemporary popular culture."[314]

Marilyn's profession brings the performativity of identities and the postmodern blandness into focus. Throughout *Blonde*, Norma and Marilyn devour monographs such as *The Actor's Handbook and the Actor's Life* and *The Paradox of Acting*—both products of Oates's imagination—as well as published books such as Constantin Stanislavsky's *My Life in Art* (1925) and Michael Chekhov's *To the Actor on the Technique of Acting* (1953).[315] These texts also make it into the epigrams included in the novel. Oates comments in "Composition" on the theme of acting, so crucial to *Blonde*:

> Is there an ideal actor-personality? Does the era create its actors, and icons? Is genius in acting akin to genius in music, art, and science? Or is this "emptiness" merely incompleteness, built into our species' collective destiny? Is there, in the most impassioned actors, a hole in the heart that must be filled, and again filled, and again? Perhaps the actor is one who dramatizes our essential ontological insecurity, our anxiety about knowing who we are or should be, and whether we "deserve" to live. For these reasons, celebrity is adored, and consumed.[316]

The drunk and vomiting Carlo, aka. The Dark Prince, aka. Marlon Brando staggers into the Blond Actress's bathtub on page 530 of Oates's novel and into Marilyn's love life in 1955. His appearance dramatizes this notion of an absent center. Brando had studied with Lee Strasberg at the famous Actors Studio and presumably subscribed to Method acting, the reaching into personal experiences for the emotions needed in scenes and roles. Oates dwells in the bathroom scene on prime-time Brando's famous body to outline surface rather than depth. Like Marilyn, Brando moves in a setting of shallow water, tile, glass and shiny surfaces, including the "arrogant glisten" of the actor's skin.[317]

The Playwright, *Blonde*'s thinly disguised Arthur Miller, ponders the role of actors and acting as he picks up "Norma's Bible," the dog-eared *Actor's Handbook* that weaves its advice across the pages of Oates's novel. The Playwright asks himself: "Is the subtext of the actor's 'acting' always and forever our own buried (and denied) 'acting'?" Norma responds with the aphorism she has copied onto the title page: "The actor is happiest only in his sacred space: the stage."[318] Though the aphorism is a bitter pill to swallow for the Playwright, it explains the inability of Norma/Marilyn to grasp the notion of "performance." The Playwright tries to appease his fiancée, who worries about Cherie in *Bus Stop*: "*You're an accomplished actress, you 'perform.' As a dancer dances on stage, and walks off. As a pianist performs, a public speaker. Always, you're greater than your roles.*" But Marilyn remains puzzled, unconvinced: "*Sometimes I don't know what people mean: 'Performance.'*"[319] She lives her life in scenes or takes, as when the Lee Strasberg figure demands sex in his Actors Studio office. Marilyn goes into the Magda character she is rehearsing at the Studio and either "*wasn't there*" or reaches a climax "*only just for the scene, you know? And then the scene was over.*"[320] This experience is twice removed; it surfaces in a dialogue between the jealous Playwright and the evasive Blond Actress during their courtship. "The truth of an actor is 'dialogue,'" the Playwright thinks. "The truth of an actor is the truth of only a fleeting moment."[321] Surrounded by actors, plays, theaters, studios, and film making, Marlon, Miller and Marilyn dramatize Oates's vision of postmodern subjectivities, adrift in images, reflections and performances.

This fluidity extends as well to Oates's choice of genre. She begins her "Author's Note" by insisting that "*Blonde* is a radically distilled 'life' in the form of fiction."[322] She repeats in "Composition" that *Blonde* does not promise "a factual transcription of the life of the woman known as 'Marilyn Monroe.'" She adds emphatically: "I hope this will be understood."[323] Like Mailer in his novel biography, Oates fictionalizes the biographical and historical sources she consults. Unimpressed reviewers or rescuers notwithstanding, Oates invites her readers into a free-for-all Marilyn country and allows herself to merge genres and voices. She indulges in melodrama when Marilyn becomes "The Fair Princess" or "The Beggar Maid," while Brando and others pose as "The Dark Prince." The purple prose of these sections blends with the poems Marilyn writes into the pages of *Blonde*, and with the stereotypes that appear in Oates's re- or unnaming of characters important to the Blond Actress: "the Ex-Athlete" for Joe DiMaggio and, of course, "the Playwright." Documentary material contributes to Oates's portraits of the people circling the Blond Actress: husbands, drama coaches, make-up artists, hairdressers, doctors, the Rat Pack, the Kennedys, and more. Oates mixes the fairy tale, the mystery novel, and conspiracy theory when the Sharpshooter does away with the Burning Princess in August of 1962. In fact, *Blonde* becomes a B movie. As Laura Miller writes in her *New York Times* review of the novel, Oates's "subject is of Cinemascope proportions, an undisputed titan in America's mythic imagination, so she can't be too vulgar or grandiose."[324] Like

Marilyn herself, *Blonde* is a mess, part potboiler and part philosophy, like the actress an (un)appetizing hybrid performing on the postmodern screen.

If we are all, as Denzin suggests (with Beaudrillard), "voyeurs adrift in a sea of symbols,"[325] Oates presents to her readership a feminine, even feminist gaze. Previous novelists-biographers, from Zolotow to Mailer to Summers, may have perpetuated degrading myths relating to Marilyn through what McCann labels "their voyeuristic mode of presentation and their sexist interpretation of her life."[326] Oates looks at Marilyn from within and without, though this distinction tends to evaporate. Oates writes in "Composition": "In *Blonde*, Norma Jeane is our guide. She is the ubiquitous voice of the novel, even when the reader may not think she is speaking. Her dissolving self allowed her the gift, or the curse, of 'seeing' herself through others' eyes. . . ."[327] In short, Oates hopes to present Norma Jeane or Marilyn as the star(let) saw herself and the world. And Marilyn and Joyce Carol see eye to eye on issues of gender and power. "The harshness of certain male portraits will not go unnoticed," Oates writes in "Composition." She adds that she writes from the perspective of Norma/Marilyn, who came down hard on herself as well.[328]

Despite Yves Montand's indiscretions with Marilyn, his wife Simone Signoret saw the actress's depressions from a feminist perspective. Also Gloria Steinem edited both *Ms. Magazine* and Miss Monroe into feminist texts. In *(Woman) Writer: Occasions and Opportunities* (1988), Oates nonetheless claims the more general perspective the parenthesis of her title highlights. "Subject matter," she writes, "is clearly culture-determined, not gender-determined. And the imagination, in itself genderless, allows us all things."[329] If we return to Marlon Brando in Marilyn's bathtub, Oates's imagination allows us, of course, to peek through the keyhole in the first place. The two stars had a fling in 1955, but Brando never talked to the press about Marilyn, dead or alive—thus the friendship and loyalty between "Carlo" and the Blond Actress in Oates's novel. In watching Carlo's glistening body in the bathtub scene, Oates and her readership nonetheless occupy a feminine position, much like the camera lingering on young Brando's torso in Elia Kazin's adaptation of *A Streetcar Named Desire*, released in 1951. Through Marilyn and Oates's eyes, we see "a beautifully sculpted male body with distinct chest muscles, perfectly shaped male breasts and nipples like miniature grapes, a peltlike covering of dark hairs in a swirl at his chest and thickening at his groin."[330] As Laura Mulvey argues in "Visual Pleasure and Narrative Cinema" (1975), the star-as-spectacle creates narrative trouble by delaying plot movement so as to allow the desiring gaze of the audience sufficient time for visual consumption.[331] Though Mulvey theorizes the roles of female stars and ungendered spectators, Marlon Brando occupies in *Streetcar* as well as in *Blonde* the position of desired object, with Oates and her readers enjoying a narrative pause. When the plot resumes with Carlo vomiting in the bathtub and simultaneously cursing Marilyn, the gaze turns from feminine to feminist and paves the way for the "harshness" of the male portraits that follow. Brando redeems himself with white lilies, roses, carnations, and gardenias expressing his gratitude and friendship. Though Marilyn's heart and body belong to Miller, Oates's readers are thrilled.

Vicious males nonetheless litter Oates's pages and the Blond Actress's road to success. Though she lands a role in *Scudda-Hoo! Scudda-Hay!* without an audition (except the encounter on Mr Z's white rug), her problems with Hollywood power brokers continue. After the nude calendar episode, she appeases a series of angry studio executives in predictable, if unmentionable, ways. Oates's company of powerful males includes the President of the United States, who behaves in a fashion that makes the antics of Peter Lawford, Frank Sinatra and the Rat Pack pale in comparison. In *Black Water* (1992), her novel about Chappaquiddick, Oates had already exposed Ted Kennedy, but at the Carlton Hotel in New York, his big brother the President does not even interrupt his phone calls while Marilyn attends to his needs. This violation paves the way for still other invasions—the passing on of Marilyn to Bobby, and the (fictional?) Sharpshooter, who in Oates's final chapter sinks a six-inch needle into the heart of the Kennedys' whore.

The cover of the original *Blonde* whets reader appetites by showing Marilyn or a look-alike from the back and by retrieving from the black background only a blond head and pale shoulders. The illustration promises a new angle on the Marilyn mystery, which the darkness enveloping the figure suggests. As spectators, we see the world from Marilyn's perspective: an apocalyptic void. Glued to her back or crouched on her shoulder, we partake in the nightmare Marilyn performed. We devour her, save her, or look at her. Despite hostile rescuers and reviewers, Oates's millennium Marilyn explodes lines between biography and memoir, reader and writer, savior and voyeur, victim and victimizer, reel and reality, male and female, black and white and so on and so forth. And in her newest outfit, sewn on again, this postmodern performer appears in gothic splendor. She moves straight from the grave into the unholy mess that Joyce Carol Oates, her readers, and her blondes, of all colors, inhabit.

Ethnic Marilyn

Marilyn Monroe is white. Her hair is white, her face is white, she has a white poodle, her dress is white and blows up to show her white legs and her white panties. In *Marilyn* (1973), Norman Mailer calls her "every man's love affair with America, Marilyn Monroe who was blonde and beautiful and had a sweet little rinky-dink of a voice and all the cleanliness of all the clean American backyards."[332] All strawberry and vanilla ice cream to Mailer, Marilyn embodies cultural and social representations of whiteness from the 1950s into the 21st century. Like the white whale in Herman Melville's *Moby Dick* (1851), she dramatizes both a specific American cultural history and universal human qualities. Joyce Carol Oates explains her own Marilyn project with a Melville reference:

> I suppose I had in mind something like *Moby-Dick*. There was actually a white whale, and Melville was writing in meticulous detail about whales. And part of that novel that's so wonderful, I think, is the reliance upon the objective world. It's very catalogued and very beautifully written. But then it's mythic, and one would not think that Moby Dick was just any whale. So I guess Marilyn Monroe became my Moby Dick, so to speak; I'm working with mythic structures and images and much that is imagined.[333]

As an American icon, Marilyn shares an elusive quality with the whale. Oates needed 738 pages to harpoon the star, and monographs about Marilyn keep coming. Obviously, she is as hard as the whale to track down and write up—and as white. Like the whale, she becomes obsession, attraction and terror. In the world they both inhabit, white becomes red, like blood or like lips, and blackness waits beyond the horizon for everybody—most certainly for Marilyn.

Betty Grable, Jayne Mansfield, Marilyn, and other bombshells signal Hollywood notions of race, because not just gentlemen but also movie tycoons prefer blondes. Though Justine Elias in "Blond Confusion" (2003) discusses attempts to deconstruct the Hollywood blonde, "Blond Revisionism" so-called, blond actresses have since silent film days participated in privileged constructions of whiteness.[334] Richard Dyer discusses in *White* (1997) both cinema and photography as "media of light" that tend to favor white people and white actors in a "technological construction of beauty and pleasure."[335] David Ehrenstein, who writes on film for *Variety* and *The Advocate*, still mentions Hollywood's longest-living blonde in explaining what this skin and hair color means on screen: "Lightness, the infinite, the unattainable, a kind of creamy, all enveloping, sensual something or other. . . . In her last few movies, Monroe got blonder and more gorgeous than ever, and that's how she is remembered."[336] Oates stresses in *Blonde* the impact of racialized cinema on Norma Jeane Baker, who consumes the Hollywood ideal and eventually becomes one. In the darkness of a movie theater, Norma Jeane learns to dream:

> And these women, too—they were close enough to be touched, they were visions of yourself as in a fairy-tale mirror, Magic Friends in other bodies, with faces that were somehow, mysteriously, your own. Or would one day be your own. *Ginger Rogers, Joan Crawford, Katharina Hepburn, Jean Harlow, Marlene Dietrich, Greta Garbo, Constance Bennett, Joan Blondell, Claudette Colbert, Gloria Swanson*. Like dreams dreamt in confusing succession their stories melded together.[337]

Idols like Mary Pickford and Lilian Gish also linger in the office of Twentieth Century Fox President Mr. Z and his aviary of stuffed birds, which "were beautiful & lifelike not seeming to grasp that they were dead."[338] As she begins her movie career, Norma Jeane Baker turned Marilyn Monroe also performs the discourse of whiteness produced and distributed in Hollywood.

The scene with a barely disguised Darryl Zanuck and the girl he calls Blondie links Oates's novel to Dyer's *White*. Before entering the Fox President's office, the Blond Actress has worked hard on her whiteness:

> I woke early & did my exercises & ironed this suit & showered only afterward & applied Arrid to my underarms which are clean-shaven daily . . . . I have powdered myself with talcum powder smelling of lilac I have spent 40 minutes on my make-up & this sharkskin suit . . . . My hands are soft from lotion & my hands are manicured & glamorous yet not showy, I think It is not my fault about the peroxide I was ordered by the Studio to have my hair bleached "platinum blond" it was not my decision but I said nothing of course.[339]

Whiteness is no longer a given but a cultural ideal, a fantasy that nobody may fully inhabit. Norma Jeane's own whiteness cracks after the visit in Mr Z's office and the sexual services exchanged for her first movie part. Her make-up is streaked and red menstrual blood stains her white sharkskin skirt: "I was trying to walk, & nearly fainted inside my clothes I was bleeding & it felt distant my body numb & distant."[340] Norma Jeane's soiled and lifeless appearance mocks the cultural obsession with glamorous whiteness and presents it as an impossible Hollywood dream. In Dyer's words, "Whiteness as an ideal can never be attained, not only because white skin can never be hue white, but because ideally white is absence: to be really, absolutely white is to be nothing."[341]

The association between whiteness and absence explains Marilyn's unending popularity. Over the decades, she has functioned as a blankness ready for inscription, whether the text she became dealt with sexual desire, female liberation, American body politics, or 21st-century miseries. Her status as empty signifier connects her to whiteness as the norm and explains her universal appeal. Unmarked, ahistorical, disinterested, she supports a conception of white objectivity, what Dyer calls "white people . . . as everything and nothing."[342] This function emerges in *The Seven Year Itch* (1955), in which Marilyn plays "The Girl," or in other roles, where she has no existence outside of being "the blonde."[343] This basic anonymity appears as well in Oates's description of Marilyn promoting the *Itch*, a focal scene in all Marilyn accounts:

> The Girl with No Name. The Girl on the Subway Grating. The Girl of Your Dreams. It's 2:40 A.M. and glaring-white lights focus upon her, upon her alone, blond squealing, blond laughter, blond Venus, blond insomnia, blond smooth-shaven legs apart and blond hands fluttering in a futile effort to keep her skirt from lifting to reveal white cotton American-girl panties and the shadow, just the shadow, of the bleached crotch. . . . She's not a dirty girl, nothing foreign or exotic. She's an American slash in the flesh. That emptiness. Guaranteed. She's been scooped up, drained clean, no scar tissue to interfere with your pleasure, and no odor. Especially no odor.[344]

With the repetition of "blond," "white" and "girl," Marilyn advertises not only her recent movie but also the connection between whiteness and purity. Unlike the historically marked African American body, her figure exists outside of space and time to suggest the centrality of whiteness to American identity and nationhood. In her blue eyes, history disappears: "*I'm only an American. Skin deep. There's nothing inside me, really.*"[345]

Almost floating on the subway grating, Marilyn becomes the Angel of America. Dyer analyzes the connection of blondness to Christian iconography and demonstrates in *White* the glow of white women such as Gish and Pickford in visual representations. To be a white woman is to suggest spirituality and transcendence, as Marilyn does with her heavenly body and hair. In one scene in *Some Like It Hot* (1959), Tony Curtis, Jack Lemmon, and Marilyn Monroe all wear black dresses, but Sugar, the Monroe character, stands out with blond hair lit from all sides, so that her head, in Dyer's view, becomes a "ball of light."[346] To Mailer, she is not just "every man's love affair with America" but also "our angel, the sweet angel of sex." "She gave the feeling," he writes, "that if you made love to her, why then could you not . . . move into tender heavens where your flesh would be restored."[347] Marilyn is more than Marilyn, more than white. She is transcendence, redemption and the Promised Land. She signals Christianity, Manifest Destiny, and a New Jerusalem, populated by whites.

But Marilyn is nobody and looking for somebody. Everybody needs a Da-da-daddy, as we know, and in the all-white America of *Blonde*, only Jews have a history and a race. Her nude calendar photographer is Jewish, she learns, and the Blond Actress has never known about Jews and Judaism and race and wonders what it feels like to be "chosen." She stares at her mysterious photographer: "In Otto Öse's dark-socketed eyes she saw a soulfulness, a depth, and a history lacking in her own eyes, which were a clear, startling blue." Like the white Americans in Toni Morrison's *Playing in the Dark: Whiteness and the Literary Imagination* (1992), she makes up for her lack with an other, in Marilyn's case with Arthur Miller. In a courtship scene between the Playwright and the Blond Actress, she dreams up a synagogue, a temple perhaps, on Wilshire Boulevard, and the language of Hebrew, "so strange and wonderful" that to Norma Jeane "it was the voice of God." The Playwright gets uneasy: "Religion meant little to him except as a mode of ancestor respect, and that he took with a grain of salt. He wasn't a Jew who believed that the Holocaust was the end of history or the beginning of history, even that the Holocaust 'defined' Jews. He was a liberal, a socialist, a rationalist."[348] Unperturbed, Marilyn finds an identity in his Jewishness: "He was her Abraham. . . . She'd been baptized a Christian and would unbaptize herself and become a Jew. *In my soul I am Jewish. A wanderer seeking my true homeland*."[349] With books like *The Shame of Europe*, Jewish recipes and a Jewish wedding, she seeks to alleviate her own void, only to reinscribe ethnic difference. Miller and his Jewish background become her version of the Dark Prince rescuing the Fair Princess, an exotic stranger that allows her to "go native" and temporarily erase her whiteness. By trying to pass for Jewish, she reveals the fluid boundaries of whiteness, a variability affordable only within "a socially guaranteed whiteness."[350] Unlike her Playwright husband, who inhabits a complex and contradictory Jewishness, she freezes his Jewish identity into essence and stasis. In the end, her racial anxiety remains. Whiteness equals no mark,

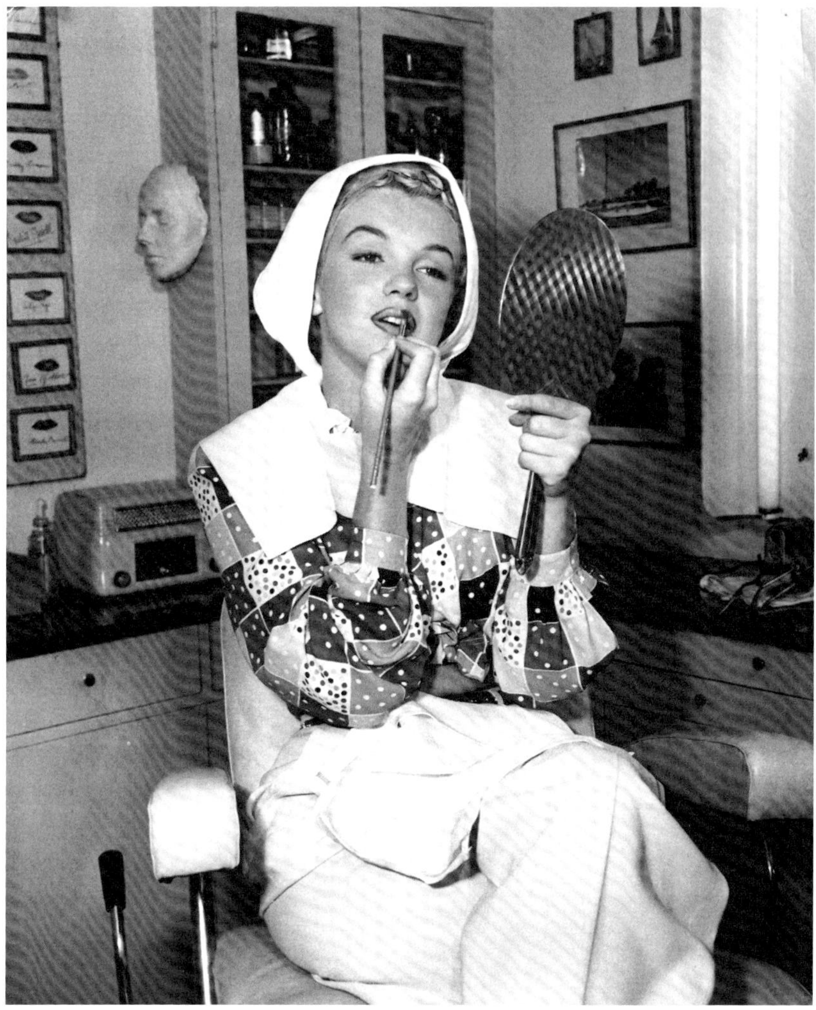

Ethnic Marilyn

no history, no community—a generic existence, with nothingness always around.

As Arthur Miller found out, Marilyn means doom. Though movie titles such as *Gentlemen Prefer Blondes*, *Platinum Blonde* and *Blonde Venus* suggest that blondes are winners, another line of films associates blondes with death. The silent drama *Blonde Vampire* (1922) begins a tradition of blond destruction. As Justine Elias and others note, femininity in general and blondes in particular often get symbolically dirty in the movies, with Alfred Hitchcock's Kim Novak, Eva Marie Saint and Tippi Hedren as examples of sexually mysterious and (self-)destructive women. "The fascinated men who try to rescue them," Elias writes, "do so at the risk of their own souls." As Rose in *Niagara* (1953) Marilyn contributes to this tradition of blond vampyres, which her own consumption of pills, champagne, lovers and husbands reinforced. Dead Marilyn figures prominently in the biographical literature about the star—also in Oates's *Blonde*, where death begins and closes the text in the shape of a messenger boy and a sharpshooter, who inserts his needle into her white flesh. In between these scenes, blood oozes across the pages to link Marilyn with danger and destruction. To be white, universal, in Dyer's phrase a "subject without properties," calls up anxieties and misgivings.[351] To be nobody is also to be dead. For the premiere of *Niagara*, Marilyn appears in a red sequined dress with white shoulders and chest mostly bare. "Five hours was the minimum the makeup people spent on her for these occasions," the newborn star explains in *Blonde*. "Like preparing a cadaver."[352] A ghost from the 1950s, Marilyn still haunts us, dead and white.

Dead or alive, Marilyn Monroe seems extremely white, the "exceptional, excessive, marked" white that coexists with what Dyer calls "ordinary whiteness."[353] Oates agrees: "Like Cherie in *Bus Stop* she appears so much paler than her companions, she might be a mannequin or a clown."[354] Her silky, shiny hair and skin evoke spirituality and transcendence, but also carnival and distance. It allows white people a "space of ordinariness" in which they may celebrate their status as unremarkable and average human beings. Marilyn is popular because she is extreme, not-us, while Norma Jeane is forgettable, ordinary. At the same time, the extreme whiteness of Marilyn Monroe denounces race as biology and destiny. She subverts established racial categories by stretching whiteness as far as it goes. Like a French feminist, she rejects social and symbolic codes with excess, with overflow, with laughter, and like a white trickster, she assumes the liberating role through joking. A trickster-artist of sorts, she crosses or overturns the boundaries that hold her. Like the trickster, she is a shape-shifter who cannot be categorized. Erratic and contradictory, she represents all options, and through her "misrule" explodes stability and familiarity.[355]

She explodes as well the patience of directors, producers, and fellow actors. Marilyn insisted on retakes—again and again and again—and drove everybody up the wall in quest of perfection. In *Blonde* this effort to reach the ideal becomes hysteria:

> The Beggar Maid's curse! To repeat to repeat to stammer & repeat & begin again & again begin & stammer & repeat & retreat & lock herself away & return at last only to repeat & repeat repeat to get it perfect to get whatever it is perfect to get perfect what is not perfectable to repeat & repeat until it was perfect & unassailable so when they laughed they would be laughing at a brilliant comic performance & not at Norma Jeane, they would not be aware of Norma Jeane at all.[356]

Through a hysterical performance, the Blond Actress expresses some sort of resistance.[357] Like Freud's nineteenth-century hysterics, she uses her body to articulate repressed dissatisfaction. As Elizabeth Bronfen suggests in *The Knotted Subject: Hysteria and Its Discontents* (1998), this sort of simulation reveals a discrepancy between self and self-representation and highlights performative aspects of identity. By insistently bringing the performance of her roles into focus, Marilyn intervenes in the power formations of Hollywood in particular and American culture in general. She inserts, so to speak, a gap between the roles she accepts and those she resists, with Norma Jeane in the first category and Marilyn Monroe in the second.

The hysteric performance displays the star's frustration at being imprisoned in cinematic and cultural signs—woman, idol, blond bombshell, whatever—without breaking her dependence on the linguistic and institutional structures that define her. Hysteria, Bronfen explains, does not cut or undo the knot, but "preserves the knot in all its ambivalence and inconsistency."[358] Dyer finds that Marilyn participates in 1950s discourses of female sexuality, including the so-called *Playboy* discourse that promotes sexuality as "natural." He also detects her efforts to resist: "Monroe embodies and to a degree authenticates these discourses, but there is also a sense in which she begins to act out the drama of the difficulty of embodying them."[359] In his analysis of *The Prince and the Showgirl* (1956), the first effort of the newly formed Marilyn Monroe Production Company, Dyer finds that the Showgirl character (Monroe, of course) represents disruption as well as resolution or a return to equilibrium. In short, she means both trouble and no trouble.[360]

Though Oates counteracts her feminist impulses by ignoring the Blond Actress's agency and self-determination, she whirls up issues of race and gender in feminist-postmodernist fashion. Oates announces the whiteness of her protagonist with the title *Blonde*, with Marilyn's white wardrobe, her creamy-white skin, her white telephone. Blondeness signals whiteness, the white man's prize, Eldridge Cleaver's ultrafeminine woman. She usually gets stuck with the image of "White Marilyn," a passive woman men adore. Marilyn seemingly fits the man-made stereotype Klaus Theweleit identifies in *Male Fantasies*: the "White Woman" who services her male partner and retreats into domesticity.[361] Unfortunately, Marilyn does not belong at home, in *Blonde* or elsewhere. Even during the idyllic summer with Arthur Miller in Connecticut, she fails miserably as a housewife. In Oates's version, she drops a whole tray of appetizers once she finally makes it downstairs to meet her new husband's friends. She comes closer to Theweleit's other male fantasy, the "Red Woman," the one who disturbs masculine ideals of self-control, dignity, and moral rectitude.

Marilyn appears in *Niagara* as a "Red Woman" in the character of Rose, who gets killed off at the end for her sexuality and adultery. In *The Woman in Red* (1984), Kelly Le Brock substitutes for Marilyn at the Manhattan subway grating, dark hair on bare shoulders and red dress blowing up to her waist to reveal red panties.[362] Oates gets a similar effect by stressing Marilyn's casual nudity, the ease with which she poses for the Miss Golden Dreams calendar, and her habit of sleeping and walking around the house *au naturel*. The menstrual cramps and oozings, the miscarriages, the abortions, and the operations spill blood all over Oates's pages and Marilyn's white clothes and ensure that the Blond Actress changes from "White Woman" to "Red."

Marilyn even turns black. As bell hooks argues in "Madonna: Plantation Mistress or Soul Sister?" white women entertainers like Sandra Bernhard, Madonna, and others appropriate African American culture to spice up their performances, while women stars of color like Tina Turner, Aretha Franklin and Donna Summer flaunt their "blonde ambition."[363] Racial boundaries vibrate, in short, when Marilyn and Madonna inhabit a sexual space usually reserved for women of African descent. In *Undressing Cinema: Clothing and Identity in the Movies* (1997), Stella Bruzzi comments upon the "extreme fetishisation of clothes" and the "significance of appearance to the heroes' identities" in blaxploitation films and thus suggests still another connection between Marilyn and blackness.[364] Marilyn articulates her function as dark other in the section of *My Story* where she accuses her admirers of projecting their own "lewd thoughts" onto her. They "whitemask" themselves, she argues, and call her lewd instead.[365] Like women of color, Marilyn finds herself cast as the always already fallen woman, her body signifying sexual experience and lust.

The constant bleaching of Marilyn's hair is not exclusively related to publicity and aesthetics. Julie Birchill asks in *Girls on Film*: "What does it say about racial purity that the best blondes have all been brunettes (Harlow, Monroe, Bardot)? I think it says that we are not as white as we think. I think it says that Pure is a Bore."[366] Apart from the intriguing flavor of the "non-blonde Other," hooks finds that Marilyn and Madonna from the margin uphold the aesthetic markers of dominant culture. Coded as non-white in their quest for blond hair and pale skin, they have, in hooks's view, "much in common with the masses of black women who suffer from internalized racism and are forever terrorized by a standard of beauty they feel they can never truly embody."[367]

Blonde stresses the constructedness of white feminine beauty. Oates spends pages and pages on Norma Jeane's make-up sessions, her ironing of clothes and, later, on Marilyn in the hands of assistants and beauticians. She focuses especially on "Whitey," the make-up artist responsible for creating Marilyn Monroe out of drunk and drugged raw materials. In the *Something's Got to Give* stage of the Blond Actress's career, the Allan "Whitey" Snyder figure has his work cut out for him:

> Whitey's deft fingers and cotton swabs soaked in astringent. His soothing ointments, his eyelash curlers and tweezers and tiny brushes and colored pencils, his pastes, rouges, powders working their magic, or almost working their magic. This morning he's been laboring for hours and she was only partway MARILYN MONROE in the mirror.[368]

As the appropriately named Whitey produces White Marilyn with considerable effort and occasional success, Oates mocks the beauty ideal in the process of its (de)construction. The Blond Actress who struggles to become the Blond Actress inhabits a space outside mainstream aesthetics, where she vacillates between hooks's plantation mistress and her soul sister. In "Fabulousness as Fetish: Queer Politics in *Sex and the City*," Christy Turner discusses the flamboyance of Samantha, the serial's Marilyn character, as a raced construct, indebted to black queer culture.[369] In Bruzzi's words, "the pursuit of fashionability has, primarily by those who despise it, been characterised as a repetitive tussle between exclusion and inclusion."[370] Marilyn should know.

Like privileged white ladies, the star has her labor performed by slaves such as "Nico," her masseur, or Whitey, who "had grown stout and ashy-skinned and -haired in the arduous service of MARILYN MONROE."[371] But the protagonist of *Blonde* knows herself from the Studio system and its masters a good deal about the peculiar institution.[372] In depicting the contracts, sales, and sexual services of Twentieth Century Fox, Hollywood, Strasberg's Actors Studio, as well as the husbands, friends, fans, and enemies who cross the Blond Actress's path, Oates relies on images of bondage and slavery that position the troubled star in racialized terrain. In *Of Women and Their Elegance* (1980), Mailer voices Marilyn's dread at having to appear with Miller at Sir Laurence and Lady Olivier's dinner party for them at Terence Rattigan's residence. Amy Greene, the wife of her partner in Marilyn Monroe Productions, delivers the news: "'Everybody in England will be there, my darling,' she said." Marilyn feels nothing of Amy's enthusiasm: "My heart sank. Everybody who was curious about Arthur and me. It would be a slave auction. 'Look at their teeth.'" She declares that she has absolutely nothing to wear: "'That slave girl doesn't carry her clothes right,' they'd say."[373] In

W. J. Weatherby's *Conversations with Marilyn* (1976), Marilyn and Weatherby's New Orleans girlfriend of African descent, Christine, occupy the same space in his heart and life.[374]

If the quintessential white woman changes to red, to black and back to blond again, Oates stresses like Mailer, Weatherby and other Marilyn observers her gift for comedy. Cast as dumb blonde, sex goddess, or the girl next door, the Blond Actress distances herself from enclosing categories with a comic twist. In performing traditional femininity, she creates an alternative space, a feminine hyperreal where issues of race and gender are exaggerated and problematized. Judith Halberstam argues in *Female Masculinity* (1998) that masculinity "becomes legible as masculinity where and when it leaves the white male middle-class body."[375] White femininity may best be read or theorized from a distance as well. Like Halberstam's notion of masculinity outside male bodies, the spaces in *Blonde* between Norma Jeane and Marilyn, between the woman behind the mirror and the magic friend, between White, Red, and Black Marilyn, and between the bombshell and the *comedienne* open up for new constellations of race and gender. Oates's Marilyn ends up as mere body, the victim of Kennedy and FBI inscriptions, but she herself dreams up an alternative scene. In "We Are All Gone Into the World of Light," the last section of *Blonde*, the Fair Princess burns: peroxide hair aflame, naked body aflame, eyes aflame, belly aflame. As she dives into the dark, she lights up everybody. In the illuminated, technologically beautiful crowd, orphans and parents, stars and fans, whites and blacks all perform the monstrous, hybrid and fertile forms of American identities.

Natural Marilyn

Marilyn travelled across the U.S. to escape the Hollywood sublime and adopted in Lee Strasberg's Actors Studio in New York the Russian-inspired approach to her craft. In movies such as *Niagara* (1953), *The River of No Return* (1954), *Bus Stop* (1956) and *The Misfits* (1961), she also explores American frontiers and borders, from Canadian waterfalls and rivers to isolated Nevada deserts. With her kaleidoscopic identities and bodies, she maps a country in flux and the people who confront or conform to disappearing American landscapes. In "On the Road Again: Metaphors of Travel in Cultural Criticism" (1993), Janet Wolf notes that the imagery of movement links up with hegemonies of class and gender, not to mention race and space.[376] As a collection of American identities, Marilyn inhabits in Canada, Arizona, Montana or Nevada a body and a terrain that articulate the tensions within and across America. She is American Monroe, a modern cowgirl caught up in whirlwinds of challenge and change. She distances herself from the coherent, efficient stars who resolve the ideological crises they encounter or embody. Instead, she presents the "strange and awkward cases" that Martin Barker in *Contemporary Hollywood Stardom* (2003) associates with the "unfinished business" of star studies.[377]

In a reversal of American myths, Marilyn fled in 1954 from Los Angeles to New York City. She had repeatedly been cast as the Blond Bombshell of Hollywood and now left behind in California her contract with Twentieth Century Fox and the tycoons controlling her. In New York she joined Lee Strasberg and his actors, whose Method confirmed her "natural" mode of performance and prepared her for the frontier world of subsequent movies. First among "The Naturalists" and the founder of the Moscow Art Theater in 1897, Constantin Stanislavsky developed in *An Actor Prepares* (1936) the aesthetic of acting that would dominate twentieth-century theater and film. In "When Acting Is an Art," Stanislavsky proposes an organic fusion of an actor with the role at hand: the successful actor needs to dig into emotional soil in the unconscious in order to harvest the role from within. This instinctual method of acting plugs into feelings that take possession of the actor according to "the laws of normal organic life." Stanislavsky explains: "Since we do not understand this governing power, and cannot study it, we actors call it simply nature."[378] At the Actors Studio, Strasberg popularized Stanislavsky's theories and refined his concept of "affective memory" by dividing it into the recall of sensations and the recall of feelings. He schooled famous post-war actors like Marlon Brando and Paul Newman and taught them that no imitations of human beings were necessary, since actors must learn to create out of themselves. As James Naremore states in *Act-*

ing in the Cinema (1988), Method actors developed "an introspective, neurotic style" that differed completely from Chaplin's theatricality.[379]

When Marilyn became Strasberg's protegée, she remained or became a neurotic and a naturalist. Like other striking figures on film, she looked "natural" and caused critics to discuss her in terms of personality rather than craft.[380] Stanislavskyans at the Studio learned to be open and relaxed, "as loose as animals in the wild," and supported their acting method with references to the "natural" human being. They needed to use their bodies as instruments and let movements and gestures grow "naturally" from emotions within. Biological "symptoms" like fatigue or hunger became central to the naturalist actor, as Marilyn would learn from her own body as well.[381] Shooting *The Misfits* in Nevada, she took a troubled path in terms of marriage, drugs, and alcohol and battled in vain a wilderness inside and out there. The western environment she sought to transform in turn transformed her. As Blake Allmendinger puts it in *Ten Most Wanted: The New Western Literature* (1998), "women who joined men, with the intention of improving frontier society, ended up experiencing the same degradation."[382]

In a famous publicity shot for *Niagara*, Marilyn merges with the Falls to suggests the connection between untameable nature and femininity gone wild. During a honeymoon in Canada, Marilyn's character, Rose, cheats on her middle-aged husband George Loomis (Joseph Cotton) with a younger man. Together, this couple hatches a plan to murder George, a plot that backfires when the grieving Rose finds in the morgue not her mentally unstable husband but her handsome lover. Thrown into temporary derangement by this sight, she is hospitalized and suffers restlessly as the town bells chime the song intended to signal her husband's liquidation. After her release from the Niagara Falls hospital, she attempts to leave town but is tracked down by George, who has killed his wife's lover amidst the roar of the Falls. Another honeymooning couple, Ray and Polly Cutler from Toledo, Ohio, get wrestled out of their cheerful complacency to become reluctant witnesses to the events whirling around them. Rose ends up dead, murdered by her jealous, revengeful husband underneath the silent town bells. In the nick of time, Polly Cutler (Jean Peters) escapes death by drowning, as George Loomis deposits her on a rock formation seconds before the boat he has hijacked gets sucked into the Falls.

The movie blurb promises "a fascinating portrait of human passion and nature's power that rushes at you with the force of Niagara itself." Obviously, Rose is the force of nature that no one can contain. The ranch-style honeymoon motel advertised as Modern Housekeeping Cabins, located at the edge of the Falls, suggests the precarious balance between order and chaos that dominates the film. In one revealing scene, Polly Cutler discovers Rose and her lover in a passionate embrace, the Falls swirling all around them. The ideal '50s wife immediately steps away from the edge and the sight, while her husband freezes her with his camera to ensure her safety and his control.

Despite his efforts, Polly Cutler and Rose Loomis turn into mirror images. Jean Peters's character embodies the domestic cheerfulness, good looks, and regulated sexuality of the suburban wife, while Marilyn's suggests the wild, unregulated nature that unbalances the whole community. In the scene when the Cutlers arrive at the vacation camp, Rose upsets the manager's plan by remaining in the room the other couple had booked. When Mr. Loomis and his wife's lover have had their fatal encounter at the Falls, she has handed over the room to Mrs. Cutler, who naps in her bed when the wronged husband seeks his revenge. Polly Cutler screams and raves in a complete departure from her regular normalcy, long after the murderer has escaped. Her own husband does not believe her story and firmly tells his troubled wife to "get organized." His unusual choice of words in comforting Polly suggests the problem. At any moment, order may give way to chaos, contained only through acts of will. The wilderness within threatens especially through women's bodies—prone in beds and deck chairs or splashed with liminal mist or men's desires throughout the movie. Twice, George Loomis tells Polly Cutler about passion and will-power. At the motel, where the manager constantly sweeps in a vain attempt to control the goings-on, George advises Polly not to let love "get out of hands." If so, he warns, nothing "can keep it from going over the edge." After the murder, he makes a last try for order, away from the tantalizing Rose, who has caused his near-insanity and crime. Asking Polly not to reveal that he is alive, he says: "At least I could go on from there—get a job—get organized!" But he can no longer control Polly, himself or his wife.

Natural Marilyn has to go, because she threatens order. She represents change and a disconcerting liminality, suggested by the mist that envelops all around her, by her suitcase, and by her well-fitted travel suit. George follows her into the Niagara Falls bell tower, adjacent to the railway station, and makes sure she falls down several floors after a passionate physical struggle. Flat on her back, legs and mouth open, she is available for her devastated husband, who spends the whole night fingering the red lipstick that had highlighted her sexuality. Interestingly, he too is locked in, allowed to escape only when the guard unlocks the front door the next morning. In the end, he perishes in the Falls, while Rose stays dead and controlled. The city bells no longer articulate desire. They will ring out the time on the hour and thus give structure to the chaos that had threatened the orderly town. Dead on the cement floor, Rose foreshadows the transfer of nature into bourgeois indoor space, the "hypernatural landscapes" of contemporary hotels and shopping malls filled with trees, ferns and waterfalls.[383] As Todd Gitlin explains in "Domesticating Nature," the bourgeois living room traps dangerous or disappearing elements of nature and keeps in check the threats from the environment.[384] Dead and decorative, Natural Marilyn suggests both the vanishing wilderness so tempting to tourists and the wild frontiers where men become savages and die.

Richard Dyer and Lisa Cohen have connected the introduction of Cinemascope in the '50s to suburban sprawl and architecture, and to the body of Marilyn Monroe, whose curvaceous figure and horizontal walk suited perfectly the new widescreen technology. The poster illustration of *River of No Return*, in which Natural Marilyn reappears, takes as its subject the final scenes of the film, where Marilyn's character is sprawled horizontally on a saloon bar desk. The camera takes in every detail of her face, breast, waist, hips and sequined shoes, which match her tight-fitting, opening red-and-yellow gown. Most horizontal of everything, however, is the torrential river of the movie title, where most of Marilyn's activities occur. In terms of tech-

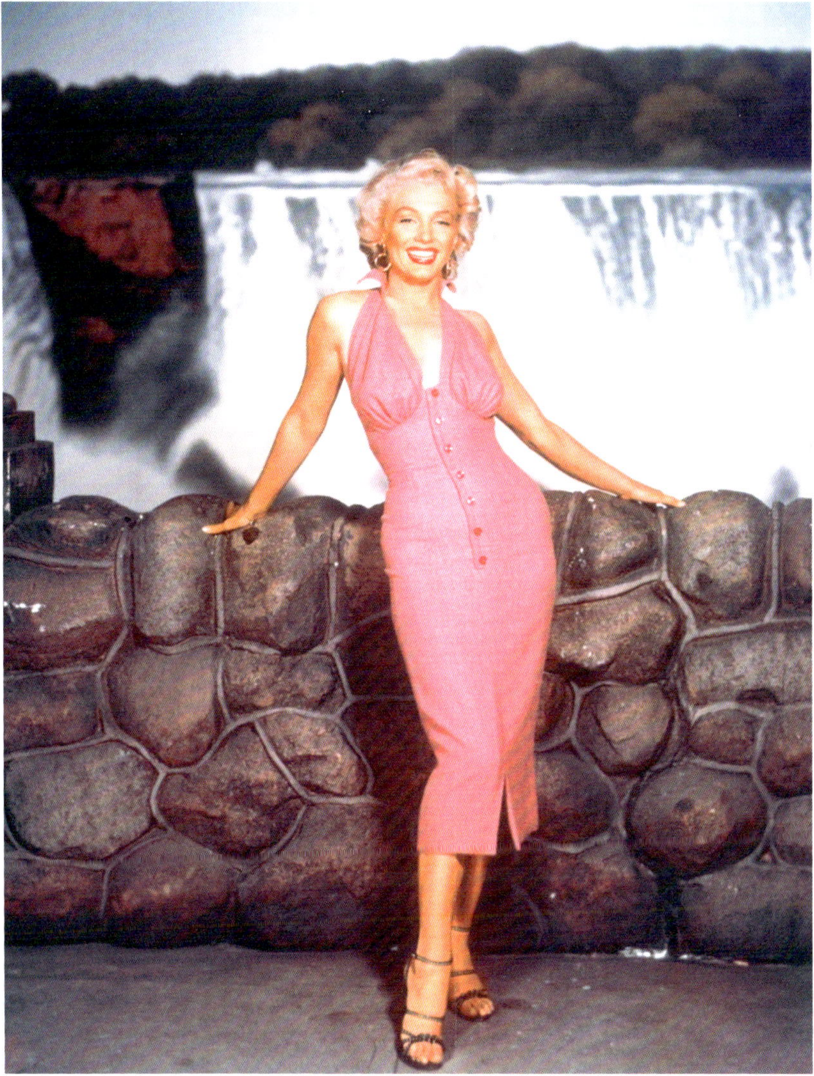

Natural Marilyn

nique and theme, she again becomes a segment of nature that must be tamed or eliminated to re-establish order and (masculine) control.

Though *Niagara* was shot in Niagara Falls and *River of No Return*, in the Banff and Jasper National Parks, all Canadian locations, Natural Marilyn dramatizes the American restlessness associated with

Western expansion and frontier life. Marilyn's character in *River*, Kay, works as a showgirl in a gold prospectors' camp in the scenic Northwest. She meets up with the rugged Matt Calder (Robert Mitchum), a widower with a dubious past about to begin a new life with his young son, Mark. Their log cabin life is threatened first by Indians and later by pretty-boy gambler Harry Weston (Rory Calhoun), who robs and pistol-whips the Calders and take off with their horse and only gun. Kay postpones her wedding to Weston in Council City to take care of the Calders and joins them on the journey down the river of no return she had begun with her sweet-talking fiancé. The film lavishes narrative energy on the river sequence, the raft replacing the log cabin as a mythic American space. With her close tie to young Mark, Marilyn becomes a differently gendered Huck Finn, new to the river of no return but with the natural gifts to navigate it.

A series of accidents during shootings suggest that nothing about *River* was tame. Marilyn almost drowned when her high waders took in water, but Mitchum and the film crew came to her rescue. Stuntman Norman Bishop recalls how he and a colleague got both Marilyn and Mitchum off the raft: "The goddam thing got stuck on a rock. It was bounding and setting to turn over any second." Off the set, Mitchum and Marilyn inspired "a string of bawdy anecdotes" that still circulates. Mitchum attempted to tell Marilyn about "anal eroticism," while his stuntmen sought to demonstrate more concretely Mitchum's lecture. Disgusted with rude innuendos, Marilyn let herself slip in the river and spoke long-distance to Darryl Zanuck about "considerable pain." Though x-rays showed no fracture, Marilyn insisted on a plaster cast and crutches and soon had director Otto Preminger "oozing studied courtesy." The schedule was so delayed that Mitchum dubbed the project Picture of No Return.[385] Wilderness Marilyn would not be tamed.

As a Western, *River* casts the landscape as protagonist, but Marilyn dominates the wide screen. Though she changes out of the velvet gowns highlighting breasts and buttocks, her blue jeans and wet tops ensure that her body stays in focus. The cinematography that captures the beauty of the river, the mountains, the wooded areas and Marilyn includes her shape and character in the wilderness geography.[386] She arrives at the log cabin seconds after Native Americans have appeared on the mountain tops surrounding the Calders' cabin in classic Western style, and she brings with her the danger that sets in motion all the violence. Like the natives, the mountains, the horses and the land, she inspires the "aesthetics of possession" characteristic of homesteader Matt Calder's vision.[387]

In the natural world, Kay suggests both the kinship and the otherness that human beings experience in contemplating nature.[388] As an ex-convict, Matt Calder recognizes in Kay the wildness and the passion that earlier caused him to shoot a man in the back. To stay in the wilderness, she lets go of clothes, money and a partner. When she arrives with Weston at the Calders' cabin, her suitcase continues down the river, while Kay makes no move to retrieve it. Her maternal instincts link her with father and son in a natural bond. With Matt Calder castrated by the theft of his gun, she feeds both her companions with berries, expertly gathered on the river slopes. At the same time, she is unmistakably other. She invades the masculine world of the Western and causes Matt Calder to lose his gun. She stays outside the civilizing space of the cabin. She plays her guitar and combs her hair, thus suggesting a displaced sexuality not lost on Matt. She tries to steal the raft, and she calls Matt a murderer in front of his son.

Kay is an object of the male gaze, as when Matt watches her singing from a cabin window, but she escapes the frame. Instead she links up with the Native Americans. Throughout *Return*, Natural Marilyn's white make-up looks like war paint. In *The Seven Year Itch*, she echoes the mythical young squaw who lured warriors away from work and wives before English settlements. In *River*, she wears a war mask of make-up that signals her difference. Sent up to Canada to interview Marilyn, L.A. reporter Jim Bacon called her "Dracula's Daughter" and found her wild: "Her hair was in tangles," he wrote. "She had cold cream all over her face, and her eyebrows were smeared." Out in the wilderness, Whitey Snyder, her make-up assistant, finally told her: "Get that crap off your face. You scare people."[389]

Marilyn/Kay activates conventions of American nature writing as she travels down the river of no return. She awakens the sense of wonder, in the tradition of the mythical and "fabulous creatures" that populated early views and descriptions of nature. Posing on the raft in skin-tight blue jeans, Marilyn causes spectators to marvel at Creation and divine Design. She appeals as well to ecologists linking all aspects of the natural world, as she herself links up with children, animals, natives, trees, and river currents. With her frontier outfit, she suggests a specifically American landscape and discourse. In the tradition from Thoreau to Dillard, she provides sufficient "residual wilderness" to distance Americans from the "over-tidy categories and conventions" dominating European models. She is an American Eve, escaped from history into the wilderness.[390] She sets off universal themes of landscape description such as nature's abundance, mystery, and power, and she suggests to the Calders and to everybody else "our relief and pleasure at not being alone on the earth."[391]

Though Preminger highlights the river, its torrents and falls, it becomes a familiar prop as the raft glides by pines and mountains and Marilyn strikes the poses her blue jeans and boots allow. No erotic sparks fly between Marilyn and Mitchum, who in pre-fame days had worked next to her first husband, Jim Dougherty, at Lockheed. And Natural Marilyn belongs in barrooms. Her blue jeans do not snuggle her body like her bar girl's velvet, and the boots are less becoming than the sequined shoes she leaves behind. In the final scene, when Matt sweeps her off the saloon bar and carries her into his buggy, Kay goes "home," but her shoes and her audience look abandoned. Unlike Rose, who must die for civilization to live, Kay is packaged and delivered to a world of domesticity, love, and masculine dominance. She is entertainment nature, after all, as complacent as Niagara Falls in cyberspace. As David Orr reminds us in "Virtual Nature" (1996), the two-dimensional simulation of natural reality is safe.[392] Virtual nature offers control, not liberation. Like the other characters in this romantic Western, Marilyn offers to spectators a dream restored, a nostalgic visit to a vanished world. She herself has vanished, as we know, but she still decorates our mental and physical space with her exotic charm and wildness.

The "anxiety of belatedness," characteristic of those exploring a vanishing American wilderness, permeates *The Misfits*, Arthur Miller's belated gift to Marilyn. Set in Reno, Nevada, the film presents a "Last Frontier," where a group of cowboys and one splendid divorcée, Marilyn's character Roslyn, seek survival and renewal in a Western environment. It also communicates Miller's "complete ethnic rush," which Stan Godlovitch associates with urban tourists exploring provincial locales.[393] As in *Niagara* and *River of No Return*, Marilyn acts in a frontier narrative stressing conflicts between natural and cultural spaces. Miller dismantles notions of Nevada as a wilderness retreat that allows American heroes an escape from history. As a resource manager of sorts, Miller insists that economic developments outside the region influence this sparsely populated and remote area.[394] Nevada becomes a map of modern America, and Natural Marilyn embodies its tensions and conflicts.

The Misfits accentuates biology and nature partly because it was the last film Marilyn and Clark Gable ever completed. As James Naremore reminds us, biology is central to acting and frequently adds to performances, like De Niro's weight gain in *Raging Bull* (1980), Brando's, in *Apocalypse Now* (1979), and Christian Bale's weight loss in *The Machinist* (2004). In *The Misfits*, Clark Gable looks old and sick, though his character Gaylord drives into the sunset with Roslyn in the end. W. J. Weatherby, who followed *The Misfits* in Nevada and received from Miller a copy of the published script dedicated to Gable, saw little of Gable's hearty, joyful trademark smile in the desert: "He had been as tired as he looked." Marilyn was hospitalized during the shooting, her red eyes and drawn looks hidden beneath make-up and unfocused camera lenses. Weatherby speculates about her reaction to the loss of father figures immediately after their time in Nevada: "Miller—Gable: it was all loss."[395] As Jean Luc Godard explains in comparing painting to cinema, film shows and exploits the decay of performers; the medium "seizes life and the mortal aspects of life." "The person one films," he notes, "is growing older and will die. We film, therefore, a moment when death is working." Montgomery Clift, who drank heavily (in Marilyn's company) at night and between shootings, also looked worse for wear, though his "ravaged face," in Naremore's phrase, suited well his rodeo cowboy role.[396] And Jane Tompkins stresses in *West of Everything* (1992) that death waits behind every cactus or mountaintop in classic Western scripts.

Everything Western in *West of Everything* finds its way to Miller's script. Death lurks in the desert sands, in the Reno divorces, in the hordes of wild horses depleted to fifteen or six, in the death of the West and the death of the Western, in the deaths of illusions and dreams, in Marilyn's red-rimmed eyes and Gable's wrinkled face. The lost cowboys speak not with words, but with action: barroom brawls, rodeo acts, guns, lassoes, hunting. In Miller's words, the land "seems undisturbed in its silence, a silence that grows in the mind until it becomes a wordless voice." When real men talk in *The Misfits*, they prefer one-liners and sentence fragments. "Be glad to come by and do your chores," Gay says to Roslyn, "plainly." "If you liked." Roslyn's friend Isabelle (Thelma Ritter) has become a man's man of sorts, due to her age, her single life style, and her decades in Nevada, "the leave-it state." As she explains, the slogan there is "anything goes, but don't complain if it went." When Roslyn comments on the desert landscape, "How quiet it is here!" Gay responds: "Sweetest sound there is." Gay and his partner Guido (Eli Wallach) "ride in silence" past "two Indians on brown and white paints riding slowly behind a small herd of cattle off to the right."[397] The silent landscape merges with the barely noticed Indians and the cattle. All elements of the Western contribute to the scene: the land, the men, the silence, the Indians, the horses, and the cattle. We are in the West, but Tompkins reminds us that "the Western doesn't have anything to do with the West as such." The genre stages a fight between culture and nature, between civilization and frontier, but the drama of the West highlights "men's fear of losing their mastery, and hence their identity, both of which the Western tirelessly reinvents."[398]

Classic Western scripts portray men alone in a masculine world, but Natural Marilyn is everywhere. In *River of No Return* she stayed in her place: in the saloon, on the raft, in the arms of Robert Mitchum, or in the pioneer "home" beyond the ending. Also Roslyn-Marilyn starts out contained, or framed. Guido looks up at the attractive new arrival in the window of her boarding-house, and the spectators also see her framed in a mirror and locked into the script to be memorized for the divorce proceedings. She belongs in town—high heels, city husband and all—and walks or rides from one designated space to the next: from divorce court to the local bar to a cabin in the desert. Once she has set up a household with Gay, she changes from tight slips and suits into western shirts, blue jeans, and braids, but she still conforms to frontier gender roles. She loves her new garden and brightens the indoor space with curtains and feminine knick-knacks. She dreams of a garden and a kitchen in the wilderness, an exterior domestic space with home-grown carrots and a cowboy with a spade.[399]

But Roslyn upsets the ways of the West, unlike Isabelle, who knows the rules. "I love Nevada," she tells Roslyn. "Why, they don't even have mealtimes here. I never met so many people didn't own a watch. Might have two wives at the same time, but no watch. Bless 'em all!"[400] Isabelle resists ideas of courtship and romance and refuses to search for a man she once liked. When Roslyn asks, "Could you find him if you—," she immediately interrupts: "Dear girl, you got to stop thinkin' you can change things." Roslyn's face turns red from "a mystifying flood of protest," but she meets with no understanding of her desire for influence. All talk comes to a halt: "She suddenly finds the three of them looking at her in silence, looking at her as though she had challenged them in some secret way." Roslyn is Marilyn loose in the West, where her female body unbalances masculine systems of control. Her response to this world is physical, like the mystifying flood coloring her face. She represents a different kind of knowledge. "How do you know? I mean, how do you *know*?" Guido asks her when she asks about his wife. Miller writes in his script: "Guido is stumped by her veering thought. Resentment mars his face."[401] Gay cannot read Roslyn either. From the cabin doorway, she faces the horizontal Western landscape, "the endless hills, the horizon, the empty sky." But Roslyn's gaze is vertical. She looks at the birds and finds them "small" and "brave" to venture out at night. Gay has no comment: "M-m." When Roslyn asks, "You think I'm crazy?" he seems confused: "I just look that way 'cause I can't make you out." He watches her body "through a mist emanating from her," thus associating her with liminality and the break-down of order. She is physical and natural. Gay kisses "her speaking mouth" to silence and holds her, but Roslyn-Marilyn dances out the doorway.[402]

By letting Natural Marilyn loose, Miller revises Western scripts. Without her, the cowboys know what to do and go hunting with dogs, cars, or airplanes all over the Last Frontier. Roslyn accepts biology and death, but unlike the men, she cannot kill. Soon after a comment on mortality, she "flies into a warm, longing solo dance among the weeds, and coming to a great tree she halts and then embraces it, pressing her face against its trunk."[403] Life and death intertwine naturally, but men may not interfere with biology and destiny. When Montgomery Cliff's character, Perce Howland, gets stabbed in a rodeo bull fight, she objects to his courting of death and confronts Gay: "But if he died . . . . you'd feel terrible, wouldn't you? I mean for no reason like that?" He responds, Western style: "we all got to go sometime, reason or no reason. Dyin's as natural as livin'; man who's too afraid to die is too afraid to live, far as I've ever seen." But Natural Marilyn does not accept death for profit and begins to see the landscape as "only a sterile white alkali waste." Riding through it after the rodeo, she hears "the murderous beating of wind against the car."[404]

Roslyn throws a hysterical fit to stop the men from killing horses, and the gender war about nature ends. She had earlier voiced her protest when Gay put aside his spade and grabbed his gun, to shoot the rabbit nibbling at their lettuce. Up in the mountains, the men go after the five horses left on the vanishing frontier, but Natural Marilyn disturbs them. Gay, Guido, and Perce "sense Roslyn's eyes on them, and this knowledge is like a raging sea on which they ride, falling and rising within themselves, yet outwardly even more relaxed than if all were calm under them."[405] Roslyn unfolds as a feminine force of nature when the men discuss how much money the captured mare might bring in as dog food. She writes with her body on the white land accustomed to male inscription: "She has swerved about. Her shadow sketches toward them. Forty yards away, she screams, her body writhing, bending over as though to catapult her hatred." Her shadow inscribes a new text on the sand, as threatening as any enemy clouding the horizon.[406] She will not accept the masculine West: "Man! Big man! You're only living when you can watch something die! Kill everything, that's all you want! Why don't you just kill yourselves and be happy?" Roslyn looks at each man in turn and "beyond them to imagined others." She takes on the whole western frontier and its cowboys past and present. Guido responds for them all: "*She's crazy!*" Roslyn has turned his world upside down and shaken loose the predatory beast inside him: "His eyes seem peeled back, fanatical, as though he had been seized from within by a pair of jaws which were devouring him as he stands there."[407] He looks and acts like an abused horse and calls up Tompkins in *West of Everything*: "The abuse of horses is part of a sadomasochistic impulse central to Westerns which aims at the successful domination of emotions, or the fleshly mortal part of self, and of the material world outside the body." With horses, Marilyn's body, and his own emotions galloping, Guido reveals the longings of the West and the hidden bodies of its heroes.[408]

Natural Marilyn has upset the logic of the West and the marketplace by insisting on life and truth, but the anxiety of belatedness haunts Miller's script. The West is no longer there—the cowboys and horses have all retreated, and nature has turned into trucks, airplanes, and canned horseflesh. As Gay looks back, he sees only vanished dreams:

> Squinting against the wind, his eyes hover on the high mountains, full of wish, almost expecting the sight of the hundreds, the full herds clambering into the open, the big horses and the sweet mares that gentled so quickly, the natural singlefooters, the smooth gallopers that just swept the ground under them, hardly touching it . . . .[409]

Gay feels nostalgic not only about the landscape and the horses flying across the horizon but also about the masculine dominance that Tomkins and others relate to both. He had struggled with the stallion and won and thus shown everybody that he had what it took. But he has let go of autonomy and independence by letting the horses run and by succumbing to a woman on his turf. The men have lost and know it. The West and the Western are dead.

The Misfits links up with revisionist Westerns challenging American wilderness ideals. These new frontier narratives no longer accept the idea of a Virgin Land where real men might reclaim Paradise, but portray the white hero as incapable of dominating the landscape. Out West, he no longer finds the redemption he craves and loses his dignity or his life in nature. Miller begins this revisionist trend not only by rewriting the narrative of conquest but also by voicing his social criticism.[410] The emasculated cowboys kill horses for canning and thus highlight the workings of capitalism and industrialism. Against this background, Roslyn speaks for nature and an agrarian economy, where men do not kill horses for profit. She becomes the national conscience, allied with the men's unconscious shame and despair. Her screams and convulsions speak the body, like the hysterical women of nineteenth-century asylums and psychiatrists' journals.

She also performs hysteria. Natural Marilyn acts, and her unconvincing braids and blood-shot eyes remind us that the nature she embodies no longer exists. At the end of Miller's script, we reach a classic Hollywood ending, where Gay and Roslyn ride together towards a big star in the sky. The Lone Ranger is gone, and the couple heads towards "home" and a baby. But the ride is "bumpy," and nature recedes behind "the streaks and the dust of the windshield." The highway leads towards '50s suburbia, and up in the air, Guido's airplane roars and reinforces the vertical lines relating to an urban choreography and the visual aesthetics of film noir.[411] *The Misfits* ends with the sky, the stars and the silence, but Gable and Marilyn ride into their futures and certain doom.

Natural Marilyn is artificial, since she inhabits a virtual body, once more a screen for male desires. To save their marriage, Miller tried to write up a new Marilyn, but he produced instead his own nostalgia. He created an Eve, a natural woman sent into Western terrain to comfort men and replenish the Earth. He knew, however, that both the American Eden and Marilyn were lost forever, and only his desire remained on the screen. As Natural Marilyn fades into the sunset and the fuzz of the camera, we part from a virtual woman in a virtual West. The cowboys are fakes, and their masculinity reduced to simulacrum long before her arrival. Underneath the myth of abundance, conquest, and Manifest Destiny appears the revisionist Western's "horror story of human and environmental ruin."[412] Natural Marilyn is nothing but Dracula's daughter, Miller's nightmare, and a Hollywood dream designed to relieve American anxieties.[413]

IV Performing Marilyn

Be Marilyn!

In "The Building of Popular Images: Grace Kelly and Marilyn Monroe" (1991), Thomas Harris finds that the most successful stars have an appeal that may be catalogued into set personality traits and mannerisms. Publicists would, in Marilyn's case, circulate her breathy voice, her plunging necklines, her horizontal walk, her half-closed eyes and lubricated mouth, and the off-stage "Monroeisms," the famous one-liners that linked a humorous approach to sex with her screen persona. Such "discursive prioritizations" or core characteristics that constituted Marilyn as cliché evoke the "illicit male sexual desire" and the "attainability" that Harris associates with her star image, but they have also proved irresistible to the host of impersonators who would follow the original sex goddess.[414] Not only has Marilyn's "media-drenched image" become an American stereotype, or archetype; the blond or megablond actress has landed within a tradition of American entertainment.[415] From the 1950s, Hollywood began impersonating Hollywood, its star system and its stars. In *The Frenzy of Renown: Fame and Its History* (1986), Leo Braudy writes that impersonation "implies that personal style is a costume that, if distinctive enough, can be turned into a commodity. Mae West began her career impersonating Eva Tanguay, just as many have now made careers impersonating Mae West."[416] Both Mae West and Marilyn have become cultural codes, what Roland Barthes calls "implicit proverbs" or social utterances.[417] Most people know Mae West, and everyone knows Marilyn.

Marilyn impersonated Mae West, Betty Grable, Jean Harlow, and especially Marilyn Monroe. Biographers and observers include in their accounts of her life that she expertly turned "Marilyn" on and off depending on mood and circumstance. In *Conversations with*

Marilyn (1976), journalist W. J. Weatherby, who met with the star on several occasions, describes a bar scene with a dishevelled Marilyn: "This last time, she had no makeup on, as usual, and her hair needed washing. There was a faint body odor which I found exciting, but which many people wouldn't have." After a middle-aged man in a mailman's uniform has followed the two out of the bar to talk to Marilyn, she changes: "The encounter seemed to have done her good. She beamed and looked much more like Marilyn Monroe."[418] "'Being' Marilyn," Lisa Cohen explains, "required a constant negotiation between distance from and proximity to her own star image."[419] Moreover, Marilyn made a career out of impersonating impersonators, in the shape of the secretaries, waitresses, actresses, and showgirls she portrayed on film—all service-oriented jobs requiring a "scripted" personality for their successful execution.[420] With her recognized comic approach to these roles, as well as the excess and masquerade of her performances, Marilyn impersonated Marilyn and inspired the impersonators in her wake.

In *Be Marilyn!: A Glamorous Guide to Living Blonde* (2000), Marilyn impersonator Gailyn Addis offers to would-be blondes her own approach to be(com)ing Marilyn.[421] On the front cover of this Barbie-pink book, a mirror adorned with a see-through photo of Gailyn-as-Marilyn allows a prospective Marilyn to blend her own reflection with Gailyn's and Marilyn's in a dizzying dance of identities. The back cover informs readers that Gailyn Addis interrupted her (unspecified) studies in Los Angeles when her resemblance to original Marilyn was discovered, and, with her "knack for impersonation," she "parlayed" a successful career for herself. Her "remarkable portrayal of Marilyn Monroe has captivated audiences from Las Vegas to Bangkok." Addis's *c.v.* includes a long list of credits in films, TV appearances and music videos. The blurb describes her most recent project:

> The world can't seem to get enough of her, and professional Marilyn Monroe impersonator Gailyn Addis knows why. In *Be Marilyn!*, Gailyn Addis guides you through all aspects of recreating the unmistakable Marilyn image, from placing the mole to the famous walk to achieving that perfect platinum hair. She even lets you in on the brilliant—and sometimes bizarre—

> beauty secrets of the woman who has been imitated by everyone from Cindy Crawford to Madonna. . . .

Readers might not know that Marilyn started out with "flat" lips, but Addis recognizes the actress's own skill at "transforming them into that famous pout" and demonstrates her own with a tapestry of pouting pink lips on a pink background inside both front and back covers of *Be Marilyn!* For Marilyn, for Gailyn, and for us, transformation/impersonation is the name of the game: "Whether you just want to look a little more like Marilyn every day, or you're considering making a living at being Marilyn, *Be Marilyn!* tells you how to walk, talk and live like the sexiest blonde of all time."

To talk like Marilyn, breathy voice aside, is to confess. In *Intimate Strangers: The Culture of Celebrity* (1985), Richard Schickel credits Marilyn with initiating "a new era of bold confession." After the nude calendar scandal that she handled so expertly, celebrities might profitably expose their indiscretions. "Properly handled," Schickel writes, "they could enlist public sympathy, help explain and justify one's weaknesses and more recent errors." No longer just a bimbo, Marilyn had, in Norman Mailer's view, "become a protagonist in the great American soap opera." Confession, in short, meant self-promotion, publicity, and success.[422] In her Marilyn manual, Gailyn Addis imitates this mode of self-presentation by treating her audience to secrets of her trade and her less glorious moments as a Marilyn look-alike. In "My Show Belongs to Daddy," she gives advice to prospective impersonators on audience participation. To highlight her act and draw applause and laughter, she usually invites a middle-aged "Daddy" on stage: "Just how physical you want to become is up to you. . . . I personally feel that it's best to have as little physical contact as possible but make it seem like you're doing a lot." This scheme occasionally fails. Once, a shy, gentle-looking man turned into an octopus; another audience participant escaped from the "Daddy" chair, chased Addis across the stage, and grabbed her: "We were squaring off like two wrestlers in an all-star wrestling match."[423] In a section on Marilyn's films, Addis mentions "The Girl" in *The Seven Year Itch* (1955), who "makes a middle-aged man of average appearance feel special again." Addis confesses:

"I hate to admit it, but that last sentence could practically be the job description for Marilyn impersonators."[424] Like Marilyn, she has endured her share of car salesmen, department store managers, baseball players, and cruise ship tourists, as she explains in "Types of Gigs," before making it to military bases in Okinawa and Sasebo, Japan. But Addis endorses a more conventional morality than did the original '50s version. Though her gigs suggest financial struggles and hardships, she remains prim: "When a girl does a take on Marilyn by allowing herself to hang out all over the place . . . it looks extremely campy and makes a farce of the Monroe image."[425]

The many sections in *Be Marilyn!* about posture, attire, and proper behavior makes the book a course in self-presentation and self-promotion. Painted, propped up, or hemmed in, the female body becomes a surface on which to write a victim's story of vulnerability, but as with original Marilyn, it constitutes as well a site of power. In *The Frenzy of Renown*, Braudy discusses the post-World War II media search for faces and bodies that might represent an increasingly complex American reality with recognizable simplicity: "public without seeming ambitious, private without being disdainful—a hero with some tinge of the victim. . . . " Marilyn fit the bill, especially in the hero/victim department, and subsequently lent her figure, and her expertise, to those eager to learn the tricks of the trade from a professional.[426] In a performative culture, Addis draws on Marilyn to thrust her young, female readership towards visibility and control. The question is, she writes, "why *not* be like Marilyn, if only for the fun of it. Or for a new image. Or to do it professionally. Why should glamour be so elusive? For women of the new millennium, anything goes!"[427] Women need a make-over to become real. Braudy explains in discussing a 1920s female impersonator :

> the key to success in the eyes of the world is a self-conscious awareness of the inadequacies of the body and a blithe belief that, no matter how extreme, they can be easily corrected into a "more photographic" and thereby more real image. Charting one's evolving visual self through such images, clipped from magazines or pasted into family albums, promised a control through self-objectification: The body might not be for sale, but it was certainly on display.[428]

The impersonator holds the key to perfection through an inevitable distance from the original body that allows for clarity and revision. In the 21st century, the quest for perfection and self-empowerment involves a re-writing of Marilyn to make her more active and powerful. In the "Types of Gigs" chapter, "Marilyn" talks back to clients asking her "Who was better, Jack or Bobby?" She handles agents, stylists, foreign hosts, and local tourist boards with steely assertion.

Addis also adopts the humor of her precursor, whose "Monroe-isms" sprinkle the pages of *Be Marilyn!* and infiltrate Addis's prose. The humorous tone helps her, as it did Marilyn, across bumpy issues, or trivialities such as diets and weight control. In her "Underneath It All" section, Addis begins with a Marilyn quote: "I'd rather be really dressed up or really undressed. I don't bother with anything in between." This "racy talk," as Addis puts it, allows Marilyn and the Marilyn impersonator to discuss their naked bodies, which hide in the folds of their humor. "Having a healthy appetite and being no immediate threat to Kate Moss," Addis writes, "I take comfort in the fact that Monroe was and is considered beautiful for her full figure." She bonds with readers by promoting "those of us who aren't planning on sprouting into six-foot-tall, Twiggy-like runway models any time soon." Her use of hyperbole suggests concern, as does the caption underneath a photo of Addis in a white '50s-era swimsuit: "Her whole body had a touch of overripeness—how Renoir would have adored her!"[429] Like the swimsuit, the humor smoothes over unfortunate bulges and veils showgirls' hunger for success and what they must do to get it. It introduces as well an ingredient in the Monroe recipe as essential as the breathy voice, the blond curls, the pouting lips, and the beauty spot.

Both the cover mirror that allows readers to indulge in dreams of (being) Marilyn and the many photographs of Addis inside the pink binding communicate that *Be Marilyn!* accepts or celebrates narcissism. Over three pages in the "Applying the Makeup" section, we face fourteen passport-sized photos of the author, who also uses first person pronouns in most of her sentences: "I apply an under-eye moisture cream" or "I take a natural-toned shadow and highlight slightly above my eye crease just under my brow bone to create the illusion that my natural eye crease is higher than it really is."[430] In transforming herself into Marilyn, Addis indulges in detailed descriptions of her own features: "As I pull back my hair and look at my face's shape, it is clear that my face is not as wide and round as Marilyn's. . . . Although I do have a small widow's peak, it is not as pronounced."[431] With such self-absorption, Addis positions herself, and her readers, in front of a mirror, much like Marilyn herself in the famous *How to Marry a Millionaire* shot, where she admires herself in a mirror reflected in other mirrors. In her scarlet gown, creamy white arms cradling her face and hair, she looks at herself in narcissistic delight while offering herself as spectacle to the audience watching her. Both Gailyn and Marilyn endorse the voyeurism that Laura Mulvey and others identify with spectatorship, but they dramatize simultaneously the cinematic structures that cast women as objects of the look.[432] In both scenarios, they subvert their roles as objects, not only by highlighting the look, the looks, and the looking, but also by bearing the gaze themselves. In the process, they posit women as "alienated spectators" while also usurping the power of the gaze.

Impersonators looking at stars establish the "scopophilic contact" Mulvey identifies with spectatorship. Studying Marilyn's form and mannerisms, Addis actively takes control of the star and freezes her into the parts she needs: the make-up, the costumes, the body, the magic. Her own distance from Marilyn, in time and in shape, contributes to the pleasure and the power of looking. In an opposite move, she identifies with Marilyn's screen image, developed, in Mulvey's phrase, "through narcissism and the constitution of the ego." In accordance with Lacan's account of the mirror phase, the unity of the image reflected in the mirror pleases the young child, who lacks coordination and ego boundaries. The recognition, in short, is a misrecognition, but it begins the process of identification that also characterizes film spectatorship. In Mulvey's words, "it is the birth of the long love affair/despair between image and self-image which has found such intensity of expression in film and such joyous recognition in the cinema audience."[433]

Though Mulvey's analysis of visual pleasure has given way to more flexible theories of gendered spectatorship, the identification with the screen image remains strong both in *Be Marilyn!* and in the "lost audience" Jackie Stacey explores in *Star Gazing* (1994). As a female fan of '40s and '50s movie stars, Betty Cruse writes to Stacey about her fascination with Marilyn:

> Monroe appealed to me deeply and desperately, little girl lost with the body of a desirable woman. She lit up the screen with her performances, the glamour, her movements were so exciting. Watching her made me feel she was in some way lonely and vulnerable, she was my cult figure, I felt like me, she was running away from herself.[434]

As Stacey notes, the spectator recognizes her own vulnerability and fear in a more glamorous version of herself. This identification with a star intensifies in imitation and copying practices outside the movie theaters, aimed, in Stacey's words, "at the transformation of the spectator's own identity." Stacey describes the female fan, who resembles Addis in *Be Marilyn!*: "In front of a reflection of herself, the spectator attempts to close the gap between her own image and her ideal image, by trying to produce a new image, more like her ideal."[435] This transformation frequently involves a copying of hairstyles, as in Patricia Ogden's case: "Now Marilyn Monroe was younger [than Doris Day] and by this time I had changed my image, my hair was almost white blonde and longer and I copied her hairsyle [*sic*], as people said I looked like her."[436] In "Gentlemen Prefer You!" Addis devotes several pages to Marilyn's hairstyle and hair color, and to her own. She concludes in a passage ripe with identification:

> I personally feel that the hair is the most important part of the look. I'm certain it is the most scrutinized. Audiences will be studying it carefully, wondering, "Is that her *real* hair?" People frequently ask me, "Is that *your* hair?" I answer, wide-eyed, empty-headed, and in my full Marilyn voice, "Of course it is . . . and I have the receipt to prove it!"[437]

The passage signals the closeness as well as the distance of Mulvey's visual pleasure, the negotiation between similarity and difference that characterizes female spectators. In fact, impersonators engage in active spectatorship by copying their models and, as in the Marilyn-Gailyn case, highlighting the importance of the performing body.

As misidentification or misquotation, impersonation entails an element of subversion by stressing physicality as a crucial sign of femininity.[438] It also undermines a naturalized femininity by mentioning the work involved in be(com)ing a woman. Readers of *Be Marilyn!* may wear themselves out with make-up application, hair dyeing, shopping, sewing gowns and gloves, diets, and dancing lessons, and they need energy to market themselves. They must put together a professional package "consisting of pictures, résumé, bio, videotape, press clippings, and letters of reference," which they will have to mail out to "as many entertainment agents, party planners, meeting planners, event consultants, and convention service companies" as they possibly can. Addis consoles them: "You can live without the rest, but without photos and video, you won't even get out of the starting gate. It takes time, so don't be discouraged."[439]

Impersonators circulate stars like Marilyn, who have become "epic commodities" with lives and bodies familiar to audiences.[440] As spectators, they also link up with stars through consumption of clothes, accessories and other consumer products. In "The Star and the Commodity," Barry King acknowledges that "stars have a key role in imparting significance to material objects."[441] Stacey identifies stars as "consumable feminine images" that women might scrutinize and reproduce, like the fan imitating the Marilyn look: "I even bought a suit after seeing her in *Niagara*."[442] In "The Economy of Desire: The Commodity Form in/of Cinema," Mary Anne Doane discusses the female spectator in her role as consumer, since "the cinematic image for the woman is both shop window and mirror, the one simply a means of access to the other."[443] The impersonator, as spectator *par excellence*, seeks proximity to Hollywood stars especially through the purchase and consumption of glamorous goods. In her "Captivating Costumes" chapter, Addis goes over Marilyn's films and public appearances in terms of her outfits, from the red dress in *Niagara*, the white halter dress in *The Seven Year Itch* to the "controversial" "Happy Birthday Mr. President" gown or the "infamous" one of gold lamé, which she reproduces paper doll fashion, with no body inside. Addis proudly imitates the pink, strapless

"Diamonds Are a Girl's Best Friend" gown with the big bow on the back, arm-length gloves, and "tons of faux diamond jewellery." She writes of department stores and second-hand shopping adventures and prints a list of Marilyn dress patterns, including Simplicity's white *Seven Year Itch* and the pink strapless (# 8393).[444]

Consumption links Marilyn, impersonators, wannabes, fans and spectators into a post-feminist community of women. Through the star image, Addis addresses this sisterhood of young women eager for glamor, or for careers as impersonators: "Never has fashion been so *unglamorous*. . . . Hats, gloves, brooches, and heels are something for school plays. . . . But Marilyn, wonderful Marilyn, brought an approachability and warmth to the glamour that eludes so many of us."[445] She addresses a circle of women like "us" directly in her pink guide to "Living Blonde": "If you're in the mood for a little adventure, you're on the right track."[446] Her tone is intimate, hinting at conspiracy and secrets shared. She confides to us that "auditioning for these roles can be nerve-racking." Only preparation helps her be Marilyn in front of casting directors: "Call them, tell them who you are and what you do, and ask if you can submit your package."[447] Like the "lost audience" of fans from the 1940s and '50s, women in Addis's text bond in their admiration for Marilyn and their own dreams of success. They also sign a contract with one another to help Marilyn survive. Like the Elvis fans who spot the King alive and kicking, Marilyn's blond and glamorous successors lend their time, and their bodies, to keeping the star among us.

Impersonators and fans consume to get closer to a Hollywood icon, but they also wish for transcendence through the ideal other. In *Star Gazing*, Stacey identifies a "psychic economy" of spectatorship that projects onto stars desirable traits that audience members may lack and the undesirable qualities they reject.[448] In this moral exchange, which includes the incorporation of star qualities into a fan's conception of self, the star becomes a religious icon. Marilyn lends herself to worship because of her tragic life and death, which epitomizes Christian suffering and redemption. According to Braudy's *The Frenzy of Renown*, suicide recurs in contemporary discussions of celebrity, because it "crystallizes conflicts about fame and aspiration that in previous eras might be represented by the saint in the desert . . . .” Especially an artist’s suicide activates emotional and religious responses, because it indicates a “grander spirit” escaping the trivialities and sufferings of lesser beings. “In a world without much sainthood,” Braudy writes, “suicide confers a transcendence. It is an assertion of the self, but one that seems not selfish but selfless.”[449] King argues that the “profound indexicality” of stars who have become signifiers of our desires and rebellions “finds its apotheosis when the bearer of meaning meets with an early death.”[450] A contested suicide like Marilyn’s brings to the star either sainthood or martyrdom. It also gives her the power that impersonators and fans desire, since suicide means control. Suicide allows a star acting in a story not her own to grab the script and direct it herself, to usurp her own image.[451] With Marilyn as a powerful spiritual presence, she bestows on impersonators considerable status and spirituality. Their quest for proximity and resemblance leads them to Hollywood and Heaven. Pete Townshend explains: “Put more celestially, when we pursue perfection, we are searching for God.”[452]

In the film *Finding Graceland* (1998), a troubled male character, Byron Gruman (Johnathon Schaech), asks a Marilyn impersonator (Bridget Fonda): “What is it about impersonators that makes everything you say sound like philosophy?” Fonda’s character responds: “I don’t know. Everybody needs guidance. What difference does it make if you get it from Jesus, Buddha or Elvis?” Part disciple and part oracle, the Marilyn impersonator acknowledges the fluid boundaries between stars and religious figures that make fans seek them out.[453] Bridget Fonda studied not only Marilyn herself but also the Marilyn impersonator. As we learn in *Be Marilyn!* Fonda consulted a proud Gailyn Addis to prepare for the role: “She was particularly interested in knowing about life on the road, whether I felt like Marilyn twenty-four hours a day, seven days a week, and if I ever ‘fell for’ Elvis impersonators.” In return, Addis watched Fonda dissect Marilyn’s dance moves and reconstruct her “You’d Be Surprised” routine to perfection.[454] The original Marilyn merges with the professional actress and the reverential impersonator.

Richard Dyer explains in *Stars* that “specialness” combines with “ordinariness” in Hollywood discourses and representations of stardom.[455] In *Graceland*, religious and secular symbols merge, in a *pi-*

etá, a candle light vigil at Graceland, a businessman-turned-Elvis, or Christ, and a healing Marilyn-Madonna, adored by male leads and the impersonator-spectator community at large. Also the most famous Marilyn impersonator of all impersonates an oracle. In an interview following *Confessions on a Dance Floor* (2005), Madonna dressed like a gypsy woman in red, purple and gold, while the glittering background veils matched her colorful outfit and hair. From an elevated chair worthy of a goddess, her face an impenetrable mask, she dispensed words of wisdom to the world. "What did you learn from success and fame," the interviewer asked. "What can you teach us?" Madonna spoke of responsibility and transcendence and seemed to be impersonating herself.

Marilyn played Marilyn most of the time, specifically in *Life* magazine, where she posed as Theda Bara, Lillian Russell, Clara Bow, Marlene Dietrich and Jean Harlow, and as two versions of herself.[456] In "The Horizontal Walk: Marilyn Monroe, CinemaScope, and Sexuality," Lisa Cohen announces her own preference among subsequent impersonators: "Jane Russell was the first and most spectacular impersonator of Marilyn Monroe, and for me her version of her costar in *Gentlemen Prefer Blondes* remains the most intriguing of all."[457] The two stars appeared together as a set of gorgeous twins, most famously when they imprinted breasts and buttocks in Hollywood Boulevard cement. In *Gentlemen*, Russell substitutes in court for Lorelei Lee, the Marilyn character, who is accused of stealing a diamond tiara. She brilliantly impersonates her blond buddy: platinum hair and red-lipped pout, sexy voice and facial expressions, eyes sucking up the men of law, horizontal walk and whirlwind dancing. Sure enough, "Lorelei" leaves court with her case dismissed and a reputation for flawless Marilyn impersonation.

Actress and impersonator Catherine Hicks declares in *Be Marilyn!* that "Marilyn was like the sister I never had. The acting was like exhaling, like I released something." On a Blue Moon Talent, Inc. webpage, she claims to "have a special place in her heart for playing Marilyn." She lists "countless events as this screen siren," including "a recent run in, [*sic*] 'The Tribute' interacting with facsimiles of 'The Rat Pack'" and several Marilyn dresses, including a "heatwave costume" consisting of "tropical black and white skirt, bathing top, and black hat."[458] Originally a New York actress known for playing Dr. Faith Coleridge in the soap *Ryan's Hope*, and for her theater roles as Cherie in *Bus Stop* and Maggie in *After the Fall*, Hicks starred in the 1980 ABC movie *Marilyn: The Untold Story*. Addis writes to prospective impersonators: "Hicks had to gain weight, which she did by eating more that her share of doughnuts for breakfast. Her hair had to be bleached and her breasts padded." Hicks herself declared, "I don't know if I'd like to be voluptuous all the time, but I did feel a certain extra femininity that was fun, and it was a joy to have my dress billowing in the breeze." Hicks played Marilyn on Manhattan and in the pool for *Something's Got to Give*, where she dispensed with the bathing suit, Marilyn fashion. Addis informs us that only "overseas audiences" got to watch.

In *Marilyn & Bobby: Her Final Affair* (1993), TV soap star Melody Anderson impersonates Marilyn in love with the Kennedy brothers. Despite an initial disclaimer, the film dramatizes Anthony Summers's conspiracy theory with a plot "inspired" by Marilyn Monroe and Bobby Kennedy as public figures. Summers's goddess lives and dies in a web of intrigues and crimes involving the Teamsters, the Mafia, the FBI, President Kennedy and his Attorney General. *Marilyn & Bobby* offended reviewers, and Marilyn impersonators shy away from the film, or its subject matter. "Marilyn's relationship with the Kennedys is a subject that won't be undertaken in this book," Addis writes in *Be Marilyn!* "So it's up to the viewers to decide for themselves on this one."[459] William C. Uchtman from Henderson, Tennessee, made his decision. In "The Earth's Biggest Movie Database," he rescues both Marilyn and Melody: "I have seen several blonde actresses play Marilyn but Melody Anderson is the best so far. She looks more like her and plays her better than anyone else ever has."[460] Her Marilyn's breathy whispers, clingy eroticism, and vulnerable sweetness suggest Marilyn as the victim of forces beyond her control and inspire all knights except Camelot and his brother.

In the HBO movie *Norma Jeane & Marilyn* (1996), Ashley Judd and Mira Sorvino share the task of becoming and living as Marilyn. The movie recounts the familiar story of Norma Jeane Baker, the orphan tossed about in foster homes before reaching the Hollywood limelight. Stressing her Gemini personality, the production casts Judd and Sorvino as two separate actresses with two different bodies and separate strategies for survival and success. The film employs the Marilyn index that begins with the troubled childhood and moves through ambition and success to vulnerable pill popper and isolated superstar. *Time* magazine reviewer Ginia Bellafante writes that Judd's Norma Jeane comes across as "a feminist out of a Camille Paglia fever dream—a firecracker of a young woman fully aware of her ravaging sex appeal and ready to use it." Though Bellafante criticizes Sorvino for her insufficiently tortured Marilyn figure, she cannot blame the Harvard-educated actress for the flawed script: Judd and Sorvino share embarrassing scenes hammering home the split personality of the star.[461] *Norma Jeane & Marilyn* predictably highlights Marilyn's marketable body, with a disrobed Judd ensuring the coveted high ratings. The HBO film includes all the clichés and body parts that belong in the Marilyn package, though Judd and Sorvino have wrapped the blond actress with professional expertise.

Jeanne Carmen, who claims to have been Marilyn's roommate before the Brentwood bungalow, tries harder than most to copy the original. At seventy-something, Carmen sports platinum hair and matching sequin earrings, jacket and shoe buckles, paraphernalia that paved the way to a *Be Marilyn!* photograph. The caption introduces Carmen as "a B movie goddess and sexy pinup girl who was a close friend of Marilyn in the years before she died. It was said that when the two were together, they looked like sisters."[462] Earlier photos of Carmen, splashing in California waves or barbecuing in nothing but an apron, confirm that in terms of hair and chest, she performed an acceptable Marilyn.[463] Later facelifts notwithstanding, she joins the sisterhood of Marilyn wannabes, impersonators and actresses. Blond, buxom, or not, these Marilyns search for the original and form a hierarchy of their own, from desperate housewives to haughty megastars.

Madonna's Marilyn

At the top, Madonna has most conspicuously and successfully recreated Marilyn. In 1985, she performed like Marilyn in "Diamond's Are a Girl's Best Friend" in her own "Material Girl" song and video. With copied steps and props, she re-enacted Marilyn's classic number and created herself as a new provocative icon.[464] Dressed in the famous pink gown and loaded with jewelry, she surrounds herself with chandeliers and adoring chorus boys and struts through the walkway formed by the male dancers, who shower her with gifts. In interviews, Madonna stressed intertextual connections: "Marilyn was made into something not human in a way, and I can relate to that. Her sexuality was something everyone was obsessed with, and that I can relate to." She added: "And there were something about her vulnerability that I'm curious about and attracted to."[465] On the set for the video production, Sean Penn remarked: "You think you're Marilyn Monroe, don't you?"[466] Madonna was not amused, but other Marilyn acts followed. She appropriated Marilyn's hair and make-up for the movie *Who's That Girl* (1988) and dressed like her in the video version of "Justify My Love" (1990). In photo spreads, she carefully copied the Marilyn look.[467] At the 1991 Oscar ceremony, Madonna arrived (with Prince) dressed in a white, sequined gown with matching gloves. She resembled Marilyn more than ever: cherry-red lips, bare shoulders, soft platinum curls. Her "Sooner Or Later" performance not only celebrated Marilyn but copied her, in terms of voice, mannerisms and erotic appeal. Though she shed nothing more than a white stole, she delivered the Best Original Song winner in an "undeniably scorching" performance.[468]

Several entertainers advertise themselves as both Madonna and Marilyn impersonators. Holly Beavon, for example, presents herself as a singing and dancing Monroe and Madonna look-alike, with classic appearances from "Diamonds," "Girl from Little Rock," and "Happy Birthday" to "Like a Virgin," "Ray of Light," and "New" Madonna on her repertoire. Her photo gallery also depicts Holly Beavon photographed as Holly Beavon, to complete the postmodern twirl of identities the Marilyn-Madonna connection inspires.[469]

In his Madonna monograph, J. Randy Taraborrelli draws on the Marilyn legend with intertextual references throughout this "intimate biography." Like Marilyn's biographers, he sets out on a quest for authenticity: "While it may not always be easy to find the real Madonna among the hocus-pocus of public relations she manufactures to hide her true self," he states in his "Author's note," "she's there just the same. In pursuit of her, one only has to be perceptive enough to look beyond the thick smoke, away from the confusing mirrors. There hides the real woman."[470] But in scratching Madonna's surfaces, he finds Marilyn instead. Taraborrelli constructs Madonna from Marilyn factoids, but he rewrites the Marilyn tragedy with a Hollywood ending.

Both women developed a volcanic sex appeal, and used it. In "Big Break," Taraborrelli interviews Mark Kamins, a fashionable DJ who helped Madonna get a record deal. "She was always sexually aggressive, and it wasn't just her image," Kamins recalls. "She used her sexuality as a performer, but it's also how she got over off stage." Michael Rosenblatt, then a Warner Bros. executive, thought Madonna's first tape not outstanding, but he remembers the young woman on the make: "Here was this girl sitting in my office, radiating a certain *something*. Whatever it was, she had more of it than I'd ever seen. I knew that there was this star sitting there." In line with George Cukor's remark that Marilyn Monroe stepping into a room "was an occasion," Taraborrelli stresses Madonnas appeal, occasionally sanitized into "charisma." In the "Drama Queen" chapter, ex-manager Camille Barbone recalls Madonna's flair for PR: "Once you met her, you either loved her or hated her. She was really her own best advertisement."[471] Both Marilyn and Madonna spent hours in front of mirrors and fans. Madonna's ex-lover Norris Burroughs remembers her narcissism: "Everything was all about her, her wants, her needs, her thoughts, her desires . . . but, still, you got swept away by it. She was just so fascinating to watch and be around." Madonna seduced Burroughs with one remark: "You get your gorgeous Brando body over here."[472]

As a recycled Marilyn, Madonna dreamt from childhood of fame and fortune. She managed to create herself rags-to-riches fashion, and became another blond Cinderella rising from the ashes, middle-class background notwithstanding. Taraborrelli notes her mother's absence and her father's distance. Marilyn fantasized about stripping in church and loved the Manhattan wind machine, and young Madonna lifted up her skirt and flashed her panties. In Taraborrelli's words, "The youngster seemed to be learning that a little flash, mixed with a bit of exhibitionism, could go a long way towards pleasing people."[473] Guided tours now lead tourists to Madonna's first New York apartment on East 42nd St., where she combined hard work with sexual favors. Like Marilyn, she did not look back. "You take what you can and then move on," she says in Taraborrelli's *Madonna*. Camille Barbone calls her a "sponge": "She soaks up what she can and drains you in every way and then goes on to her next victim."[474]

The name issue came up as soon as Madonna landed her first film role. Her co-star in *A Certain Sacrifice* (1979, 1981) explains: "She had already adopted the practice of using one name, thinking of how the great stars of yesterday would become known by a single name at the height of their fame. Marilyn, Dietrich, Gable, Garbo, Liz, Brando. I guess Madonna wanted her name added to the list of one-name legends."[475] The film was forgettable and did not advance her career. Like Marilyn, Madonna modelled in the nude to pay her bills. On February 12, 1979, photographer Martin Schreiber, then teaching a course at the New School in Greenwich Village, paid her $30 to pose naked for one and a half hours. Madonna did not care either and did not regret. As Schreiber remembers, "I thought to myself, after she leaves here she will never again think of these pictures."[476] Abortions and several marriages recur in both women's lives. Madonna struck out on her own, with more success than Marilyn Monroe Productions, but with similar consequences for her new marriage to Sean Penn.[477] In terms of publicity, Penn became DiMaggio, who avoided the limelight and resented his wife for courting it. In terms of his career, he became a frustrated Miller, who did not write for years and deeply resented Marilyn's staff.

More ingredients in the Marilyn recipe spice Taraborrelli's *Madonna*. Like Marilyn, Madonna faced huge crowds in Japan, where one thousand troops in the airport had to hold back the 25,000 fans eagerly awaiting her 1987 *Who's That Girl* tour. To promote the film version, Madonna posed as Marilyn on various magazine covers, perhaps to use her precursor's personality instead of her own. In Taraborrelli's version of Madonna, the two stars merge, as in the detailed account of Madonna's affair with John Kennedy, Jr., who revealed an inherited weakness for Marilyn. For one thing, he placed a platinum blond Drew Barrymore wearing the "Happy

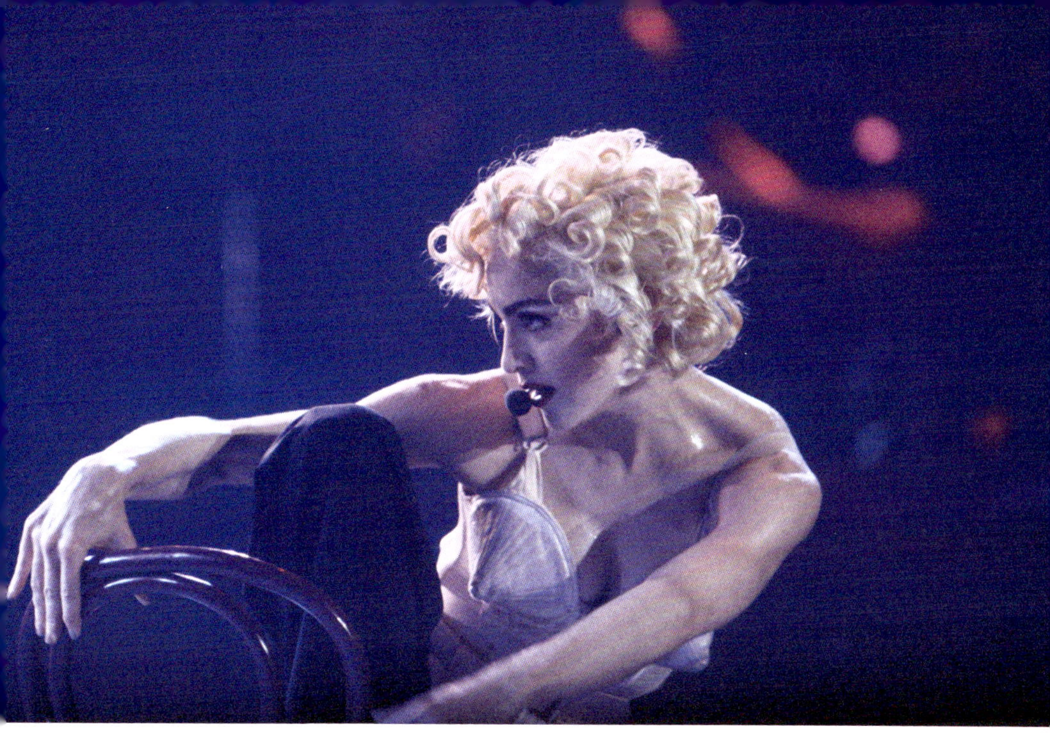

Madonna impersonating Marilyn

Birthday" gown on the cover of his new magazine, *George*.[478] Once again, Jackie stepped in. In "Jackie Refuses to Meet Madonna," Taraborrelli stresses his point: "Jack Kennedy ended up with Marilyn Monroe and, somehow, John ended up with Madonna. I don't know which scenario most upset Jackie: her husband with Marilyn, or her son with Madonna."[479] Not to be outdone, Madonna put on a tight gown and a blond wig and re-enacted "Happy Birthday, Mr. President" on *Saturday Night Live* in 1993.

Troubles intensified in the lives of both superstars. They had to disguise themselves to walk the streets or go into restaurants—with faded dresses, with wigs, with sunglasses. Madonna tries to look in disguise like Marilyn disguised. Both do not always look like stars. Marilyn called in Whitey with brushes, chalk, and lipstick to make her resemble Marilyn, and Madonna frowns at her reflection, which in 1996 reveals "an exhausted woman with an imperfect complexion." Taraborrelli provides the details:

> Clearly visible was a network of lines around her mouth, a web of wrinkles around her eyes. Sitting at her dressing table, she would begin the careful

> application of make-up. Her eyes would not leave her image until she was satisfied that her public mask was perfect. However, as she would later recall, it would take her longer, with each passing day to achieve her goal.[480]

Lonely hotel rooms, late-night phone calls, and a growing emptiness inside complete the Marilyn epic. Neither goddess can relate to "normal" people. Both have lost themselves in images and headlines; both are terribly isolated, and both have suffered from "abysmal" relationships with men. With indistinguishable lives and thoughts, Marilyn and Madonna have become one miserable Venus.[481] But Taraborrelli rewrites the tragedy. Marilyn could not hold Camelot and died, but Madonna marries the white British knight. In the end, Guy Ritchie sweeps his princess off her feet and out of trouble, if only for a while.[482]

Ritchie takes Madonna into a gay world, where she already knows her way around. In "Just What Sort of a Guy Is Guy Ritchie," Mark Simpson of the *Independent* labelled his two films, *Lock, Stock & Two Smoking Barrels* and *Snatch* "gay porn for straight males" and Ritchie himself "the pre-eminent example of a rising phenomenon: the homo-hetero." Simpson asks: "Could it be that Guy Ritchie—who lives with the woman famously described as a gay man trapped in a woman's body—is a gay man trapped in a straight man's body?"[483] In his lines and elsewhere, Madonna appears with Ritchie as a gay icon. Taraborrelli discusses a series of Madonna's woman-identified or lesbian relationships, and she constantly turns up in gender-bending contexts, including music videos like *Vogue* (1990), *Justify My Love* (1990), and *Erotica* (1992). Films such as *In Bed With Madonna* (1991) and *Truth or Dare* (1991), and her book *Sex* (1992) have distinct homoerotic contents. Photos show Madonna in drag, as when she wears a three-piece suit, with a monocle. In *Justify My Love*, she blends gay male S & M, Marilyn, and James Dean. As Reena Mistry writes, "With her constant image changes, parodies of blonde bombshells such as Marilyn Monroe, her assertion of female power and sexuality, and her appropriation from gay/queer culture, the popular music icon Madonna can be seen as the virtual embodiment of Judith Butler's arguments in *Gender Trouble* (1989)."[484] Also Marilyn is available for queer politics, though her alliance with heterosexual desire tends to cover up her homosexual connections. As a trickster, she projects a shifting, uneasy personality along with a "persuasive and amusing prankster and sexual polymorph."[485] Drag performers routinely put on blond Marilyn wigs, tight dresses, high heels and beauty spots to wiggle their way to carnival floats, parades, and bit parts in movies, music videos and TV commercials.

Gay Marilyn

Transvestites adore Marilyn. As a gay icon, she is everywhere, as in the *Time* magazine article listing actresses who have played Marilyn under the caption "NOT JUST DRAG QUEENS".[486] In "Wishes Come True: Designing the Greenwich Village Halloween Parade," Jack Kugelmass discusses the multiplicity of voices and identities that have contributed to the success of New York City festivals in general and Greenwich Village parades in particular.[487] At the annual Village Parade, which he calls "New York's answer to Mardi Gras," the public staging of dreams and fantasies results in a world turned upside down and inside out. Audiences cheer with catcalls drag and drama queens displaying elaborate costumes and colors: "vivid reds, golds, purples, and others intended by their creators to dazzle against the black backdrop of the night."[488] In the ludic atmosphere of New York's "gay mecca," Marilyn serves as a last-minute option for more conventional participants, who lean towards "the irreverent and the lascivious."[489] Ross Berman, a fashion stylist who missed his first parade because he spent the night applying the make-up for his Connie Francis drag costume, dismisses Marilyn for more challenging possibilities:

> "We wanted to be 'conceptual,' but not be Lana Turner, Marilyn Monroe, or Jane [sic] Mansfield. We wanted to do something that would sort of be camp and sort of fun and sort of more accessible to people, because we felt that it would be a very accessible thing to be flight attendants, where they have not met Marilyn Monroe or Joan Crawford."[490]

In this statement, Marilyn and other stars are suspended between the ordinary and the exceptional. Choices like her come to mind

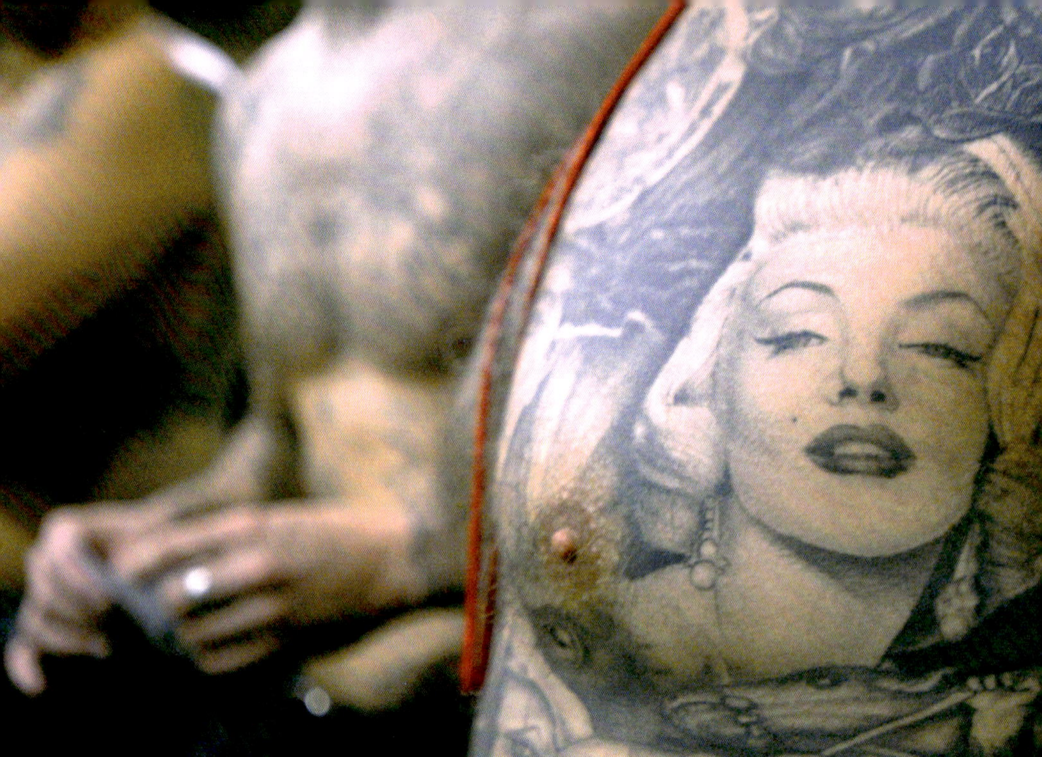

Gay Marilyn

quickly, only to be discarded. This tension is crucial to Richard Dyer's definition of charisma, in which the charismatic figure embodies central features of a culture, intensified and therefore exceptional. He links stars to "specific instabilities, ambiguities and contradictions in the culture," reproduced in scripts, screen images and star promotion. Marilyn's blend of experience and innocence thus situates itself in the flux of moral and sexual contradictions in ´50s America, when she "seemed to 'be' the very tensions that ran through the ideological life."[491] He suggests that conflicted stars like Marilyn embody and intensify the contradictions that especially marginal groups experience in relation to dominant culture and thus begins to explain the attraction in gay culture to Marilyn's image of femininity and excess.

With the "powerful sense of irony" that Kugelmass identifies in carnivalesque events, Marilyn joins with figures like Queen Kong, transvestite nuns, and folks on "Condom Ferry" to mock the arbitrariness of gender and the emptiness of role playing.[492] She highlights the centrality of image to identity formations, especially in relation to the construction of femininity, which becomes parody, or masquerade. As Joan Riviere writes in "Womanliness as a Masquerade (1929)," observers may find "the mask of femininity taking curious forms." Riviere first theorized "womanliness" as a mask intended to hide a female masculinity offensive to the surrounding culture, such as ambition, success, or intellectual achievements. In a radical move, she equates womanliness with masquerade: "My suggestion is not, however, that there is any such difference; whether radical or superficial, they are the same thing."[493] Stephen Heath explains in "Joan Riviere and the Masquerade": "In the masquerade the woman mimics an authentic—genuine—womanliness but then authentic womanliness is such a mimicry, *is* the masquerade ('they are the same thing'); to be a woman is to dissimulate a fundamental masculinity, femininity is that dissimulation."[494] To dramatize a marginalized femininity or a lack of masculinity, the gay community attaches itself to the highly visible, tension-filled and constructed image of Marilyn Monroe, a repository of male heterosexual authority and fantasy. With femininity that spills into parody, the "queen of desire" has through her excessive performance, or masquerade, a subversive potential attractive to drag queens.[495]

Marilyn moves among transvestites and cross-dressers in films like *Some Like It Hot* (1959). In "Shots in the Dark: Why the Lure of the Old-timers Is Still so Strong," Graham Fuller praises "the deviousness of Tony Curtis's impersonation," which he compares to Kyle MacLachlan performing Cary Grant with "suaveness, unflappability, and appeal as a gay icon."[496] In Linda Cohen's analysis of *Gentlemen Prefer Blondes* (1953), Marilyn Monroe and Jane Russell finally marry not their grooms but each other. From the opening scene, the two showgirls in hot red sequined dresses mirror each other as they sing and dance "We're Just Two Girls from Little Rock." In the final scene aboard a transatlantic liner, the two best friends enter the dining room wearing matching wedding gowns and singing a chaster version of the number. Cohen continues:

> While the soundtrack blends the "Little Rock" theme first with the wedding march and then with "Diamonds Are a Girl's Best Friend," the girls process toward their grooms. This is a double wedding, and here come the brides.

> In the final shot of the film, as the music swells, the camera tracks toward the two women, excluding the grooms who now flank them, and presenting us (and, importantly, them: they exchange a quick, knowing glance in that moment) with a brief but radiant vision of how a girl might marry Marilyn.[497]

Under the caption "How to Marry Marilyn Monroe," Cohen warns (or promises) her reader: "And now we're crossing over." Criss-crossing between sexualities, genres and voices, and between academic writing and parody, she writes: "I have to confess, I haven't kissed or even met my MARILYN." However, "if I were to marry Marilyn Monroe, I'd do it in white, the way Jane Russell does at the end of *Gentlemen Prefer Blondes*. I would. I do. And if luck is with me, she'll be my bride forever more."[498]

The gay theme resurfaces with Elton John and "Candle in the Wind." Susan J. Hubert notes that his doubling of Marilyn and Diana involves no lesbianism, but she still stresses the gay connection: "Part of the impact of 'Candle in the Wind' 1997 is that it was performed by Elton John, a popular music superstar, and based on a hit song of the 1970s and 1980s. John, an openly gay man, was a friend of Diana's; both were involved in fundraising for persons with HIV/AIDS, and John's role at the funeral served to bring Diana's advocacy to the forefront."[499] As the most "media-hounded" women of the twentieth century, Marilyn and Diana combine in their image constructions femininity with subversion.[500] Both the queen of desire and the queen of hearts embodied ideal notions of femininity, complete with emotional instability and incessant exposure to the male gaze. Both epitomized as well the destructive powers of dominant ideologies and power structures, among Hollywood tycoons or in the Royal Family. Objections to John's lyrics, to his arrival at the funeral with his partner, David Furnish, and to his wig, tune in on the subversive potential of song and performance, which also Diana's mourners recognized. A message left outside Kensington Palace read: "Queen of the Coloured Hearts, Queen of the Devastated, Queen of the Unloved Ones, Queen of the Unknown, Love from the Unknown."[501] Both Marilyn and Diana, dead and alive, signify dominant culture as well as its fabulous or abject other. They are madonnas and monsters, a tension-filled site attractive to minorities. In Taraborrelli's biography of Madonna, her dance instructor Christopher Flynn introduces his teenaged student to gay clubs and bars and "the more provocative aspects of Michigan nightlife." She asks him during stretching exercises at his studio: "Look at women like Judy Garland and Marilyn Monroe. These women are gay favorites, aren't they? I wish I knew what it is about them. Is it the glamour? Is it their behaviour?" "I think it's because they're so tragic," Flynn responds.[502]

Lisa Cohen and Elton John share a gay/lesbian gaze with other spectators. In her later work with a gender perspective, Laura Mulvey finds that a female spectator takes a masculine position and, through cross-gender identification and desire, puts on "transvestite clothes," though somewhat uneasily, since her masculinization remains problematized.[503] In "Film and the Masquerade," Mary Anne Doane criticizes both the metaphor of the transvestite and the tendency in film criticism to operate with a binary notion of gendered spectatorship, which insists on a female suspension between masculine and feminine viewing positions. Instead of this sexual mobility, she brings in Riviere's notion of masquerade, the flaunting of femininity that works against trans-sexual identification and insists on femininity as a mask, as representation only. In this way, Doane allows for multiply eroticized spectators, in the French feminist theory formations she draws on associated with bisexuality.[504]

With a cultural studies or sociological dimension in *Star Gazing*, Stacey also backs more elastic theories of spectatorship by stressing the place of fantasy in cinematic pleasures. As a staging of desires, fantasy allows for multiple, cross-gender identifications and makes possible fluid notions of cinematic spectatorship that dismiss sexual difference as determining the identification and involvement of audiences. In her examination of British women's responses to the stars of their youth, Stacey locates forms of "*intimacies between femininities*" that do not result in lesbian object choices but nonetheless go beyond identification without erotic components: "The intensity and the intimacy found in these memories repeatedly strike the reader as signifying more than simply the 'desire to become.'" Instead, Stacey writes, "they involve some sort of homoerotic pleasure in which the boundary between self and ideal produces an endless source of fascination."[505]

Performing Marilyn may thus involve what José Esteban Muñoz calls "disidentification," a reading or viewing strategy that enables marginalized groups such as gay/lesbians, poor people or non-whites—the "Coloured Hearts," the "Devastated" or the "Unloved Ones" of "Queen" Diana's wreath, to reclaim what is not theirs.[506] Through emotional proximity to certain aspects of dominant culture representations and distance to others, minority audiences use disidentification in order to write themselves into dominant cultural domains. In Muñoz's words, disidentification describes "the survival strategies the minority subject practices in order to negotiate a phobic majoritarian public sphere that continuously elides or punishes the existence of subjects who do not conform to the phantasm of normative citizenship."[507]

In *Gentlemen Prefer Blondes*, this disidentification occurs both on the script and on the spectator level. Within the narrative, Lorelei Lee, the Marilyn character, disidentifies with romantic notions of love and marriage by claiming that diamonds are a girl's best friend. She highlights, in short, the trading of bodies and funds implicit in bourgeois marriage and sets up a minority culture of glamorous disobedience with Jane Russell's Dorothy. Russell, in turn, disidentifies with law and order by impersonating the Marilyn character in court and by throwing off her fur coat and performing her way to the judge's case dismissal. In both disidentification scenarios, fabulousness takes center stage. In Cristy Turner's explanation of the term, fabulousness borrows from black queer culture and conspicuous consumerism. It is embodied "in a web of cultural markers that signify status, wealth, style, confidence, attitude, glitter, and panache against the banal backdrop of everyday existence."[508] Fabulousness allows for outrageous performances that destabilize constructions of race, class and gender. Russell certainly undermines conventional notions of identity and justice, first with a simulated personality and then by shaking her glittering attributes in court and taking control of masculine rituals. Dorothy and Lorelei's fabulous performances, aboard the liner and beyond, form an alliance with alternative communities and sexualities, as they simultaneously veil and display their own marginality.

Gentlemen Prefer Blondes positions itself in the "writing gay, casting straight" tradition that in Stephen Maddison's view includes Tennessee Williams's Blanche in *A Streetcar Named Desire*.[509] This "textual gender bending" presents gay scripts and roles in heterosexual disguises and works with "messy, uncontainable female characters" and other "camp representations" that address the gender instabilities and possibilities of the script and makes disidentification possible. Accordingly, Marilyn as Lorelei playfully invites spectators to read her "in drag." She masquerades, exaggerates and messes up sexual conventions and in the process creates a space of gender possibilities. She makes possible a Samantha Jones in the HBO TV series *Sex and the City* (1998-2004), herself a Marilyn impersonator of sorts. As Turner puts it, "her campy failed femininity opens the possibility for feminist and other disidentificatory audiences to embrace Samantha as a queer icon, beyond constricting, conventional notions of gender."[510]

In *Of Women and Their Elegance* (1980), even Norman Mailer gets into gender trouble. He writes in drag, so to speak, by speaking in Marilyn's voice and claiming her body as his own. Focusing on Marilyn in New England, where she stayed with Amy and Milton Greene, her partner in Marilyn Monroe Productions, Mailer invades Marilyn and gains access to her skin, her private parts, and her sexual partners. His Marilyn autobiography swirls up homoerotic, homosexual, transvestite and transsexual possibilities. Indeed, Marilyn Mailer thrives in the carnivalesque atmosphere of urban parades:

> I must have looked like I belonged in the circus (which deep down I do) for I was holding a red drink next to my extra-blond hair—it was extra-blond that day—and I was wearing sky-blue slacks with an electric-green blouse that, come to think of it, was as dirty as the fake old palm trees.[511]

With her extra-bright colors and artificial surroundings, this Marilyn functions as Mailer's ambassador in Gay Mecca, where impersonation floats in the air. Milton Greene buys her a white ermine coat and she becomes Jean Harlow. He introduces her to Marlene Dietrich, and, as Mailer writes in ventriloquist fashion, "for a little while I felt just like her."[512] Various identities and sexualities merge or dissolve within Mailer's Marilyn, as vacuous as ever. "I guess I have no personality of my own," she tells Mailer's readers. "Maybe that is why I am an actress. I feel like I can be anybody else for a little while."[513] For now, at least, she is Mailer.

Hybrid Marilyn competes with Schizophrenic Marilyn. Mailer introduces his split personality theory with Marilyn's acting teacher, Abraham Robert Charles, who houses two complete personalities, known as Abe and Bob. Mr. Charles explains to Marilyn: "Say, for instance, that when I, Charley, see a woman putting on lipstick, maybe it's the Abe in me who thinks he'd like to kiss her, and it's Bob who can feel her putting it on her lips. Maybe Bob is a little bit of a closet faggot even though Abe is straight."[514] The Marilyn we meet among Mailer's women knows that "it was Bob all the way," but she lives a double existence herself. Abe putting on lipstick and Bob feeling it on his lips is "nothing," she declares, "to what I did with my twin personalities when it came to being photographed." Marilyn poses in front of cameras as both subject and object, the split gaze of beautiful women in general and this star in particular: "If one of me sat there looking into the lens, the other personality really got into the head of the photographer. I always felt as if it was my eye telling his finger to click the shutter."[515] But in *Of Women and Their Elegance*, her gaze belongs to Daddy. We recognize Mailer's mouse in the woman who declares: "In those years I was scared to open my mouth (I am still petrified, alas, with strangers)."[516] Underneath lives his monster. At night, this Marilyn belongs among the ghosts, murderers and nightmares of her past: "They hung outside the door like a smelly wolf I'd once seen walking back and forth. His cage smelled of rotten meat."[517] Mailer's monster allies herself with death and burial by imagining herself underground in a wet graveyard. She has an internal space that does not show itself to others and confronts two Marilyns in front of the mirror: "I just kept thinking of my two personalities, wondering which was the murderer in me."[518] Underneath these lines, a Milton Greene photo shows Joanne Woodward with her face divided into a white angelic and a black demonic half. *Of Women and Their Elegance* hammers home the split in Mailer's view of (elegant) women and blends his love and loathing with other anxious masculinities and gender scenarios.

Marilyn belongs to Mailer. She dresses like his favorite dumb blonde, white fur and all, and she acts like her. She has not heard of Degas, or Paphos, or "damask," and she confuses "Bordeaux" with "Bordello."[519] She is catty, like all his women, and competes for male attention with Napoleon's Josephine, Ava Gardner, Elizabeth Taylor, and Amy Greene. She cannot cook or clean, and she lounges around naked amidst dirty clothes and empty champagne glasses. She shows Mailer's hatred of Miller while showering him with love. Mailer's Miller cannot write, and he cannot protect his wife, from Hollywood, from Sir Laurence Olivier, from the Greene family, and from herself. What is more, he is a tightwad who tries to charge a fishing rod to Marilyn Monroe Productions. Marilyn Mailer socks it to him: "Arthur was getting awfully tight with a dime. It wasn't that he was thrifty, he was tight. I kept telling myself it was because he couldn't write these days. If nothing was coming in, nothing should go out. But he embarrassed me."[520] Marilyn is Mailer's dream girl, his all the way through. She peeps at Amy's underwear and shows him her own.

Since Mailer lives inside Marilyn's body, he enjoys the air blowing up his skirt during the Lexington Avenue PR session. He has finally managed to get into Marilyn's panties and uses his advantage to taunt DiMaggio, who is watching and "dying because he knew the secret of acting." Marilyn Mailer confirms that his jealousy is justified: "I guess he knew that I was feeling a little moist every time my skirt blew up. Immorality would be immortalized if I ever took those white panties off. It's true, I wanted to throw myself to the crowd."[521] Mailer has cramps like "National Emergencies" and is inside Marilyn's stomach as she starts bleeding. The mouse and the monster compete for attention: "Then it's as if half the inside of my body is eating the other half. I get headaches like migraines and throw up. Sometimes I can't keep from shrieking."[522] Marilyn Mailer is disgusted by unattractive males such as "a guy with fat lips who I once kissed at a party." Now, the guy returns "like two patties of raw hamburger."[523] Mailer wonders about making love with Prince Rainier of Monaco, but ends up with gay bar acquaintance Rod instead. While the two bar hoppers race along Sunset Boulevard and into the hills on Rod's motorcycle, the "I" of Mailer's story leans up on the handlebars while Rod takes "the proper place, if from behind, my dear." From two men inside one woman and each other, unmentionable gender constellations take over as they all reach Bel Air. Twenty people sprawled on purple couches participate in "the first Hollywood party of the sort I'd grown up hearing about."[524]

Mailer inserts Marilyn into gay culture through literary trans-sexuality, queer bars, and Hollywood festivities. Like the Madonna biographers who speculate on the pop star's relationship with manager Camille Barboni or girl-friend Sandra Bernhard, Mailer dwells on Marilyn's close friendship with Amy Greene and others. At the Greene's home in Connecticut, Marilyn spends hours in the bath-tub to wash Hollywood out of her pores. One morning, as she feels "all pink and white and wet," Amy walks in and gets flustered at the sight of her house guest. "You're really, truly, *exquisitely* beautiful," she tells Marilyn, who is pleased by the compliment: "I lay there in the water and thanked God I was beautiful enough to make Amy notice it."[525] The two women look into each others' eyes and find that both have eyes like stars. Marilyn decides that she herself has never looked happier. Back in bed, Marilyn imagines herself taking a bath in milk. She would blindfold Amy and somehow get her into the tub, where her beautiful guest would be waiting, wearing nothing but lots of lipstick. Marilyn's sexual fantasy takes off: "I'd be coated from head to toe in chocolate sauce. 'Hello, I'm your little black boy,' I'd tell her. I'm here to get you out of the tub.'"[526]

Mailer amplifies the trans-, bi-, or homosexual innuendos in describing a "sleazy" bar on the Strip, where "girls dance with girls and boys disappear into the bathroom with boys." Marilyn is looking for a ride and company for the night. She manages to get Rosalie, "a stout girl in a leather jacket and a crew cut," a member of the only women's motorcycle gang in L.A., to buy her drinks and from there considers her options. "I knew a couple of things about sex with strangers in those days," she tells us, but later backs off, because "Rosalie was a possibility then, but not a very good one." Her detailed assessment of Rosalie's sexual potential suggests her own lesbian experiences, which Mailer dwells on elsewhere. In Marilyn's voice and body, he brings up Natasha Lytess, the live-in drama coach who would throw jealous fits when her protégée dated others:

"She'd practically be my husband," Marilyn remembers. "Let's not get into it."[527]

Mailer's fantasies and Milton Greene's photos of elegant women form a woman-identified community of sorts. In *Of Women and Their Elegance*, the blond actress changes from All-American sweetheart to the drag queen of Marilyn country. But she finally escapes the ghost-writers chasing her. Though she agrees to meet Milton Greene in early September of 1962, she flies away from her date and Mailer's pages. "Of course," she whispers from the other side, "I never got to see the end of August. Or even the middle."[528]

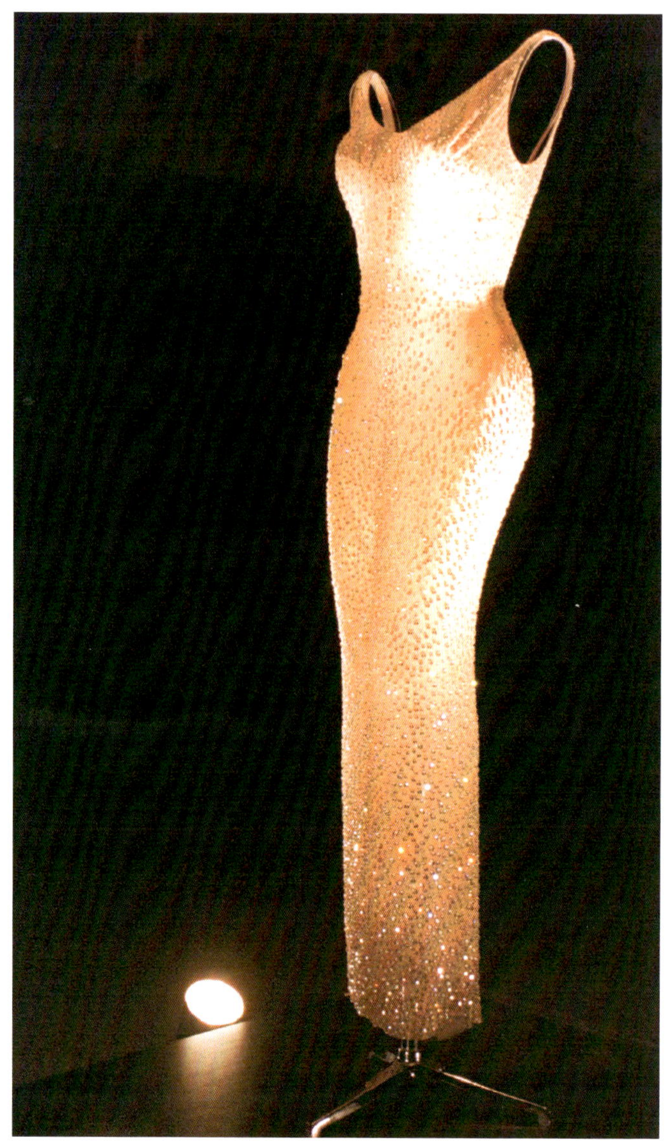

Elusive Marilyn

Postscript

In 2004, Arthur Miller's last play, *Finishing the Picture*, premiered at Chicago's Goodman Theater, directed by Robert Falls. Forty years earlier, his other play about Marilyn, *After the Fall*, became the first staged production at the new Repertory Theater of Lincoln Center and met with angry spectators and reviewers, who felt he defiled the memory of his deceased ex-wife. Writing for *The New Republic*, Robert Brustein called Miller's first account of their marriage "a shameless piece of tabloid gossip," presumably because of its hostile portrait of a drug-dependent, despondent singer closely modelled on Marilyn. "You'd think Miller would let sleeping sex symbols lie," Richard Zoglin exclaims in "Scenes from a Marriage, Part 2," his review of Miller's newest Marilyn play, but like everybody else, Miller cannot finish the picture. He returns to 1961 in Nevada, where a troubled film crew is shooting *The Misfits*, and where the play's central character, Kitty, sends the producer, her co-stars, her director, and her screenwriter-husband into crisis and despair.

Mostly off-stage and mostly mute, Kitty is still the object of everybody's dreams and designs, with the Miller figure, in Zoglin's phrase, "just one of many satellites orbiting Kitty's imploding star." Subtitled "Arthur Miller Is Still in the Thrall of Marilyn Monroe," his review credits Miller with "evenhanded and convincing" portraits of Hollywood film-making, including the thinly veiled John Huston character, Harris Yulin, and with keeping the Gable figure offstage and away from "cheesy impersonations." Nonetheless, Zoglin concludes, "people who were offended at the way Miller treated Monroe in After the Fall won't like Finishing the Picture any better." Her *Misfits* co-stars and crew romanticize her vulnerability or pity her fame, but Marilyn-Kitty remains a diseased if beautiful void filled by voices not her own, except her screams when her tormented husband invades her space. With *After the Fall* and *Who's Afraid of Virginia Woolf?*, Miller's latest rendering of the marriage stands, in Zoglin's estimate, "as one of the most ruthless and revealing in American theater history." But to Miller, 89 at the time he finished the picture, Marilyn was "still an inspiration."[529]

Marilyn also stimulated Don DeLillo enough to edge her way into *Underworld* (1997), where she inhabits some fifty years of American Cold War history. During a "dead afternoon in a dark bar" conversation between the artist Klara Sax and her African American painter friend, Acey, Marilyn crops up, not surprisingly with a reference to the Marilyn calendar in Acey's studio. As usual, Marilyn is dead, absent, and uncontainable. She exists, as for Warhol, in the plural. "On the one hand," Acey says, "you can never have too many Marilyns. On the other hand the minute Marilyn died, all the other sexpots died with her."[530] Philosophically "banned" after Marilyn, Jayne Mansfield, for example, lived on only four or five years with "nothing left but exploitation movies and heavy drinking." Marilyn-Jayne becomes in Acey's art "a white whale," forever tormenting and inspiring its haunted pursuers.[531] Marilyn is gone, but her death no longer matters to the biographers, to the fans, and to the artists orbiting the icon. "It's not Marilyn I want," Acey tells Klara, herself intent on creating art out of garbage, scraps and discarded planes, "it's fake Marilyn." "I wanted a packaged look," she continues. "I didn't want Monroe, I wanted Mansfield. All bloated lips and total boobs. I mean it was so obvious and it took me fucking forever."[532] As a ghost hovering under and over *Underworld* cityscapes, Marilyn constructs and deconstructs the artificiality of DeLillo's garbage-filled America. Marilyn-Jayne turns into a "living threatening presence," and not only because she cannot die. "Marilyn hated being Marilyn," Acey explains. "But Jayne loved it." She secretes into Cold War politics and nuclear physics: "This is a woman with a heavy flow. Atomic Jayne."[533] Jayne is simulacrum Marilyn, a "reproduced Goddess." Like pop culture Marilyn, she is "all the more strong for being unoriginal."[534]

In Terry Pratchett's tenth Discworld novel *Moving Pictures* (1990), everyone is fake, Marilyn included. The alchemists of Discworld have discovered the silver screen, which gets tested and marketed in Holy Wood, with Victor Tugelbend and the female lead, Ginger

Withel, as focal characters. References to Hollywood movies and moguls abound in Discworld, both "world and mirror of worlds" and certainly "nearly unreal." In this movie location, reality is neither digital nor an "on/off" choice, but gradual. As the narrator explains, it is a quality "that things possess in the same way that they possess, say, weight." Discworld, we learn, "is as unreal as it is possible to be while still being real enough to exist," or, to rephrase, "just real enough to be in real trouble."[535] In this extraordinary universe, Ginger Withel dreams uncannily of "red carpets and cheering crowds. And a grating. She kept coming back to the grating, in the dream, where a rush of warm air blew up her skirts. . . ."[536] Like the other actress, she does not mind acting in the nude, though she complains to Victor about the pay: "You'd be amazed what girls have to do for a lot less than ten dollars a day."[537] She finds herself surrounded not just by men but by Method actors. Rock star Rock keeps asking for his motivation for a scene and influences his co-stars, who experience acting as close to daydreaming: "It was like your own life fading away and something else filling up the space."[538] As with Marilyn, acting becomes a shortcut to identity, an escape from being no one in particular. Ginger laughs towards the sunset: "I'm going to be the most famous person in the world, everyone will fall in love with me, and I shall live forever."[539]

Like Marilyn the starlet, Ginger lives in a modest rented room that nonetheless exudes "magic." The girl has transformed it into a shrine to herself, with posters and clippings of her own image tagged to every inch of the walls. Ginger's face stares at the visiting Victor from every angle, and from the huge mirror with half-burned candles in front. "'It's like a sort of temple,' he said. 'A temple to . . . herself.'"[540] Already, the lower-eschelon stars of Holy Wood, the trolls, are imitating her. Ruby, for one, sings that "a rock on the head may be quite sentimental," but does not know quite how to proceed: "'but diamonds are a girl's best friend.' She hesitated. That didn't sound right, even to her."[541] Ginger cannot help her, or anybody else. A compulsive sleepwalker, she inspires in Victor a vision of her future: "People who used magic without knowing what they were doing usually came to a sticky end."[542] As she sleepwalks into Victor's dreams, Ginger redefines his ambition: "He pictured

Ginger, back on the beach. *I want to be the most famous person in the whole world.* Perhaps that was something new, come to think of it. Not ambition for gold, or power, or land or all the things that were familiar parts of the human world. Just ambition to be yourself, as big as possible. Not ambition *for*, but to *be*."[543]

In Marilyn fashion, Ginger enables Victor to articulate his own concerns and fantasies. She is malleable to the point of merging with other stars in Discworld. With her screen savvy, her ballooning white dress, her rising fame, and her appeal to a collective unconscious, she resembles Marilyn most, but other stars inhabit her identity. Ginger Rogers dances in somewhere, while Victor gets a response to his screen test similar to that of Fred Astaire: "Can't act. Can't sing. Can dance a little." Ginger's real name, Theda, and her rumored exotic parentage, hint at Theda Bara, the movie star who in the 1910s gave "vamp" its current meaning.[544] Dietrich and Garbo hover on the horizon, as when Ginger mysteriously asks to be left alone.[545] With her fluid ego boundaries and recurrent appearances, Marilyn becomes nobody and everybody, a text available to anybody reading and writing her life as story and history. As Leo Braudy writes in *The Frenzy of Renown* (1986), "little could be read into Carter, while Reagan, like any good performer, suggested a host of possibilities and 'personal' messages that could be read as desired by any fan."[546] Ginger, Marilyn, Elvis and Reagan knew their stuff.

Marilyn's image must be situated in the flux of ideas about morality and sexuality in post-WWII America, as Richard Dyer argues, but she belongs as well in the ideological fluctuations of all the decades since then.[547] As a cultural sign, she operates with usual adeptness, since she comes across as a natural, as somebody who does not need to act when acting, as somebody naturally sexy, white, blond, American, female. She conceals, as James Naremore reminds us, that actors "produce *signs*" and manages to hide the ideological machinery working in and through her body.[548] She embodies not just the Hollywood star system but also the political, economic, technological and discursive formations of the last half of the twentieth century and the new twenty-first. Marilyn's bodies are words and images, not flesh and blood. She lives on in dumb blonde jokes, whether dumb, political, or subversive, and in neologisms. In "Among the New Words" (1999), she is sandwiched between entries on "greasecake," apparently an erotic term for "large trucks competing in beauty contests," and "marinating," a teenage term for idleness and relaxation. Marilyn turns up as a "Marilyn Monroe cocktail," in Indiana Police Chief Ronald Crytzer's usage a "drink consisting of wine mixed with painkillers (often fatal)."[549] Marilyn may live forever and finally get an Oscar for best postmodern performance. She has become an endlessly circulating discourse through which the nation, or the global community, attempts to locate itself in time and space.

Marilyn has also become "Marilyn," a perfume created by International Flavors and Fragrances. In September 2002, Deanne Stillman wrote in a *New York Times* article on the blond actress's lasting charisma that the Marilyn fragrance "takes the concept of celebrity perfume to a new level: the notion of smelling like a famous dead person—even Marilyn Monroe—is at best an odd one." The public relations manager at I.F.F., Diane Biancamano, responded in February 2003 to the Editor: "I.F.F. does not create fragrances to smell like dead people." Instead, she explains, the company perfumer selects and combines different facets of a celebrity in a new product, in Marilyn's case "glamour, sensuality and playfulness." We are, the PR manager concludes, "capturing the essence of a personality, not a dead body."[550] While scholars and perfumers and big business still try to circle Marilyn, to find her essence or to sniff her death, her glamor, or her marketing value, she playfully evaporates.

Marilyn will survive and maybe not join Elvis, but her friend and confidant Marlon Brando. After a fling in 1955 with the star he called "Angel," Brando became one of the few who never cashed in on the dead actress by telling it all. When he finished *The Score* (2001), directed by Frank Oz and co-starring Robert De Niro and Ed Norton, he was seventy-seven years old and received $ 3 million for three weeks of work. By all reports, Brando behaved as obnoxiously during production as Marilyn ever did, *The Misfits* and the unfinished *Something's Got to Give* included. He would refuse to appear on the set if the director were present, thus forcing Oz to watch his actors on an off-site monitor and send instructions by an assistant director to De Niro, who would then pass them on to Brando.[551]

Like most Marilyn biographers, Gloria Steinem imagined a Marilyn future in "Who Would She Be Now"?[552] The Brando scenario offers a glimpse of another Marilyn, still bossing everyone around, or circling above us, beyond reach, like an angel.

Notes

Introduction

1 Caryn James, "The Women Behind the Myths," http://nytimes.com/2005/02/09/bios.html
2 Alvah Bessie, *The Symbol* (1966; London: Bodley Head, 1967); Norman Mailer, *Marilyn* ([New York]: Grosset and Dunlap, 1973), *Of Women and Their Elegance* (New York: Simon & Shuster,1980), "Strawhead," *Vanity Fair* (April 1986): 58-67; Berniece Baker Miracle, *My Sister Marilyn: A Memoir of Marilyn Monroe* (Chapel Hill: Algonquin, 1994); Norman Rosten, *Marilyn: A Untold Story* (New York: Signet, 1973).
3 Hans Jørgen Lembourn, *Diary of a Lover of Marilyn Monroe* (New York: Arbor House, 1979); Graham McCann, *Marilyn Monroe* (London: Polity, 1988), p. 38.
4 McCann, *Marilyn Monroe*, pp. 190, 39, 42.
5 Jackie Stacey, *Star Gazing: Hollywood Cinema and Female Spectatorship* (New York: Routledge, 1994), p. 9.
6 Gloria Steinem, *Marilyn Monroe/Norma Jeane* (1986; New York: Signet, 1988).
7 Mailer, *Marilyn*, p. 15.
8 Qtd. McCann, *Marilyn Monroe*, p. 9.
9 Marilyn Monroe, with Ben Hecht, *My Story* (New York: Stein and Day, 1974), p. 135.
10 Greg Johnson, "Interview with Joyce Carol Oates on 'Blonde'" (2000), http://www.usfca.edu/fac-staff/southerr/blonde.html; Joyce Carol Oates, *Blonde: A Novel* (2000; New York: Ecco, 2001).
11 Constantin Stanislavsky, *An Actor Prepares*, trans. Elizabeth Reynolds Hapgood (London: Geoffrey Bles, 1936), pp. 82, 85.
12 Arthur Miller, *The Misfits* (New York: Penguin, 1961).
13 Johnson, "Interview," p. 4.
14 *Ibid.*
15 S. Paige Baty, *American Monroe: The Making of a Body Politic*. Berkeley: U of California P, 1995.
16 Sarah Churchwell, *The Many Lives of Marilyn Monroe* (London: Granta Books, 2004), p. 14. See also A. O. Scott's review, "Marilyn as Metaphor," http://www.nytimes.com/2005/03/06/books/review/006SCOTTL.html
17 Churchwell, p. 14.
18 Johnson, "Interview," p. 5.

19 Vladimir Nabokov, *Lolita* (1955; New York: Berkley Books, 1985), p. 11.
20 See Anthony Summers, *Goddess: The Secret Lives of Marilyn Monroe* (London: Victor Gollancz, 1985), p. 5.

Chapter I: Text

21 S. Paige Baty, *American Monroe: The Making of a Body Politic* (Berkeley: U of California P, 1995).
22 Edwin P. Hoyt, *Marilyn: The Tragic Venus* (1965; London: Robert Hale, 1967), p. v; Norman Mailer, *Marilyn* ([New York]: Grosset and Dunlap, 1973), p. 9.
23 Fred Lawrence Guiles, *Legend: The Life and Death of Marilyn Monroe* (New York: Stein and Day, 1984); Anthony Summers, *Goddess: The Secret Lives of Marilyn Monroe* (London: Victor Gollancz, 1985); Barbara Leaming, *Girl-Woman* (New York: Crown, 1998); Joyce Carol Oates, *Blonde: A Novel* (2000; New York: Ecco, 2001).
24 Victor Adam, *The Complete Marilyn Monroe* (London: Thames and Hudson, 1999).
25 Lucinda Ebersole and Richard Peabody, ed., *Mondo Marilyn* (New York: St. Martin's, 1995), p. 18.
26 Michiko Kakutani, "BOOKS OF THE TIMES; Girl-Woman: The Interior Marilyn," www.nytimes.com, December 18, 1998.
27 Marilyn Monroe, with Ben Hecht, *My Story* (New York: Stein and Day, 1974).
28 Monroe, p. 142.
29 Laura Miller, "Joyce Carol Oates's Marilyn," *The New York Times Book Review*, April 2, 2000, p. 8. In *Marilyn Monroe: A Life of the Actress* (1986; New York: DaCapo, 1993), Carl E. Rollyson, Jr., states that despite her "inertia and timidity," Marilyn "was nevertheless dynamic and inventive in working out her own career" (p. 68).
30 Mailer, *Marilyn*, p. 41.
31 Monroe, p. 28.
32 *Ibid.*, p. 66.
33 Miller, *Timebends*, p. 370.
34 *Ibid.*, p. 490.
35 Mailer, *Marilyn*, p. 20.
36 Adam, p. 180.
37 Mailer, *Marilyn*, pp. 15, 43.
38 *Ibid.*, p. 16.
39 *Ibid.*, p. 19.
40 Adam, p. 180.
41 Gloria Steinem, *Marilyn Monroe/Norma Jeane* (1986; New York: Signet, 1988), p. 132.
42 Mailer, *Marilyn*, p. 78.

43 *Ibid.*, p. 76.
44 *Ibid.*, pp. 23, 37, 43.
45 Mike Gold, "The Loves of Isadora," *New Masses* 4 (March 1929), p. 20.
46 Mailer, *Marilyn*, p. 33.
47 Summers, pp. 318-19.
48 Graham McCann, *Marilyn Monroe* (Cambridge, UK: Polity, 1988), p. 191.
49 Summers, pp. 368, xvi.
50 *Ibid.*, p. 368.
51 Steinem, p. 26.
52 *Ibid.*, p. 27.
53 *Ibid.*, p. 26.
54 *Ibid.*, p. 25.
55 *Ibid.*, p. 12.
56 *Ibid.*, p. 66.
57 *Ibid.*, p. 179. Steinem is quoting Andres Dworkin here.
58 *Ibid.*, p. 12.
59 *Ibid.*, p. 7.
60 *Ibid.*, p. 8.
61 *Ibid.*, p. 8.
62 *Ibid.*, pp. 28-29.
63 *Ibid.*, p. 147.
64 *Ibid.*, p. 157.
65 *Ibid.*, p. 153.
66 *Ibid.*, p. 118.
67 *Ibid.*, pp. 99-100.
68 *Ibid.*, pp. 9-10.
69 *Ibid.*, p. 159.
70 *Ibid.*, pp. 19, 144.
71 *Ibid.*, p. 88.
72 *Ibid.*, p. 132.
73 *Ibid.*, pp. 10-11.
74 Baty, pp. 5-6.
75 *Ibid.*, p. 23.
76 Guiles, p. 311.
77 Baty, p. 119.
78 *Ibid.*, p. 9.
79 *Ibid.*, p. 5, note 6.
80 Monroe, p. 126.
81 Richard Ben Cramer, *Joe DiMaggio: The Hero's Life* (2000; New York: Touchstone, 2001), p. 42.
82 *Ibid.*, p. 181.
83 Sam Shaw and Norman Rosten, *Marilyn among Friends* (London: Bloomsbury, 1987), p. 38.

84 Gay Talese, "The Silent Season of the Hero" (1966), in David Halberstam, ed., *The Best American Sports Writing of the Century* (New York: Houghton Mifflin, 1999), p. 4.
85 Cramer, p. 175.
86 *Ibid.*, pp. 175, 248.
87 *Ibid.*, p. xi.
88 Maria Testa, *Becoming Joe DiMaggio* (Cambridge, Mass.: Candlewick Press, 2002), pp. 4-5.
89 *Ibid.*, p. 24.
90 *Ibid.*, pp. 48, 49.
91 Cramer, p. x.
92 *Ibid.*, p. 241.
93 *Ibid.*, p. 45.
94 Halberstam, "Introduction," p. xxvii.
95 Talese, p. 16.
96 In *Of Women and Their Elegance* (New York: Simon & Schuster, 1980), p. 38. For other comments on DiMaggio, see pp. 59, 92.
97 Neil Norman and Jon Barraclough, *Insignificance: The Book* (London: Sidgwick and Jackson, 1985), p. 56.
98 *Ibid.*, p. 106.
99 *Ibid.*, p. 107.
100 McCann, *Marilyn Monroe*, p. 46.
101 Oates, *Blonde*, p. 474.
102 Roger Kahn, *Joe and Marilyn: A Memory of Love* (New York: William Morrow, 1986), p. 247.
103 *Ibid.*, p. 269.
104 Talese, p. 4.
105 Cramer, pp. 110-11.
106 Talese, p. 7.
107 Monroe, p. 140.
108 Halberstam, "Introduction," p. xxi.
109 Cramer, p. 60.
110 Halberstam, "Introduction," p. xxi.
111 Kahn, p. 256.
112 Cramer, p. 293.
113 Talese, p. 16.
114 Cramer, p. 194.
115 *Ibid.*, p. 367.
116 Norman and Barraclough, p. 88.
117 *Ibid.*, p. 89.
118 *Ibid.*, p. 106.
119 *Ibid.*, p. 109.
120 This outfit appears as a collector's item in Curtis Hanson's film *Wonder*

Boys (Paramount, 2000).

121 Cramer, pp. 203-04.

122 See, for example, Lisa Cohen, "The Horizontal Walk: Marilyn Monroe, CinemaScope, and Sexuality," *The Yale Journal of Criticism* 11.1 (1998), p. 268: "Monroe's sexuality combined naturalness and artificiality (or performance, or technology), as well as privacy and display."

123 Monroe, p. 136.

124 Cp. Cohen, p. 268: "No one simply mentions her three failed marriages. All are eager to testify to the fact that she was a slob; that she didn't know how to cook; that her car, her home, her hotel rooms, and above all her body, were always in disarray."

125 Monroe, p. 136.

126 Guiles, p. 219.

127 Cramer, p. 352.

128 Guiles, p. 229.

129 Monroe, p. 140.

130 Guiles, p. 206.

131 Shaw and Rosten, p. 10.

132 Cramer, p. 139.

133 *Ibid.*, p. 151.

134 Kahn, p. 246.

135 Qtd. Cramer, p. 370.

136 *Ibid.*, p. 369.

137 Talese, pp. 18-19.

138 Qtd. Guiles, p. 223.

139 Cramer, p. x.

140 Nostalgia permeates as well obituaries on DiMaggio published in Europe. See, for example, Klaus Justesen, "USA sørger" [The U.S. in Mourning], *Jyllands-Posten* 10 March, 1999, Section 1, p. 18, and Jørgen V. Larsen, "Profession: Joe DiMaggio," *Politiken* 14 March, 1999, Section 1, p. 12.

141 Guiles, p. 213.

142 Talese, p. 19.

143 Cramer, pp. ix-x.

144 *Ibid.*, p. 394.

145 Guiles, p. 69.

146 Arthur Miller, *After the Fall* (1964), in *Collected Plays* II (New York: Viking, 1981), pp. [125]-242.

147 Arthur Miller, *Timebends: A Life* (1987; London: Methuen, 1999).

148 Miller, *Timebends*, p. 307.

149 Cp. McCann's biography, which discusses the jealousy between Mailer and Miller. McCann quotes Pauline Kael, who in 1973 writes a review of Mailer's biography of Marilyn: "Miller and Mailer try for the same things: he's catching Miller's hand in the gentile cookie jar" (p. 33).

150 Baty, p. 6.
151 Miller, *Timebends*, p. 299.
152 *Ibid.*, p. 299.
153 *Ibid.*, p. 302.
154 *Ibid.*, p. 302.
155 *Ibid.*, p. 306.
156 Marie Louise Pratt, *Imperial Eyes: Travel Writing and Transculturation* (London: Routledge, 1992).
157 Miller, *Timebends*, p. 307.
158 Steinem, p. 153.
159 Miller, *Timebends*, p. 307.
160 *Ibid.*
161 *Ibid.*, p. 366.
162 *Ibid.*, p. 356.
163 *Ibid.*, pp. 370-71.
164 Julia Kristeva, "Woman Can Never Be Defined," in *New French Feminisms*, ed. Elaine Marks and Isabelle de Courtivron (New York: Schocken, 1981), p. 137.
165 Miller, *Timebends*, p. 371.
166 *Ibid.*, p. 378.
167 *Ibid.*
168 *Ibid.*, p. 381.
169 *Ibid.*
170 McCann, *Marilyn Monroe*, p. 49.
171 Norman Rosten, *Marilyn: An Untold Story* (New York: Signet, 1973), p. 88.
172 Miller, *Timebends*, p. 413.
173 Rosten, pp. 44-45.
174 Miller, *Timebends*, p. 423.
175 *Ibid.*, p. 448.
176 *Ibid.*, p. 460.
177 *Ibid.*, pp. 460-61.
178 David Miller, *Dark Eden: The Swamp in Nineteenth-Century American Literature* (Cambridge: Cambridge U P, 1990), pp. 211-12.
179 Rosten, pp. 88-89.
180 Miller, *Timebends*, p. 482.
181 *Ibid.*, p. 483.
182 *Ibid.*, p. 485.
183 Miller, *Fall*, p. 127.
184 Miller, *Fall*, p. 228.
185 *Ibid.*, p. 230.
186 *Ibid.*, p. 234.
187 *Ibid.*, p. 238.

188 *Ibid.*, pp. 238, 239.
189 Rosten, p. 86.
190 Barbara Johnson, "My Monster/My Self," *Diacritics* 12 (1982), p. 3.
191 Qtd. *ibid.*, p. 3.
192 *Ibid.*, p. 7.
193 Miller, *Timebends*, p. 527.
194 Johnson, p. 3.
195 Graham McCann, "Biographical Boundaries: Sociology and Marilyn Monroe," in *The Body: Social Process and Cultural Theory*, ed. Mike Featherstone, Mike Hepworth, and Bryan S. Turner (London: Sage, 1991), p. 331.
196 Adam Kirsch, "The Great Disconcerting Wipeout," *The New Republic* (October 5, 2009), online: http://www.tnr.com/article/books-and-arts/the-great-disconcerting-wipeout.
197 Joyce Carol Oates, "On the Composition of Blonde." Unpublished xerox copy, June 1999.
198 Oates, *Blonde*, p. 541.
199 *Ibid.*
200 Rosten, pp. 38, [39].
201 Miller, *Timebends*, p. 599.
202 *Ibid.*
203 http://www.nytimes.com/2002/08/15/arts/theater/15BLUE.html
204 http://www.playbill.com/news/article/print/80864.html

Chapter II: Body

205 Norman Rosten, *Marilyn: An Untold Story* (New York: Signet, 1973), p. 36.
206 Mabel Elsworth Todd, *The Thinking Body: A Study of the Balancing Forces of Dynamic Man* (1937; Princeton, N.J.: Princeton Book Co.), 1968.
207 Richard Dyer, *Stars* (1979; London: British Film Institute, 1998), pp. 30-31.
208 Graham McCann, *Marilyn Monroe* (London: Polity, 1988), p. 88.
209 *Ibid.*, pp. 1-2.
210 Carl E. Rollyson, Jr., *Marilyn Monroe: A Life of the Actress* (1986; New York, Da Capo, 1993), p. 56.
211 Arthur W. Frank, "For a Sociology of the Body: An Analytical Review," in *The Body: Social Process and Cultural Theory*, ed. Mike Featherstone, Mike Hepworth, and Bryan S. Turner (London: Sage, 1991), pp. [36]-102.
212 Graham McCann, "Biographical Boundaries: Sociology and Marilyn Monroe," in Featherstone *et al.*, p. 332.
213 *Ibid.*, p. [325].
214 *Ibid.*, p. 326.
215 *Ibid.*, p. 327.

216 McCann, *Marilyn Monroe*, p. 215.
217 Berniece Baker Miracle, *My Sister Marilyn: A Memoir of Marilyn Monroe* (Chapel Hill: Algonquin, 1994), p. xiv.
218 Rollyson, Jr., p. 58.
219 Frank, p. 51.
220 *Ibid.*
221 *Ibid.*, p. 52.
222 *Ibid.*, p. 69; Judith Halberstam, *Female Masculinity* (Durham, NC: Duke U P, 1998). See also Jean Noble's *Masculinities Without Men: Female Masculinity in Twentieth-Century Fictions* (Vancouver: U of British Columbia P, 2003).
223 Frank, p. 55.
224 *Ibid.*
225 *Ibid.*, p. 56.
226 Norman Mailer, *Marilyn.* ([New York]: Grosset and Dunlap, 1973), p. 15.
227 Rollyson, Jr., p. 159.
228 See, for example, Anthony Summers, *Goddess: The Secret Lives of Marilyn Monroe* (London: Victor Gollancz, 1985), pp. 195-96.
229 Mailer, *Marilyn*, p. 75.
230 *Ibid.*
231 Oates, *Blonde*, p. 158.
232 *Ibid.*, p. 214.
233 *Ibid.*, p. 215.
234 Rosten, p. 9; cp. pp. 10-11: "She seems so very fragile and alone. . . ."
235 McCann, *Marilyn Monroe*, p. 205.
236 Rollyson, Jr., p. 39; McCann, *Marilyn Monroe*, p. 147.
237 Oates, *Blonde*, p. 10.
238 Qtd. in Rollyson, Jr., p. 66.
239 Mailer, *Marilyn*, p. 209.
240 *Ibid.*
241 Oates, *Blonde*, pp. 214, 215.
242 *Ibid.*, pp. 43-44.
243 Mailer, *Marilyn*, p. 78.
244 *Ibid.*, pp. 78, 79.
245 Frank, p. 56.
246 Oates, *Blonde*, p. 227.
247 Rollyson, Jr., p. 41.
248 McCann, *Marilyn Monroe*, p. 204.
249 Frank, p. 61.
250 *Ibid.*, p. 62.
251 *Ibid.*, p. 63.
252 Mailer, *Marilyn*, p. 48.
253 *Ibid.*, p. 157.
254 *Ibid.*, p. 48.

255 Rollyson, Jr., p. 17.
256 Mailer, *Marilyn*, p. 121.
257 Arthur Miller, *After the Fall* (1964), in *Collected Plays* II (New York: Viking, 1981), p. 225.
258 Frank, p. 61.
259 Rollyson, Jr., p. 63.
260 *Ibid.*, p. 75.
261 Oates, *Blonde*, p. 10.
262 Rollyson, Jr., p. 6.
263 Mailer, *Marilyn*, p. 43.
264 *Ibid.*, p. 79.
265 Frank, p. 80.
266 *Ibid.*
267 Oates, *Blonde*, p. 375.
268 See Hélène Cixous, "The Laugh of the Medusa" (1976), in *New French Feminisms*, ed. Elaine Marks and Isabelle de Courtivron (New York: Schocken, 1981), p. 258.
269 Rosten, p. 17.
270 This anecdote is widely circulated. See, for example, Rosten, p. 29.
271 *Ibid.*, p. 24.
272 Rollyson, Jr., p. 52.
273 Frank, p. 80.
274 *Ibid.*, pp. 80, 81.
275 *Ibid.*, p. 83.
276 Qtd. in Henry M. Sayre, *The Object of Performance* (Chicago: U of Chicago P, 1989), pp. 96-97; for a photo and a discussion of *Eye Body*, see pp. 74-75.
277 *Ibid.*, p. 81.
278 Bryan S. Turner, "Recent Developments in the Theory of the Body," in Featherstone *et al.*, p. 4.
279 Lisa Cohen, "The Horizontal Walk: Marilyn Monroe, Cinemascope, and Sexuality," *The Yale Journal of Criticism* 11.1 (1998), p. 259.
280 Turner, p. 29.
281 *Ibid.*, p. 28.
282 *Ibid.*, p. 29.
283 *Ibid.*
284 McCann, "Biographical Boundaries," p. 331.
285 McCann, *Marilyn Monroe*, p. 193.

Chapter III: Marylin Performing

286 Joyce Carol Oates, "On the Composition of Blonde," unpublished xerox copy, June 1999, p. 1.
287 Graham McCann, *Marilyn Monroe* (London: Polity, 1988), p. 165.

288 Oates, "Composition," p. 1.
289 Michiko Kakutani, "Darkening the Nightmare of America's Dream Girl," www.nytimes.com, March 31, 2000.
290 Fred Lawrence Guiles, *Legend: The Life and Death of Marilyn Monroe* (New York: Stein & Day, 1984); Anthony Summers, *Goddess: The Secret Lives of Marilyn Monroe* (London: Victor Gollancz, 1985); Carl E. Rollyson, Jr., *Marilyn Monroe: A Life of the Actress* (1986; New York: Da Capo, 1993).
291 Norman Mailer, *Marilyn* ([New York]: Grosset and Dunlap, 1973); Marilyn Monroe, with Ben Hecht, *My Story* (New York: Stein & Day, 1974).
292 Kakutani, www.nytimes.com, March 31, 2000.
293 Diana Trilling, "The Death of Marilyn Monroe," in *Claremont Essays* (New York: Harcourt Brace World, 1964), p. 243.
294 *Ibid.*, p. 237.
295 Joan Mellen, *Marilyn Monroe* (New York: Pyramid, 1973); Gloria Steinem, *Marilyn Monroe/Norma Jeane* (New York: Signet, 1986).
296 Molly Haskell, *From Reverence to Rape* (Harmondsworth: Penguin, 1974).
297 Oates, "Composition," p. 1.
298 *Ibid.*, pp. 1, 2.
299 Mailer, *Marilyn*, p. 15.
300 See, for example, John Berendt's *Midnight in the Garden of Good and Evil* (1994), Don DeLillo's *Underworld* (1997), Philip Roth's *American Pastoral* (1997), Tim O'Brien's *In the Lake of the Woods* (1994), and Toni Morrison's *Paradise* (1998) and *Love* (2003).
301 Joyce Carol Oates, *Blonde: A Novel* (2000; New York: Ecco, 2001), p. 37.
302 *Ibid.*, p. 50.
303 Oates, "Composition," p. 1.
304 Oates, *Blonde*, p. 648.
305 *Ibid.*, pp. 85, 15.
306 *Ibid.*, pp. 15, 16.
307 *Ibid.*, pp. 539-40.
308 Rollyson, Jr., p. 5.
309 *Ibid.*, pp. 8, 35.
310 Oates, *Blonde*, p. 69.
311 *Ibid.*, p. 270.
312 *Ibid.*, p. 78.
313 S. Paige Baty, *American Monroe: The Making of a Body Politic* (Berkeley: U of California P, 1995).
314 Norman K. Denzin, *Images of Postmodern Society: Social Theory and Contemporary Cinema* (London: Sage, 1991), p. 5.
315 Constantin Stanislavsky, *My Life in Art* (1924; Moscow: Foreign Languages Publishing House, 1958); Michael Chekhov, *To the Actor on the Technique of Acting* (New York: Harper, 1953).
316 Oates, "Composition," p. 2.

317 Oates, *Blonde*, p. 531.
318 *Ibid.*, p. 587.
319 *Ibid.*, p. 547.
320 *Ibid.*, p. 508.
321 *Ibid.*, p. 587.
322 *Ibid.*, n.p.
323 Oates, "Composition," p. 1.
324 Laura Miller, "Joyce Carol Oates's Marilyn," *The New York Times Review of Books* (April 2, 2000), p. 6.
325 Denzin, p. [vii].
326 McCann, *Marilyn Monroe*, p. 42.
327 Oates, "Composition," p. 2.
328 *Ibid.*
329 Joyce Carol Oates, *(Woman) Writer: Occasions and Opportunities* (New York: E. P. Dutton, 1988), p. 25.
330 Oates, *Blonde*, p. 531.
331 Laura Mulvey, "Visual Pleasure and Narrative Cinema," *Screen* 16.3 (Autumn 1975), 6-18.
332 Mailer, *Marilyn*, p. 15.
333 Charles McGrath, *et al.*, "The Real Story: Literary Fact and Fiction." *PEN America: A Journal for Writers and Readers* 1 (Spring 2001). http://www.pen.org/journal/texts/realstory.html. I am indebted to Lotta Kähkönen, Dept. of Comparative Literature, University of Turku, for this reference.
334 Justine Elias, "Blond Confusion." June 29, 2003. www.nydailynews.com/entertainment/story/96149p-87120c.html
335 Richard Dyer, *White* (New York: Routledge, 1997), p. 83.
336 Qtd. in Elias.
337 Oates, *Blonde*, p. 53.
338 *Ibid.*, p. 211.
339 *Ibid.*, p. 213.
340 *Ibid.*, p. 216.
341 Dyer, *White*, p. 78.
342 *Ibid.*, p. 39.
343 Richard Dyer, *Heavenly Bodies: Film Stars and Society* (London: British Film Institute, 1986), p. 21.
344 Oates, *Blonde*, p. 473.
345 *Ibid.*, p. 227.
346 Dyer, *White*, p. 138.
347 Mailer, *Marilyn*, p. 15.
348 Oates, *Blonde*, pp. 227, 516.
349 *Ibid.*, pp. 532-33.
350 Dyer, *White*, p. 50.
351 *Ibid.*, p. 80.

352 Oates, *Blonde*, p. 347.
353 Dyer, *White*, p. 222.
354 Oates, *Blonde*, p. 672.
355 See John Izod, "Madonna as Trickster," in *Deconstructing Madonna*, ed. Fran Lloyd (London: B. T. Batsford, 1993), pp. [49]-50.
356 Oates, *Blonde*, p. 619.
357 For a more hostile reading of Marilyn's hysterical performance, see Rollyson, Jr., p. 56.
358 Elizabeth Bronfen, *The Knotted Subject: Hysteria and Its Discontents* (Princeton: Princeton U P, 1998), p. 42. I owe this reference to Lotta Kähkönen, who also introduced me to other ideas in this section, including Marilyn's hysteria.
359 Dyer, *Heavenly Bodies*, p. 27.
360 *Ibid.*, p. 46.
361 Klaus Theweleit, *Male Fantasies* I-II (London: Polity, 1987, 1989).
362 See McCann, *Marilyn Monroe*, pp. 20-21.
363 bell hooks, "Madonna: Plantation Mistress or Soul Sister?" in *Black Looks: Race and Representation* (Boston: South End P, 1992), p. 158.
364 Stella Bruzzi, *Undressing Cinema: Clothing and Identity in the Movies* (London: Routledge, 1997), p. 98.
365 Monroe, p. 142.
366 Qtd. in hooks, p. 158.
367 *Ibid.*, pp. 158-59.
368 Oates, *Blonde*, p. 712.
369 See Christy Turner, "Fabulousness as Fetish: Queer Politics in *Sex and the City*," *S & F Online* 3.1 (Fall 2004), p. 1. http://www.barnard.edu/sfonline/hbo/printctu.htm
370 Bruzzi, p. 109.
371 Oates, *Blonde*, p. 713.
372 In describing a party in Marilyn's honor given by director Billy Wilder and producer Charlie Feldman to celebrate the completion of *The Seven Year Itch* (1955), Norman Rosten writes that "the aristocracy of Hollywood," i. e. studio heads and other "men of power," did what they could to "retain the slavery of the contract player." See Sam Shaw and Norman Rosten, *Marilyn among Friends* (London: Bloomsbury, 1987), p. 70. In *Conversations with Marilyn* (London: Robson Books, 1976), W. J. Weatherby has Marilyn reply to his comment that American women of color seem to admire her: "It's easy to understand the slave system when you've been through the star system . . ." (pp. 129, 130, 131-32).
373 Norman Mailer, *Of Women and Their Elegance* (New York: Simon & Schuster, 1980), pp. 181, 183.
374 See Lisa Cohen, "The Horizontal Walk: Marilyn Monroe, CinemaScope, and Sexuality," *The Yale Review of Criticism* 11.1 (1998), p. 272: "[Weath-

erby] ultimately makes Marilyn and Christine oddly interchangeable."
375 Judith Halberstam, *Female Masculinity* (Durham, NC: Duke U P, 1998), p. 2.
376 Janet Wolf, "On the Road Again: Metaphors of Travel in Cultural Criticism." *Cultural Studies* 7.2 (May 1993): 224-39.
377 Martin Barker, "Introduction," *Contemporary Hollywood Stardom*, ed. Thomas Austin and Martin Barker (London: Arnold, 2003), p. 14.
378 Constantin Stanislavsky, "When Acting Is an Art," in *Star Texts: Image and Performance in Film and Television*, ed. Jeremy G. Butler (Detroit: Wayne State U P, 1991), p. 21.
379 James Naremore, *Acting in the Cinema* (Berkeley: U of California P, 1988), pp. 18-19.
380 *Ibid.*, p. 1.
381 *Ibid.*, pp. 50, 51, 65.
382 See Blake Allmendinger, *Ten Most Wanted: The New Western Literature* (New York: Routledge, 1998), p. 74. Allmendinger is discussing a little-known western writer, Louise A. K. S. Clappe, who used the pen name "Dame Shirley" and inspired Bret Harte.
383 See Susan Kollin, "The Wild, Wild North: Nature Writing, Nationalist Ecologies, and Alaska," *American Literary History* 12.1/2 (Spring-Summer 2000), pp. 43-44.
384 Todd Gitlin, "Domesticating Nature," *Theory and Society* 8.2 (Sept. 1979), p. 291.
385 Summers, pp. 89-91.
386 See, for example, Laurie Shirley's review on amazon.com.
387 For the term "aesthetics of possession," see Kollin, p. 51.
388 See Richard Mabey, *The Oxford Book of Nature Writing* (New York: Oxford U P, 1997), p. [vii].
389 Summers, p. 89.
390 In *Nature Writing and America: Essays upon a Cultural Type* (Ames, Iowa: Iowa State U P, 1990), Peter A. Fritzell discusses American nature writing in relation to "America's case against history" (p. 163).
391 Mabey, pp. viii-x.
392 David Orr, "Virtual Nature," *Conservation Biology* 10.1 (Feb. 1996), pp. 8-9.
393 See Stan Godlovitch, "Evaluating Nature Aesthetically," *The Journal of Aesthetics and Art Criticism* 56.2 (Spring 1998), p. 117.
394 For a contemporary parallel, see Kollin on Alaska. She presents the idea of the writer as resource manager on p. 52.
395 Weatherby, p. 109.
396 Naremore, p. 20.
397 Arthur Miller, *The Misfits* (New York: Penguin, 1961), pp. 28, 35, 29.
398 Jane Tompkins, *West of Everything* (New York: Oxford U P, 1992), p. 45.
399 Cp. Anette Kolodny, *The Lay of the Land: Metaphor as Experience and His-*

tory in American Life and Letters (Chapel Hill, N.C.: U of North Carolina P, 1975).

400 Miller, *Misfits*, p. 35.

401 *Ibid.*, pp. 36, 39.

402 *Ibid.*, pp. 45, 43, 47.

403 *Ibid.*, pp. 39-40.

404 *Ibid.*, pp. 83, 84, 63, 92.

405 *Ibid.*, p. 125.

406 *Ibid.*, p. 126. Tompkins writes that "the desert offers itself as a white sheet on which to trace a figure. It is a tabula rasa on which man can write, as if for the first time, the story he wants to live" (p. 74).

407 Miller, *Misfits*, pp. 126, 127.

408 Tompkins, pp. 107, 123.

409 Miller, *Misfits*, p. [128].

410 See Torben Huus Larsen on "The Modern Horror Movie and the Critique of the American Landscape Narrative," *OASIS* 72 (Feb. 2006), pp. 3-4.

411 Paul Schrader, "Notes on Film Noir," in *Perspectives on Film Noir*, ed. R. Barton Palmer (New York: G. K. Hall, 1996), p. 103. I am indebted to Martin Andersen for this reference.

412 Larsen, p. 10.

413 Cp. Kollin on Alaska: "the region's role as the 'Last Frontier,' as a radically other American terrain, serves primarily to overcome US environmental anxieties by enabling the US to once again unmap and remap itself" (p. 72).

Chapter IV: Performing Marilyn

414 See Barry King, "The Star and the Commodity: Notes towards a Performance Theory of Stardom," *Cultural Studies* 1.2 (1987), p. 157, and Thomas Harris, "The Building of Popular Images: Grace Kelly and Marilyn Monroe," in *Stardom: Industry of Desire*, ed. Christine Gledhill (New York: Routledge, 1991), pp. 40, 42, 43.

415 See Paul Rudnick, "Marilyn Monroe," *Time* (June 14, 1999), www.time.com/time/time100/heroes/profile/monroe01.html.

416 Leo Braudy, *The Frenzy of Renown: Fame and Its History* (New York: Oxford U P, 1986), p. 551, incl. note 41.

417 Roland Barthes, *S/Z* (New York: Hill and Wang, 1976), p. 100.

418 W. J. Weatherby, *Conversations with Marilyn* (London: Robson Books, 1976), pp. 182, 192.

419 Lisa Cohen, "The Horizontal Walk: Marilyn Monroe, CinemaScope, and Sexuality," *The Yale Journal of Criticism* 11.1 (1998), p. 278.

420 King, p. 159.

421 Gailyn Addis, *Be Marilyn!: A Glamorous Guide to Living Blonde* (Naperville,

Ill.: Sourcebooks, 2000).

422 Richard Schickel, *Intimate Strangers: The Culture of Celebrity* (Garden City, NY: Doubleday, 1985), p. 115.

423 Addis, pp. 82-83.

424 *Ibid.*, p. 55.

425 *Ibid.*, p. 39.

426 Braudy, p. 568.

427 Addis., p. 3.

428 Braudy, pp. 569-70.

429 Addis, pp. 24-25.

430 *Ibid.*, p. 13.

431 *Ibid.*, p. 12.

432 Laura Mulvey, "Visual Pleasure and Narrative Cinema, *Screen* 16.3 (Autumn 1975): pp. 6-18. See also Jackie Stacey, *Star Gazing: Hollywood Cinema and Female Spectatorship* (New York: Routledge, 1994), p. 21.

433 Mulvey, pp. 8-10.

434 Stacey, p. 162.

435 *Ibid.*, p. 167.

436 *Ibid.*, p. 168.

437 Addis, p. 21.

438 Cp. Stacey, p. 231.

439 Addis, p. 90.

440 For the term "epic commodity," see Paul Rudnick, "Marilyn Monroe," http://www.time.com/time/time100/heroes/profile/monroe01.html

441 King, p. 149.

442 Stacey, pp. 168-69.

443 Mary Anne Doane, "The Economy of Desire. The Commodity Form in/of Cinema," *Quarterly Review of Film & Video* 11 (1989), p. 32.

444 Addis, pp. 34-35, 112.

445 *Ibid.*, p. 3.

446 *Ibid.*, p. 87.

447 *Ibid.*, pp. 86, 94.

448 Stacey, p. 230.

449 Braudy, p. 536.

450 King, p. 146.

451 *Ibid.*, p. 149.

452 Qtd. *ibid.*, p. 146.

453 The dance of hybrid identities in *Graceland* involves as well Harvey Keitel as Elvis, Elvis returned, or a businessman exorcizing the death of his wife and child by impersonating Elvis.

454 Addis, p. 105.

455 Richard Dyer, *Stars* (1979; rev. ed. London: British Film Institute, 1998), p. 43.

456 *Life*, December 22, 1958.
457 Cohen, p. 281.
458 www.bluemoontalent.com
459 Addis, p. 101.
460 http://www.imdb.com/title/tt0107517/
461 Ginia Bellafante, "Sybil in a Wonderbra," *Time* 147.21 (20 May, 1996). http://www.time.com/time/magazine/article/0,9171,984575,00.html
462 Addis, p. 95, which spells Carmen's first name "Jeane." Various other sources use "Jeanne."
463 See www.angelfire.com
464 Madonna has also recycled Frida Kahlo in *Bedtime Stories* (1994) and Martha Graham in *Frozen* (1998).
465 Qtd. in J. Randy Taraborrelli, *Madonna: An Intimate Biography* (London: Sidgwick & Jackson, 2001), p. 95.
466 *Ibid.*, p. 97.
467 See, for example, "Homage to Norma Jean," *Vanity Fair* (April 1991).
468 See www.allstarz.org/oscars/moments10.htm.
469 www.partypop.com/Vendors/3002810.htm. For a similar impersonator, see Coty Alexander's tribute to Madonna, Marilyn & Britney Spears, at www.bluemoontalent.com/coty-alexander.html
470 Taraborrelli, pp. x-xi.
471 *Ibid.*, pp. 72, 65.
472 *Ibid.*, p. 45.
473 *Ibid.*, p. 11.
474 *Ibid.*, p. 69.
475 *Ibid.*, p. 53.
476 *Ibid.*, p. 44.
477 *Ibid.*, pp. 119-20, 128-29.
478 *Ibid.*, pp. 131, 137.
479 *Ibid.*, p. 143.
480 *Ibid.*, p. 276.
481 *Ibid.*, p. 233.
482 The couple was granted a divorce on January 2, 2009.
483 Qtd. Taraborrelli, p. 328.
484 Reena Mistry, "Madonna and *Gender Trouble*," http://www.theory.org.uk/madonna.htm, pp. 1, 6. See also Ann E. Kaplan, "Madonna Politics: Perversion, Repression, or Subversion? Or Masks and/as Master-y" and Cathy Schwichtenberg, "Madonna's Postmodern Feminism: Bringing Margins to the Center," in *The Madonna Connection: Representational Politics, Subcultural Identities, and Cultural Theory*, ed. Cathy Schwichtenberg (Boulder: Westview P, 1993), pp. 149-65 and pp. 129-45; and Beverly Skeggs, "A Good Time for Women Only," in Fran Lloyd, *Deconstructing Madonna* (London: B. T. Batsford, 1993), pp. [61]-73.

485 See John Izod, "Madonna as Trickster," in Lloyd, p. 57.
486 *Time* 147.21 (May 20, 1996). http://weblinks1.epnet.com.heimdal.bib.sdu.dk
487 Jack Kugelmass, "Wishes Come True: Designing the Greenwich Village Halloween Parade," *The Journal of American Folklore* 124.414 (Fall 1991), pp. 443-65.
488 *Ibid.*, p. 445.
489 *Ibid.*, p. 447.
490 *Ibid.*, p. 454.
491 Richard Dyer, "Charisma," in *Stardom: Industry of Desire*, ed. Christine Gledhill (New York: Routledge, 1991), pp. 58, 59.
492 Kugelmass, p. 445.
493 Joan Riviere, "Womanliness as a Masquerade" (1929), in *Formations of Fantasy*, ed. Victor Burgin, James Donald and Cora Kaplan (New York: Methuen, 1986), pp. 39, 38.
494 Stephen Heath, "Joan Riviere and the Masquerade," in Burgin *et al.*, p. 49.
495 I have borrowed the term from Sam Toperoff's *Queen of Desire* (New York: HarperCollins, 1992).
496 Graham Fuller, "Shots in the Dark: Why the Lure of the Old-timers Is Still So Strong," www.findarticles.com/p/articles/mi_m1285/is_7_34/ai_n6128061/print
497 Cohen, p. 282.
498 *Ibid.*, pp. 280, 282, 283.
499 Susan J. Hubert, "Two Women, Two Songs: The Subversive Iconography of 'Candle in the Wind,' " *NWSA Journal* 11.2 (1999), p. 125.
500 *Ibid.*, p. 128.
501 *Ibid.*, p. 134.
502 Taraborrelli, p. 29.
503 See Laura Mulvey, "Afterthoughts on 'Visual Pleasure and Narrative Cinema' Inspired by *Duel in the Sun*," *Framework* 6.15/16/17 (1981), pp. 12-15.
504 Mary Anne Doane,"Film and the Masquerade: Theorising the Female Spectator," *Screen* 23. 3-4 (1982), pp. 81-82.
505 Stacey, pp. 172, 173.
506 See José Esteban Muñoz, *Disidentifications: Queers of Color and the Performance of Politics* (Durham: Duke U P, 1998).
507 *Ibid.*, p. 4.
508 Cristy Turner, "Fabulousness as Fetish: Queer Politics in *Sex and the City*," *S & F Online* 3.1 (Fall 2004), p. 1 (www.barnard.edu/sfonline/hbo/printctu.htm)
509 See Stephen Maddison, "Miss DuBois: Queer Defiance?" in *Fags, Hags, and Queer Sisters: Gender Dissent and Heterosocial Bonds in Gay Culture* (New York: St. Martin's, 2000), pp. 49-63.

510 Turner, p. 5. I am indebted to Turner for many of the concepts and references in this section.
511 Norman Mailer, *Of Women and Their Elegance* (New York: Simon & Schuster, 1980), p. 28.
512 *Ibid.*, pp. 31, 149.
513 *Ibid.*, p. 114.
514 *Ibid.*, p. 30.
515 *Ibid.*, p. 36.
516 *Ibid.*, p. 29.
517 *Ibid.*, p. 76.
518 *Ibid.*, p. 119.
519 *Ibid.*, pp. 94, 81, 74.
520 *Ibid.*, pp. 199-200.
521 *Ibid.*, p. 57.
522 *Ibid.*, p. 95.
523 *Ibid.*, p. 65.
524 *Ibid.*, p. 130.
525 *Ibid.*, p. 68.
526 *Ibid.*, p. 74.
527 *Ibid.*, pp. 121, 168.
528 *Ibid.*, p. 228. For another "ghost-written" novel that Marilyn narrates, see Sam Toperoff's *Queen of Desire* (1992).

Postscript

529 See Richard Zoglin, "Scenes from a Marriage, Part 2," *Time* 164.17 (Oct. 25, 2004), pp. 84-85. Cp. Kenneth Jones, "Almost 40 Years After *After the Fall*, Miller Addresses Marilyn Monroe in a New Play." www.playbill.com/news/article/print/80864.html. Arthur Miller died the following year, on February 10, 2005.
530 Don DeLillo, *Underworld* (1997; London: Picador, 1999), p. 474.
531 *Ibid.*, p. 475.
532 *Ibid.*, p. 474.
533 *Ibid.*, p. 484.
534 *Ibid.*, p. 490.
535 Terry Pratchett, *Moving Pictures: A Discworld Novel* (1990; London: Corgi Books, 1991), p. 9.
536 *Ibid.*, p. 90.
537 *Ibid.*, pp. 91, 129.
538 *Ibid.*, p. 136.
539 *Ibid.*, pp. 144-45.
540 *Ibid.*, p. 180.
541 *Ibid.*, p. 151.
542 *Ibid.*, p. 181.

543 *Ibid.*
544 "Moving Pictures: Annotations, Information, Quotes," p. 4. www.co.uk.lspace.org/books/apf/moving-pictures.html
545 Pratchett, p. 172.
546 Leo Braudy, *The Frenzy of Renown: Fame and Its History* (Oxford: Oxford U P, 1986), p. 567.
547 Richard Dyer, "Charisma," in *Stardom: Industry of Desire*, ed. Christine Gledhill (New York: Routledge, 1991), p. 58.
548 James Naremore, *Acting in the Cinema* (Berkeley: U of California P, 1988), p. 49.
549 See Jeannie B. Thomas, "Dumb Blondes, Dan Quayle, and Hillary Clinton: Gender, Sexuality, and Stupidity in Jokes," *The Journal of American Folklore* 110.437 (Summer 1997), pp. 277-313, and Wayne Glowka, *et al.*, "Among the New Words," *American Speech* 74.2 (Summer 1999), pp. 214-15.
550 Biancamano, Diane. "Marilyn Monroe: Essence of a Personality," *New York Times on the Web*, February 19, 2003.
551 Jess Cagle, "How to Make a Score," *Time* (July 23, 2001), p. 60.
552 In Gloria Steinem, *Marilyn Monroe/Norma Jeane.* 1986. (New York: Signet, 1988).

Works Cited

Adam, Victor. *The Complete Marilyn Monroe.* London: Thames and Hudson, 1999.

Addis, Gailyn. *Be Marilyn!: A Glamorous Guide to Living Blonde.* Naperville, Ill.: Sourcebooks, 2000.

Alexander, Coty. "Tribute to Madonna, Marilyn & Britney Spears." www.bluemoontalent.com/coty-alexander.html

Allmendinger, Blake. *Ten Most Wanted: The New Western Literature.* New York: Routledge, 1998.

Barker, Martin. "Introduction." *Contemporary Hollywood Stardom.* Ed. Thomas Austin and Martin Barker. London: Arnold, 2003. 1-24.

Barthes, Roland. *S/Z.* New York: Hill and Wang, 1976.

Baty, S. Paige. *American Monroe: The Making of a Body Politic.* Berkeley: U of California P, 1995.

Bellafante, Ginia. "Sybil in a Wonderbra." *Time* 147.21 (May 20, 1996). http://www.time.com/time/magazine/article/0,9171, 984575,00.html

Berendt, John. *Midnight in the Garden of Good and Evil.* 1994. London: Vintage, 1995.

Bessie, Alvah. *The Symbol.* 1966. London: The Bodley Head, 1967.

Biancamano, Diane. "Marilyn Monroe: Essence of a Personality." *New York Times on the Web*, February 19, 2003.

Bigsby, Christopher. *Arthur Miller.* London: Phoenix, 2009.

Braudy, Leo. *The Frenzy of Renown: Fame and Its History.* New York: Oxford U P, 1986.

Bronfen, Elizabeth. *The Knotted Subject: Hysteria and Its Discontents.* Princeton: Princeton U P, 1998.

Burgin, Victor, James Donald and Cora Kaplan, ed. *Formations of Fantasy.* New York: Methuen, 1986.

Bruzzi, Stella. *Undressing Cinema: Clothing and Identity in the Movies.* New York: Routledge, 1997.

Butler, Judith. *Gender Trouble: Feminism and the Subversion of Identity*. New York: Routledge, 1989.

Cagle, Jess. "How to Make a Score," *Time* (July 23, 2001): 60.

Chekhov, Michael. *To the Actor on the Technique of Acting*. New York: Harper, 1953.

Churchwell, Sarah. *The Many Lives of Marilyn Monroe*. London: Granta Books, 2004.

Cixous, Hélène. "The Laugh of the Medusa." In Marks and de Courtivron. 245-64.

Cohen, Lisa. "The Horizontal Walk: Marilyn Monroe, CinemaScope, and Sexuality." *The Yale Journal of Criticism* 11.1 (1998): 259-88.

Cramer, Richard Ben. *Joe DiMaggio: The Hero's Life*. 2000. New York: Touchstone, 2001.

DeLillo, Don. *Underworld*. 1997. London: Picador, 1998.

Denzin, Norman K. *Images of Postmodern Society: Social Theory and Contemporary Cinema*. London: Sage, 1991.

Doane, Mary Anne. "The Economy of Desire: The Commodity Form in/of Cinema." *Quarterly Review of Film & Video* 11 (1989): 23-33.

- - -. "Film and the Masquerade: Theorising the Female Spectator." *Screen* 23.3-4 (1982): 74-87.

Dyer, Richard. "Charisma." In: *Stardom: Industry of Desire*. Ed. Christine Gledhill. New York: Routledge, 1991. 57-59.

- - -. *Heavenly Bodies: Film Stars and Society*. London: British Film Institute, 1986.

- - -. *Stars*. 1979. Rev. ed. London: British Film Institute, 1998.

- - -. *White*. New York: Routledge, 1997.

Ebersole, Lucinda and Richard Peabody, ed. *Mondo Marilyn*. New York: St. Martin's, 1995.

Elias, Justine. "Blond Confusion." June 29, 2003. www.nydailynews.com/entertainment/story/96249p-87120c.html

Featherstone, Mike, Mike Hepworth and Bryan S. Turner, ed. *The Body: Social Process and Cultural Theory*. London: Sage, 1991.

Frank, Arthur W. "For a Sociology of the Body: An Analytical Review." In Featherstone *et al.* [36]-102.

Fritzell, Peter A. *Nature Writing and America: Essays upon a Cultural*

Type. Ames, Iowa: Iowa State U P, 1990.

Fuller, Graham. "Shots in the Dark: Why the Lure of the Old-timers Is Still So Strong." www.findarticles.com/p/articles/mi_ml285/is_7_34/ai_n6128061/

Gitlin, Todd. "Domesticating Nature." *Theory and Society* 8.2 (Sept. 1979): 291-97.

Glowka, Wayne, Brenda K. Lester, Amedeo Fedeli *et al.*, "Among the New Words." *American Speech* 74.2 (Summer 1999): 203-24.

Godlovitch, Stan. "Evaluating Nature Aesthetically," *The Journal of Aesthetics and Art Criticism* 56.2 (Spring 1998): 113-25.

Gold, Mike. "The Loves of Isadora." *New Masses* 4 (March 1929): 20-21.

Guiles, Fred Lawrence. *Legend: The Life and Death of Marilyn Monroe*. New York: Stein & Day, 1984.

Halberstam, David, ed. *The Best American Sports Writing of the Century*. New York: Houghton Mifflin, 1999.

Halberstam, Judith. *Female Masculinity*. Durham, NC: Duke U P, 1998.

Harris, Thomas. "The Building of Popular Images: Grace Kelly and Marilyn Monroe." In: *Stardom: Industry of Desire*. Ed. Christine Gledhill. New York: Routledge, 1991.

Haskell, Molly. *From Reverence to Rape: The Treatment of Women in the Movies*. Harmondsworth: Penguin, 1974.

Heath, Stephen. "Joan Riviere and the Masquerade." In Burgin *et al.* [45]-61.

Hicks, Catherine. http://www.bluemoontalent.com/catherine-hicks.html

"Homage to Norma Jean." *Vanity Fair* (April 1991).

hooks, bell. "Madonna: Plantation Mistress or Soul Sister?" In: *Black Looks: Race and Representation*. Boston: South End P, 1992.

Hoyt, Edwin P. *Marilyn: The Tragic Venus*. 1965. London: Robert Hale, 1967.

Hubert, Susan J. "Two Women, Two Songs: The Subversive Iconography of 'Candle in the Wind,'" *NWSA Journal* 11.2 (1999): 124-37.

Izod, John. "Madonna as Trickster." In Lloyd. [49]-59.

James, Caryn. "The Women Behind the Myths." http://nytimes.

com/2005/02/09/books/09bios.html

Johnson, Barbara. "My Monster/My Self." *Diacritics* 12 (1982): 2-10.

Johnson, Greg. "Interview with Joyce Carol Oates on 'Blonde'" (2000). http://www.usfca.edu/fac-staff/southerr/blonde.html

Jones, Kenneth. "Almost 40 Years After *After the Fall*, Miller Addresses Marilyn Monroe in a New Play." www.playbill.com/news/article/print/80864.html

Justesen, Klaus. "USA Sørger" [U.S. in Mourning]. *Jyllands-Posten* 10 March, 1999, Section 1, p. 18.

Kahn, Roger. *Joe and Marilyn: A Memory of Love.* New York: William Morrow, 1986.

Kakutani, Michiko. "BOOKS OF THE TIMES; Girl-Woman: The Interior Marilyn. www.nytimes.com, December 18, 1998.

- - -. "Darkening the Nightmare of America's Dreamgirl." www.nytimes.com, March 31, 2000.

Kaplan, Ann E. "Madonna Politics: Perversion, Repression, or Subversion? Or Masks and/as Master-y?" In Schwichtenberg. 149-65.

King, Barry. "The Star and the Commodity: Notes towards a Performance Theory of Stardom." *Cultural Studies* 1.2 (1987): 145-61.

Kirsch, Adam. "The Great Disconcerting Wipeout." Review of Christopher Bigsby, *Arthur Miller*. *The New Republic* (October 5, 2009). http://www.tnr.com/article/books-and-the-arts/the-great-disconcerting-wipeout

Kollin, Susan. "The Wild, Wild North: Nature Writing, Nationalist Ecologies, and Alaska." *American Literary History* 12.1/2 (Spring-Summer 2000): 41-78.

Kolodny, Anette. *The Lay of the Land: Metaphor as Experience and History in American Life and Letters.* Chapel Hill, N.C.: U of North Carolina P, 1975.

Kristeva, Julia. "Woman Can Never Be Defined." In Marks and de Courtivron. 137-41.

Kugelmass, Jack. "Wishes Come True: Designing the Greenwich Village Halloween Parade." *The Journal of American Folklore* 124.414 (Fall 1991): 443-65.

Larsen, Jørgen V. "Profession: Joe DiMaggio." *Politiken*, 14 March, 1999, Section 1, p. 12.

Larsen, Torben Huus. "The Modern Horror Movie and the Critique of the American Landscape Narrative." *OASIS* 72 (Feb. 2006): 1-12.

Leaming, Barbara, *Girl-Woman*. New York: Crown, 1998.

Lembourn, Hans Jørgen. *Diary of a Lover of Marilyn Monroe*. London: Arbor House, 1979.

Life (Dec. 22, 1958).

Lloyd, Fran, ed. *Deconstructing Madonna*. London: B. T. Batsford, 1993.

Mabey, Richard. *The Oxford Book of Nature Writing*. New York: Oxford U P, 1997.

Maddison, Stephen. "Miss DuBois: Queer Defiance?" In: *Fags, Hags, and Queer Sisters: Gender Dissent and Heterosocial Bonds in Gay Culture*. New York: St. Martin's, 2000. 49-63.

Madonna. *Sex*. London: Secker & Warburg, 1992.

Mailer, Norman. *Marilyn*. [New York]: Grosset and Dunlap, 1973.

- - -. *Of Women and Their Elegance*. New York: Simon & Schuster, 1980.

Marks, Elaine and Isabelle de Courtivron. *New French Feminisms*. New York: Schocken, 1981.

McCann, Graham. "Biographical Boundaries: Sociology and Marilyn Monroe." In Featherstone *et al.* [325]-38.

. *Marilyn Monroe*. London: Polity, 1988.

McGrath, Charles, *et al.* "The Real Story: Literary Fact and Fiction." *PEN America: A Journal for Writers and Readers* (Spring 2001). http://www.pen.org/journal/texts/realstory.html

Mellen, Joan. *Marilyn Monroe*. New York: Pyramid, 1973.

Miller, Arthur. *After the Fall*. 1964. In: *Collected Plays* II. New York: Viking, 1981. [125]-242.

- - -. *The Misfits*. New York: Penguin, 1961.

- - -. *Timebends: A Life*. 1987. London: Methuen, 1999.

Miller, David. *Dark Eden: The Swamp in Nineteenth-Century American Literature*. Cambridge: Cambridge U P, 1990.

Miller, Laura. "Joyce Carol Oates's Marilyn." *The New York Times Book Review*, April 2, 2000, pp. 6, 8.

Miracle, Berniece Baker. *My Sister Marilyn: A Memoir of Marilyn Monroe*. Chapel Hill: Algonquin, 1994.

Mistry, Reena. "Madonna and *Gender Trouble*." http://www.theory.org.uk/madonna.htm

Monroe, Marilyn, with Ben Hecht. *My Story*. New York: Stein & Day, 1974.

Morrison, Toni. *Love*. London: Chatto & Windus, 2003.

- - -. *Paradise.* 1998. London: Vintage, 1999.

"Moving Pictures: Annotations, Information, Quotes." www.co.uk.lspace.org/books/apf/moving-pictures.html

Mulvey, Laura. "Afterthoughts on 'Visual Pleasure and Narrative Cinema' Inspired by *Duel in the Sun*." *Framework* 6.15/16/17 (1981): 12-15.

- - -. "Visual Pleasure and Narrative Cinema." *Screen* 16.3 (Autumn 1975): 6-18.

Muñoz, José Esteban. *Disidentifications: Queers of Color and the Performance of Politics.* Durham, NC: Duke U P, 1998.

Nabokov, Vladimir. *Lolita*. 1955. New York: Berkley Books, 1985.

Naremore, James. *Acting in the Cinema.* Berkeley: U of California P, 1988.

Noble, Jean. *Masculinities Without Men: Female Masculinity in Twentieth-Century Fictions.* Vancouver: U of British Columbia P, 2003.

Norman, Neil and Jon Barraclough. *Insignificance: The Book*. London: Sidgwick and Jackson, 1985.

"Not Just Drag Queens." *Time* 147.21 (May 20, 1996). http://weblinks1.epnet.com.heimdal.bib.sdu.dk

Oates, Joyce Carol. *Blonde: A Novel*. 2000. New York: Ecco, 2001.

- - -. "On the Composition of Blonde." Unpublished xerox copy, June 1999.

- - -. *(Woman) Writer: Occasions and Opportunities*. New York: E. P. Dutton, 1988.

O'Brien, Tim. *In the Lake of the Woods.* New York: Houghton Mifflin,1994.

Orr, David. "Virtual Nature," *Conservation Biology* 10.1 (Feb. 1996): 8-9.

Pratchett, Terry. *Moving Pictures: A Discworld Novel*. 1990; London: Corgi Books, 1999.

Pratt, Marie Louise. *Imperial Eyes: Travel Writing and Transculturation*. London: Routledge, 1992.

Riviere, Joan. "Womanliness as a Masquerade." In Burgin *et al.* 35-44.
Rollyson, Jr., Carl E. *Marilyn Monroe: A Life of the Actress.* 1986. New York: Da Capo, 1993.
Rosten, Norman. *Marilyn: An Untold Story*. New York: Signet, 1973.
Roth, Philip. *American Pastoral.* New York: Houghton Mifflin, 1997.
Rudnick, Paul. "Marilyn Monroe." *Time* (June 14, 1999). www.time.com/time100/heroes/profile/monroe01.html
Sayre, Henry M. *The Object of Performance.* Chicago: U of Chicago P, 1989.
Schickel, Richard. *Intimate Strangers: The Culture of Celebrity.* Garden City, NY: Doubleday, 1985.
Schrader, Paul. "Notes on Film Noir." In: *Perspectives on Film Noir.* Ed. R. Barton Palmer. New York: G. K. Hall, 1996. 99-109.
Schwichtenberg, Cathy, ed. *The Madonna Connection: Representational Politics, Subcultural Identities, and Cultural Theory*. Boulder: Westview P, 1993.
- - -. "Madonna's Postmodern Feminism: Bringing Margins to the Center." In: Schwichtenberg. 149-65.
Scott, A. O. "Marilyn as Metaphor." http://www.nytimes.com/2005/03/06/books/review/006SCOTTL.html
Sedgwick, Eve Kosofsky. *Between Men: English Literature and Male Homosexual Desire*. New York: Columbia UP, 1985.
Shaw, Sam and Norman Rosten. *Marilyn among Friends.* London: Bloomsbury, 1987.
Skeggs, Beverly. "A Good Time for Women Only." In Lloyd. [61]-73.
Stacey, Jackie. *Star Gazing: Hollywood Cinema and Female Spectatorship*. New York: Routledge, 1994.
Stanislavsky, Constantin. *An Actor Prepares.* Trans. Elizabeth Reynolds Hapgood. London: Geoffrey Bles, 1936.
- - -. *My Life in Art.* 1924. Moscow: Foreign Languages Publishing House, 1958.
- - -. "When Acting Is an Art." In *Star Texts: Image and Performance in Film and Television.* Ed. Jeremy G. Butler. Detroit: Wayne State U P, 1991. 18-33.
Steinem, Gloria. *Marilyn Monroe/Norma Jeane.* 1986. New York: Signet, 1988.

Summers, Anthony. *Goddess: The Secret Lives of Marilyn Monroe.* London: Victor Gollancz, 1985.

Talese, Gay, "The Silent Season of the Hero." 1966. In David Halberstam. [3]-22.

Taraborrelli, J. Randy. *Madonna: An Intimate Biography.* London: Sidgwick & Jackson, 2001.

Testa, Maria. *Becoming Joe DiMaggio.* Cambridge, Mass.: Candlewick Press, 2002.

Theweleit, Klaus. *Male Fantasies* I-II. London: Polity, 1987, 1989.

Thomas, Jeannie B. "Dumb Blondes, Dan Quayle, and Hillary Clinton: Gender, Sexuality and Stupidity in Jokes." *The Journal of American Folklore* 110.437 (Summer 1997): 277-313.

Todd, Mabel Elsworth. *The Thinking Body: A Study of the Balancing Forces of Dynamic Man.* 1937. Princeton, N.J.: Princeton Book Co., 1968.

Tompkins, Jane. *West of Everything.* New York: Oxford U P, 1992.

Toperoff, Sam. *Queen of Desire.* New York: HarperCollins, 1992.

Trilling, Diana. "The Death of Marilyn Monroe." In: *Claremont Essays* (New York: Harcourt Brace World, 1964). 229-43.

Turner, Bryan. "Recent Developments in the Theory of the Body." In Featherstone *et al.* [1]-35.

Turner, Christy. "Fabulousness as Fetish: Queer Politics in *Sex and the City*." *S & F Online* 3.1 (Fall 2004). http://www.barnard.edu/sfonline/hbo/printctu.htm

Uchtman, William C. [Review of *Marilyn & Bobby: Her Final Affair*]. "The Earth's Biggest Movie Database." www.imdb.com/title/tt0107517

Weatherby, W. J. *Conversations with Marilyn.* London: Robson Books, 1976.

Wolf, Janet. "On the Road Again: Metaphors of Travel in Cultural Criticism." *Cultural Studies* 7.2 (May 1993): 224-39.

Zoglin, Richard. "Scenes from a Marriage, Part 2." *Time* 164.17 (Oct. 25, 2004): 84-85.